LIVING DANGEROUSLY

LIVING DANGEROUSLY
Story of a Young WAAF in WWII

Betty Farley

Ad Astra Books
Key Biscayne, Florida

Contact the author at:
bettfarley@gmail.com

This edition was prepared for publication by
Ghost River Images
5350 East Fourth Street
Tucson, Arizona 85711
www.ghostriverimages.com

Cover design by
Ghost River Images

ISBN 978-1-7326005-0-8

Library of Congress Control Number: 2018908552

Printed in the United States of America
August 2018

Contents

Dedication

This book is dedicated to my wonderful children, Norman, Franklin, Elizabeth, and Martha and also to my close friend and sister, Norma. Each one having given me unstinting support, always. Never too busy to consult.

Special thanks go to my cousin Richard Adams who has generously given me the benefit of his professional expertise, caring and encouragement from the first rough draft to the conclusion of the book. He is much appreciated.

Everlasting thanks to my son, Franklin Smith for his never ending efforts on my behalf in order to keep me computer friendly and tending the mechanical hazards encountered on the way. This and more, accomplished promptly, despite his own business demands on his time.

Last, but never least, Michael White, my publisher has to be the best possible person to create joy in the business of producing a book. It has been an absolute pleasure to work with him and learn. I am lucky to have found him, thanks to Ethel Coffee who also sings his praises.

Preface

Living Dangerously is a lively and entertaining read which will appeal to all readers interested in personal histories of World War Two. Betty Farley commences with detailed descriptions of her outstandingly happy childhood spent with her affluent and secure family in England's West Midlands.

The author then tells of joining the WAAF, (Women's Auxiliary Air Force), and her role within Special Operations. We are provided with sufficient technical detail to have an understanding of her work, and an appreciation of its importance in supporting RAF pilots in their efforts to outwit enemy aircraft.

The author's reminiscences, recalled with astonishing clarity, permit us an intimate view of her personal life as she attains womanhood whilst the world around her is in a state of wartime upheaval. It is this juxtaposition of the personal experiences alongside Farley's witnessing of vital aspects of war which serves to make *Living Dangerously* a valuable contribution to memoirs of WWII.

– Dr. Dianne Lawrence

1 – In the Beginning

LOOMING OVER THE wireless with an air of foreboding, like pillars at Stonehenge, we sat stiff backed, silently waiting, on that crisp, clear autumn night in September. The ticking clock, sounded like an amplified heart-beat, ticking away the long minutes, as they shuffled by on leaden feet. All day, tension had been building and now at last, our life changing moment was here.

The sonorous stroke of Big Ben delivered its final bong precisely on the dot of nine p.m. and Mr Chamberlain wasted no time in getting to the point. Swift as Damocles' sword, slicing through all past equivocation, the vainless, hoping for 'peace in our time' and with sad finality, he spoke those unforgettable words, "Today Britain has declared war on Germany." The long wait was over and we were committed. These few words were to change the future for all of us, forever.

Hitler had made his last pie crust (made to be broken) promise, stating, "No further territorial claims will be made." The first time after annexing Austria, we believed him. Next, came his conquest of Czechoslovakia, once again evoking strong protests, uselessly expressed by Britain and France, but it too, was ruthlessly swallowed up by the German Reich. Reluctantly, the Allies forbore taking further action, still unwilling to declare war at this juncture, they continued to nurture a vague hope for peace.

Once more soon after, Poland was threatened, unmistakable final warnings were clearly issued again, and again, but Herr Hitler, ignoring all opposition and without the slightest hesitation, defiantly marched his troops into Poland, anyway. It was the last straw! His decision left Britain no choice. We were honour bound to follow through with a declaration of war, as promised. The date was September 3rd 1939.

As we gathered around the radio, my family heard the announcement in silence, each absorbing the impact, in her/his own way. Over our heads, our parents worriedly exchanged knowing glances, remembering the 1914-1918 war, only twenty years before, but Norma, a kindergartner, and I, at fifteen, had been spared that experience. It was totally unimaginable for us. We wondered out loud, just what would happen to us? "Would the enemy be coming to England and how would they get there? How soon? What about school? Would everyone have to fight? Would we wear uniforms?" Our parents fielded responses as best they could but they too were left with their own unanswerable questions, which would also have to wait. We could only speculate.

The last war to involve fighting on our soil happened in 1066 and resorted to the use of swords and chain mail, conjuring up visions of long haired, sabre carrying warriors. Much more recently, along came World War I, before our time, of course, and not on our soil, but diligently studied in history classes. We dutifully read all required books, saw documentaries and listened to teacher's lectures, all factual stuff, but our lessons were concerned mostly with battle dates, places, and the all important outcome. Who won what? Dates were recited by rote, when one was called upon to do so, but generally it was all so impersonal and we found it all rather hard to imagine. 'Battle of Hastings 1066' usually began the litany, but nothing spells reality like a first-hand account.

Our parents, had actually lived through four long years of World War I, from 1914-1918 making war a much more personal event for them, and for us. Civilians in England then experienced deprivations, shortages of all kinds, and loss of family, and family life. They anxiously read newspapers, listened to the wireless for news of battles fought by their menfolk, always waiting for the next letter and filled with dread when it didn't appear. Forever trying to make-up, and make do, for the absence of normal family living. For the most part however, those at home were out of harm's way. We tried not to think of ways in which our island could be encroached upon as we realized the forthcoming war posed quite different threats. How vulnerable were we? Churchill was yet to make his speech about "fighting them in the fields, in the ditches" etc.(I didn't think I'd do very well in those circumstances.) He knew we didn't have much in the way of weaponry. The Home Guard pitchforks not withstanding, would hardly be a major obstacle for invading, well armed Germans, yet ill-equipped though we were, response on all sides was positive and strong. In the meantime, so many questions: so few answers.

The First War: A Backward glimpse

Those who lived through the actual fighting in WW I, like my Father, knew all too well about war's horror and deprivation and the endless bombardment in the trenches, having been on the front lines during those formative years from age eighteen to twenty two. He drove teams of six to eight horses, depending on the load, carrying heavy ammunition behind the lines in France, Belgium and later Italy. When we asked what it was like, he gave us some idea of the long hours under fire, but made no mention of shells exploding ahead, and behind him. He saw no reason to elaborate on the gruesome horrors, witnessed along the way. Victims of mustard gas, or unspeakable mutilations of men and horses alike, blown to bits all around him. Men, young men, dying agonizing deaths in the field, their anguished cries for help punctuating the boom of artillery. Nights without sleep: the bone weary tiredness. Sometimes nodding off in the saddle from utter exhaustion, hoping to escape gaping holes along the way, trusting the horse to find his way through while falling asleep, sitting bolt upright and sopping wet, at times. Craters, noisily appeared in his path, jolting him back to awareness as he struggled to block out some of the carnage, or even, just some of the noise. This part of the story was not for young ears, and many years passed before we overheard any of this, when Dad, on rare occasions, shared experiences with another war survivor, as we laid low and eavesdropped.

He did, however, tell us about the relentless rain and sopping, squelching mud, never really getting dry, the wet socks wrung out and put back on, existing all the while on a steady diet of bully beef and biscuits. The beef was a canned version of someone's concept of beef, and the biscuits resembled dog treats, but were big, square, and barely breakable with a hammer.

There were a few other stories fit for our ears, like the one about the Sgt who made a name for himself as the number one scrounger of all time. Once, behind the lines when there was no shelter from the demoralizing rain, no candles to be had anywhere, and certainly no booze, my Father came upon him by chance, at night, on a lonely stretch beyond the supply depot.

There he was, ensconced in a small tent, camouflaged with branches, well hidden from the casual observer. Finding a chink in the abundant foliage, which on closer inspection revealed the tent flap, Dad peered inside, and saw the unbelievable occupant, comfortably reclining on a real army cot (unheard of) surrounded by a flock of candles, lit up like a Christmas tree and enjoying a nightcap of scotch. Gazing into the tent, convinced that it was all a mirage, Dad watched, fascinated, as the Sgt. reached under the bed with his free arm and looking up, casually enquired," how about a drink, or perhaps a few chocolates?"

Hardly able to believe his eyes and in shock, but not too shaken to accept, he spent that night in comparative luxury, on a comfy bed with fresh sheets, swapping war stories and contemplating the irony of war, among other things: wisely forbearing to enquire too specifically into the source of so much bounty. Leaving at dawn, after a breakfast of something other than bully beef and biscuits, Dad strode with a jauntier step in dry socks yet! Even the horses seemed spryer.

A welcome break from the stark reality, and horror outside the tent: Moments like this were all too rare, and stranger than fiction.

Somehow, Dad kept his sense of humour alive 'til war's end, staying sane and human, just grateful to be home again in one skinny piece. He never went to church after that though, except for the occasional wedding or funeral. He had survived Ypres, pronounced Wipers by the irreverent Tommies, and was in at the very dawn of the vicious Battle of the Somme, the Chaplain having warned the troops beforehand that they might be the 'sacrificial unit,' but by some fluke of fate, they were stood down, long enough to survive the next wave. Dad was also in the worst of battles on the Marne to mention but three hell-holes.

But that was the last War and we couldn't envision trench war as it was then, happening again in this war. Still, there was a Maginot Line in France and a Ziegfried Line in Germany on which the Allies planned to sing the latest marching ditty, "we're gonna hang out the washing on the Ziegfried Line." That was just a bit premature, however.

After World War I came the Depression, smothering any hopes of further education for Dad.

He realized that an income must be his first priority, but jobs for veterans were few and far between, as soldiers returned en masse from the front all with similar objectives.

Jobs of any kind were scarce, particularly for my Mother who was an Art College graduate, and she found little available in the art world, so she decided to invest her savings in a baby linen shop. A boutique in today's parlance. Here, she had some chance to use her creativity, and also earn a living.

Dad on the other hand decided to form a partnership with his brother, to design and produce toys.

Although Dad and brother Harold, had enlisted together, in 1914, they were soon parted and served in different units during the war and their paths never crossed whilst in the Army. After being de-mobbed, they were so happy to be re-united, and in one piece, they decided to pool their resources and begin a small toy factory together. They researched the area to find the right property and acquire tools etc, so that in due time they were up and running within the year and established enough to be getting regular business orders. They were gradually gaining strength and assurance in their new venture, when a very large order came in from a big department Store in Manchester, for child-sized rocking horses for the Christmas season. A real boost, one that would proclaim them as serious, reliable, manufacturers of well-made toys, enabling them to grow and expand sooner than expected. The future boded well for the Payne brothers

The trouble was, the order was so large and they were so new, that their cash flow wasn't big enough to cover all expenses. Reluctantly, they took in a non-working partner as investor and shareholder. From then on, Norman and Harold started the day early, and finished late, with only a handyman to help, and after putting in long arduous hours, without a break, the day finally came, when the order was complete and ready to go. Finished and crated! Weary, but happy they slept the sleep of the just that night.

Next morning, all three partners went to the Birmingham railway station to supervise the loading. A bright yellow sun shone benevolently down, sprinkling its gold-dusted rays on their bare heads, matching their upswing mood, as the last crate was carefully stowed. The new Partner kindly volunteered to escort the shipment and readily boarded the train which was carrying the load north to its destination in Manchester. Dad and Uncle Harold waved him off, relieved to be back to normal hours again, glad to have a chance to take a breather after all their hard work. They shook hands all around, smiling happily, knowing they were all set to collect payment, and celebrate their first really profitable Christmas. They dared to speculate on a New Year filled with promise.

All went according to plan and payment was collected by their emissary. And that was IT. Nothing! Nothing, but silence! No check appeared, no happy phone call came. No sign of their Partner. Nothing! Just a large void!

The brothers held off before checking with the buyer in Manchester, unwilling to face the enormity of the apparent treachery, but face it they must, when the truth became all too sickeningly evident. The end result of months of all the grueling hard work and planning, was a disaster. Their trusted partner with the excellent references was never seen or heard from again. They had indeed been well and truly bilked.

Disheartened, with little capital left, they might have carried on to fulfill smaller orders locally, but with no reserve supplies and little capital, the brothers dismally realized their best choice would be to sell the machinery, some of it quite large and costly, then the property, and rethink a new beginning. That painfully decided, their caretaker James, undertook to clean up and put the premises in saleable condition first, but Fate wasn't finished with the brothers yet. While sweeping up, James had carelessly dropped a smouldering cigarette butt among the shavings, and that night while they slept, the ensuing conflagration reduced everything to ashes, and molten metal. The fire was visible for miles around. Prospects for the brothers were now at a low ebb.

What next? The inadequate insurance, when equally divided, provided limited capital to start afresh in some new venture, but what? The employment outlook hadn't changed and the economy was still not good. After reviewing various options, Dad decided to emulate his wife and invest what he had left in a small clothing shop, near the boutique. A capable manager was installed in each shop, paired with an assistant, leaving the owners free for other areas such as, buying, stock-taking, book-keeping and now and then, hiring extra people for busy periods.

In time, with patience, imagination, business acumen, and many unclocked hours, both projects grew and prospered, fulfilling their hopes and becoming an unqualified success, though it didn't happen overnight.

Sometime between the demise of the toy factory and the beginning of Dad's investment in the haberdashery business, Martha and Norman decided to wait no longer for a white wedding and trimmings. They had waited long enough already, expecting the toy factory to fulfill its promise expecting to celebrate both events at the same time, success of the factory and their happy union. When the former fizzled out, they realized there was no reason to delay their wedding celebration and proceeded accordingly. A few close friends and relatives would be ideal they thought. It was time for them to be together, and sharing, their lives more fully so joyously they began, making new arrangements for a simple service, cutting frills, but leaving all that was essentially meaningful and beautiful, intact.

Thus on October 19 1922 they were married in a quiet ceremony in

Birmingham, with just their closest family in attendance and one or two special friends. After the service champagne and a festive breakfast wer served. The honeymoon was brief, as they were just beginning to get established, and couldn't be spared for very long, but a few days alone in the country, not far from the coast, was just what they needed, and they made the most of it.

It wasn't until April 1924 that their first daughter appeared, (me) making us a family. As I grew I was the lucky recipient of a lone, surviving, wooden, child sized, rocking horse, a silent reminder of the road not taken, had the factory continued, I was probably then about two, and had to be lifted up to sit in the saddle, but eventually I grew big enough to climb aboard unaided, and we kept Dobbin around for many years. After a few years, Norma inherited the same steed and was impressed to hear it was designed and manufactured by her Dad and Uncle Harold at the end of WW1. But of course, Norma had yet to be born.

I had to wait a few more years, before my hopes for a live playmate were realized. When at last, my sister Norma did appear, she was worth waiting for eventually but this took time for me to discover. She was not an immediate hit, since she was too small to play with, and couldn't talk. It would take time before she could be a maiden in distress and tied to a tree, so it seemed I was doomed to continue in that role, until she grew a bit. As we became older, the difference in age mattered less and less, and with the passing years we grew close, finally evolving into best friends. Still are, despite the distance between us.

When Norma was about three or four years old our mother found time to design a pretty, hand-smocked, silk dress for a toddler and Norma became the model tot who appeared in colour on the cover of a catalogue which circulated throughout Britain. This became so successful it was then produced in quantity, to be repeated many times, gratifying the manufacturer as well as my mother. She often designed unusual things which were much admired but never found time to pursue the manufacturing aspect.

Eventually, our parents owned four shops in two towns, but as the threat of war approached, two were sold, thereby reducing the need to obtain extra petrol needed to travel back and forth. Only the original two businesses remained, both now in the same town, Oldbury. Much easier to supervise at war's onset and quite enough joint responsibility, they decided.

Both of these ventures provided our family with a comfortable and productive life. Besides, our parents seemed to enjoy working together, happily allotting themselves the tasks they were best suited for, and sharing

Norma, in tot model mode

Me with Dad about three or four years old

Me with Mom in car

their playtime with equal equanimity. They were a harmonious pair, with the occasional differences of opinion and these were aired with gusto, sometimes quite funny for Norma and me to listen to, though we didn't dare laugh aloud while it was all happening.

Like the time we were all set to go to Weston Super Mare for a holiday and all arrangements had been made weeks ago, the clothes chosen and packed, sandwiches readied for a picnic en route, and we were in the car, about forty miles from home, when my Mother suddenly, out of the ether, decided she didn't really want "to go there, "again,!" she said. "After all it was 'old hat' and we were long overdue for a real change." Dad, disbelieving his ears, screeched the tires, drawing up on a grassy verge, he flung both arms in the air, in pure exasperation and huffing out a few expletives, ignoring raised eyebrows, he asked "Where in the world *did* Madam wish to go, and why didn't she say so before?" For heaven's sake! Calmer, now that she had his undivided attention, she said she didn't realize it before, but now, she knew she wanted to go "somewhere different," this time. Busy with business details and packing, she hadn't taken time to think about her reluctance to repeat old trips, but bit by bit she realized it seemed rather hum drum, They were "too young to be stuck in such a rut" she decided. Keeping the lid on, knowing that she didn't have to go to Weston Super Mare again, she suggested some options. Sparkling amber brown eyes, alight with possibilities met with brilliant blue ones, betraying a suspicion of their old twinkle. More friendly dialogue ensued regarding a possible destination as she expressed her thoughts. Maps were spread out, conversation ensued, interspersed with remarks like, "we've been there, twice, or that's for retirees" or, "not a pebble beach, it hurts my feet." They finally agreed on Bournemouth, in a completely different area from where we usually went, and with no reservations ahead. We would have to take pot luck and hope for the best. An adventure!

By forfeiting the deposit, it was easy to undo previous arrangements. In the busy holiday season, newcomers would be delighted to find a vacancy sign in such a pretty spot, outside Weston Super Mare, but would we find anywhere as nice at our new destination? In any case, we were on our way, relieved to have the matter decided.

Arriving in Bournemouth in the late afternoon, Dad tried two possible hotels but on reaching his destination, found the dreaded, "no vacancy" sign, posted. Out came the guide book and off we set, once more headed towards the ocean, where he had seen an illustration of a place he quite liked, and looking at the illustration it seemed to be a long shot so we weren't very

Parents in Bournemouth

hopeful. We came to a halt under a tree, at the edge of a grassy lawn. There, we watched as he headed for the receptionist, crossing our fingers as he left. This looked nice, obviously a special spot, but what were our chances this late in the day? Not great! Dad slowly returned and to our utter amazement, smilingly conveyed the news that there had been a cancellation barely an hour earlier, leaving two rooms available, and who could believe it? Just perfect for us!. Fate had indeed smiled upon our venture.

Our first glimpse convinced us of our amazing luck. We had arrived at a small private hotel overlooking the ocean, where green ivy, traced leafy patterns on the fresh white walls, and at the entrance, either side of the double doorway were tubs overflowing with brightly coloured begonias. Here and there on the grass verge outside, were a few benches, mostly under the shade of a lacy tree, surrounded by bright, potted tubs of zinnias, tempting the weary traveler to linger in peace.

Inside, we were warmly welcomed and shown to our rooms, where fresh flowers adorned the well polished old bureau. Later on, after a dip in the sea opposite, we showered, changed and joined some of the other guests, for a

Norma and self, Bournemouth

chat and afterwards this was followed by an excellent dinner and it was in this ambiance enhanced by soft candlelight we were to bask every night after a busy day. The week flew by, and before leaving we agreed it had to be one of our best holidays, ever. Norma and I learned a bit about flexibility from that adventure. Changing one's mind at the last minute didn't prove fatal, after all.

Usually, the biggest difference of opinion between our parents came when it was time to decide which of the relatives was to be visited each week. My Mother had two sisters and a brother, all with families of their own and cousins to play with, for us. Dad had three brothers and a sister also with progeny our ages, but none of them lived in the same town. Our family happily rotated their visits between his or her family, to avoid leaving anyone out. This worked well most of the time, unless someone had a special event like a birthday, or they forgot whose turn was next. Then, frequently, the schedule became unglued and which family should be next was again in question, aggravating them both to the point of "words."Cross ones.

Our visits were quite important as we were one of the first to own a car then, and could make the journey more easily. On these occasions, spats flared briefly and colourfully, between our two parents, and rather predict-ably, were all over and done with, the moment we arrived on the chosen relatives doorstep exuding smiling equanimity. They had a knack of expressing frustrations flat out, hammer and tongs, till one or the other made a sugges-tion, and shortly afterwards a solution would be reached. No resentment, no aftermath and all reverted to normal,like a garden after a squall, fresh, sparkling, and ready to enjoy whatever came next. We knew the routine, often quietly speculating on a possible duration, with small secret bets on the side. Car rides in our family were never boring.

At first we lived in a well wooded residential area, ideal for children. The house had an upper and lower lawn connected by about five wooden steps, with a flourishing bank of rhododendrons along the slope between top and bottom lawns. On the far right side, next to the trellised fence were the climb-ing roses, prolific and fragrant, though alas, not to be picked by me.Flowers were my downfall and at a very early age I was known to reach through fences to pick the stray (unfortunately, prize) rose, or two, but always upon discovery I was sent next door to Dr Harper, our neighbor who grew them, with the evidence clutched in my grimy little paw to explain my crime and offer tear-ful apologies. My first penitent trip took place at age four, and my last? Well, I only do a little occasional 'pruning' now, and usually don't get found out.

At the bottom of the second lawn was a small brook, ideal for catching tiddlers. On the other, left hand side of the lawns was a wide border of perennials and bulbs producing great swaths of color and fragrance, when in season. These were occasionally mine to pick. Special permission required, of course.

While both parents were busy running their businesses, we had a house-keeper who became very special to us all. She was with us for many years, though not during the war when she married and took time out to have her own family. She returned years later, after my Mother died in 1947 at the early age of forty nine, and Dad needed her help. He was desolate. She came willingly and with pleasure. She was alone now, since her husband had died, and both her children had left the nest. Her name was Edith!

I was just a small child when she first came to us, and she was perhaps, twenty or so. She was truly wonderful, in spite of her merciless, energetic scrubbing of my hair, scalp and ears after every too frequent bath. Her bed-time stories were fabulous and original. She was quite tolerant of all my very assorted friends and their regular visits, although she wasn't very tolerant of my organized competition, held with those same friends when, inspired by me, we were all to take turns calling out any swear words we knew, or thought we did, tho' some were of our own invention. Our vocabulary was a bit limited, though enthusiastically uttered. She caught us fair and square, sitting on my little upturned play car, and swiveling on the little wheels as we performed. My sentence was dire. Banished to my bedroom, to await my parents return, in disgrace. For that one, I had cried myself into hiccups by the time they came home to administer sage and tender counsel. How I hated being sent to bed!

Our house had a front door, side door and back door. Edith proclaimed the front door was for family and friends, the side door for tradesmen and the back door for garden use, and for me and my friends, the latter being rather heavily emphasized, I noted. There was to be no over-use of the front door bell on Edith's watch.

Inside the front door, was a small vestibule then a living room and din-ing room on one side. On the other side of the hall was a small bathroom under the staircase. Further down the hall was a kitchen, big enough for a sturdy table, long couch and two leather arm chairs beside the fireplace, with a hob for boiling a teakettle, always at the ready. Beyond that, was a scullery with a big brick built-in boiler, for laundry, also two sinks, one of which had a faucet connected to a rain barrel outside, meant for washing hair, faces, watering flowers etc. The rain water left our hair and skin so soft, I always

Edith in later years, long retired

wanted one again wherever I lived, but never quite managed it. There was a big mangle, also a clothes dryer, which went up to the ceiling on a pulley in rainy weather. We had a lady who came in to do the laundry and heavy cleaning, she sang as she worked and always wore a brightly printed dress.

Her name was Alice and she wore her hair in a braid, like a crown around her head. Alas, mine was too curly to copy that.

Upstairs, was my playroom, just off the landing then up a few stairs, were Edith's bedroom, a guest bedroom, and next to that, a small loo. My parents' bedroom and bath was at the very end of the hall. A pale blue room, with pretty wall sconces and paintings it always seemed like a happy, sunny haven to go with a cut knee, puzzling questions, or even just extra hugs after a bad dream. Either parent would do when needed.

Most of my friends were boys, (with two exceptions.). Playing cowboys and Indians, was a favourite, and always exciting but I got so tired of being the one who always got tied to a tree. They maintained that 'by rights,' only a 'damsel' could yell for help. "Sheriff or Indian Chief is more my speed," I argued, but we already had those, they reminded me. I kept hoping, but no such luck. "Someone" had to get rescued!

One of the boys was Valentine Vickers whose bright red hair practically burst into flame every time he defended that impossible first name. Then there was Freddie Price and Jackie Simpson, usually on the rescue team performing deeds of valour, and a few other Indians who were addicted to fierce dances, accompanied by blood curdling war whoops, repeated often and with great gusto, causing Edith to hastily close all nearby windows with a decided thump, and a roll of the eyes.

Both rescue-team boys, my self-appointed guardians, would wait for me to come out of school, and one day on my way home I passed a new building going up. There was a square aperture, in the half built brick wall, framing a forthcoming window, just above my head from whence I heard some giggling and scuffling. Looking up, I saw two faces silhouetted against a pale sky, centred in the space were Jackie and Freddie, side by side with right arms poised in salute, fingertips pressed to their foreheads, grinning like chimpanzees. Finally, I turned and waved, and they seemed satisfied. Wonder how in the world they got up there? Best not to ask!

My best friend was Marjorie Lowe, who knew all my secrets, and took them with her to the grave when she died suddenly, at thirteen due to a weak heart valve. A devastating event for her parents, and for me as her friend, a stunning blow. But this hadn't yet occurred. There were seven more intervening years to share, and we made the most of them, before tragedy struck.

When it did strike, I was just returning home from school one day, glad it was the end of the week and there would be time to play, when I was suddenly aware of my mother's downcast face and asked what was wrong?

With her arm around my shoulder she guided me to the couch and we sat together while she explained, gently as possible, that she had some bad news for me. Nothing could have prepared me for the shock that followed when I learned that my best friend, Marjorie had suddenly died, She was my age, only twelve! How could that be?

Coming out of the blue as it did, it didn't seem quite real, and I struggled to take it in. Only the year before, we had attended grade school together and saw each other every day, and sometimes on the weekend, then at age eleven when it was time to advance, she went on to a regular High school and I, to a Grammar school. We couldn't be together as often, since we were in different towns but our friendship never faltered. It was inconceivable to me that we should never meet again. Trying to absorb it all, I retreated to my bedroom for some quiet time and though it didn't bring comfort, it gave me pause to realize how awful this must be for her parents and younger sister, so I decided to go and see them. Setting off with much trepidation and clutching a small bouquet, I made my way to Marjories's house and seeing the door was ajar, I entered to find her parents were receiving two old friends who were also paying their respects. I waited' hesitating until they turned to leave and then headed for Marjorie's Mom.

She sat upright in her chair as tears fell soundlessly and unheeded and then, almost in a whisper, she said how glad she was that I was there. As we spoke, her husband, silently passed along a handkie which she mechanically used to dry her face, though minutes later it was just as wet. We spoke of good times that Marjorie and I had shared and after a while she told me that my dear friend was only in the next room and how peaceful and pretty she looked. Would I like to go in to see her? Mindful of my promise to my mother not to do so, I said that I would rather remember her as she was. Afterwards though, I wondered if that was the best decision.

Her Dad (Mr. Lowe) was like a man in a trance as we exchanged a few words and when he stood to say goodbye, I saw how stiffly he moved, almost robotic, as he stooped to pick up his wife's hankie, as it fell in a sodden ball, unnoticed at her feet.

It was with wet eyes and a heavy heart that I returned to the comfort of my family.

But that was not to occur for several years hence. Now looking back and remembering, how it was before this sad event, I thought of Marjorie as I knew her then, vital and full of life.

She was a very pretty brunette, with lovely, melting chocolate brown eyes, and a 'widow's peak', she said it was. Marjorie was always a safe recipient to trust with private thoughts, besides being endowed with a delightful sense of humour. I remember sitting on the heating pipes on a cold winter day, in the hall at school, drinking our morning milk through a straw and making fun of our teacher's habits and mannerisms. As a mimic she was a hoot. Later, Marjorie's little sister Geraldine, known as Denie, became my sister's best friend. All four of us often went to the park together, or elsewhere, and thus the younger girls formed their own bond. This little foursome was special to all of us.

Another chum, part of my regular group, was a little girl named Janet, who planned to be a ballerina some day. She liked to stay clean, even when she didn't have to, and not even wearing her tutu, and there was Mary, with the perpetually runny nose, who somehow tagged along, invited or not. One girl a little older, named Eva Hartsawn, the only black girl in our school, was there for a very short stay before her family moved to another area. She was always alone on the playground so one day I invited her to come to my house. Other friends had been and gone, leaving Eva and me sitting on the steps between the lawns thinking up a new game when I noticed her pink palms contrasting with the dark brown skin on the backs of her hands, so I asked her, "Are you that color all over?" "Yes" she said, proudly. "So show me". Thus challenged, off came the clothes and she did show me. She was also pink under her arms. So fancy with two colours! Now it was my turn. Naturally Eva repeated my question 'Are you that colour all over?" Laughing and giggling by now, I presented my pale self to her for inspection, hamming it up a bit, but keeping a sharp eye out for Edith, just in case. I had a feeling we weren't supposed to be all bare even in a private garden, but we eluded her that time. Back went the clothes, all curiosity satisfied and mystery resolved and on to the next project, soon immersed in building a mud house for my pet toad, Fred. A messy affair for the pretty dresses we wore but we hadn't heard of jeans then. That house and garden was the scene of many adventures, mis-adventures, delights and sorrows. It was a sad day when we held separate funerals for the dead birds we had discovered. We rocked them on the swing, I have no idea why, before burial in a shoe box. These were small victims of a neighbor's cat we thought.

My sister Norma hadn't arrived in this world yet and didn't appear until about four months before my seventh birthday. She made her dramatic entry at home on Christmas Eve.

When I got up, in the very early hours of that day I was suddenly aware of unusual sounds around me in my temporary bed downstairs, I saw my Father and two of his brothers through the doorway, in a very jovial mood, little whorls of delicious smelling, spirals of cigar smoke emanating from the den, and the sound of clinking crystal glasses met my senses They were joyfully toasting the new mother and baby they said. Stemming the tide of my excited questions, like why couldn't I see the baby being born? I was hastily ushered upstairs to see the newcomer and my Mom.

I had been told more than was usual at that time, about the origin of a baby, but didn't know how a baby began, yet, nor how it emerged from the cosy place inside, but still wasn't given any more answers at this moment. In any case I was too interested in viewing my sister to pursue matters. Peering down at the new arrival was a shock. I wasn't expecting anything quite this small. My new sister was cute alright, but so tiny! I thought dolefully, it might be awhile before she could be a small indian or cowboy or even play with Fred the toad. Pity! No chance of getting to be sheriff at this rate.

Several years after Norma's arrival, when war was whispered on the wind, our parents decided in anticipation of that possibility that we could do without tiddlers in the brook and even the house we lived in and enjoyed. We just might just need a bolt hole instead, they thought. A cellar, in fact was on the list of priorities, so they decided, not without regret and many debates, that it was time for us to move on.

Our new quarters proved to be a three story edifice, right in the town. On ground level, a double fronted shop faced the street with ample living quarters behind. The second shop was conveniently located just over the bridge only a few doors away, and was the first one they owned, Mother's original boutique.

This new home possessed the 'all important cellar' extending under a large part of the structure. There was also a separate entry way at the side of the double fronted windows of the building, accessible without having to go through the shop, to enter the living areas behind, but mostly we just drove in, entering from the rear. Later though, during the war, the side entry was much in use as a means to enter the shelter of the air raidcellar.

At the rear there was also stabling for two horses, with a separate brick-built garage, plus a play area, tiled though, not the grassy lawn and flowers we were used to. The driveway was enclosed by a ten foot brick wall on two sides, and joining both, in the middle, was a big high wall of wood divided into two gates, at the end. These gates, once meant for coach-exit originally, now used for cars at the moment, and in the center of one gate there was a small door for individual entry, both kept locked usually. The long driveway came in from a side road, running parallel to the main street beyond. A useful exit for the horse and carriage, which were to appear later, better described as pony and trap, "To save petrol," Dad said at the time, when he surprised us all with the acquisition of this duo. "Any excuse for a horse" said Mom, not easily fooled.

Once inside the big gates, the garage big enough for two cars, was dead ahead and turning the corner on the left of the garage, were three stables and an open area for carriages, at present not in use though.

Our move to the little town of Oldbury with no garden, was balanced by the acquisition of our week-end cottage in the country, with a big garden, where we also spent school breaks at Easter, Whitsuntide and Teachers rest. It was hidden away in Shropshire and not on any paved road. It could only be approached by a long rocky lane, covered in honey suckle and dog roses, with one lone, goat, tethered and hidden by foliage, at the top. (always an element of surprise to the unsuspecting.)

Once, this self-same goat, Billy, made his most successful, and sudden, appearance involving my Father, who was riding his favourite highly strung chestnut horse, Ray, up the lane, sedately followed by me, seated on steady old Kitty, on a lovely sunny day. Dad reached the bend in the lane, when suddenly out popped the goat, rattling his chain ferociously behind him, and uttering his shrillest and loudest bleat. Ray true to form, reacted by promptly rearing high in the air, then plunged head down immediately after, bucking, and lashing out with his back legs, thus creating the motion of an electrified, over powered rocking chair. Dad went over the hedge so fast, like a cork from a vigorously shaken champagne bottle, he flew in a great arc. I only saw the seat of his breeches as he vanished over the high shrubbery into the field beyond. Kitty reared a few times in response to Ray's warning, but magically I stayed on, and as the shock wore off, the thought of my unseatable father coming unglued, was too much for me. Unstoppable howls of glee poured out of me. Dad's disgruntled face, hat askew, blue eyes shooting sparks, appeared over the stile as he rejoined us, just made me worse. "You might wait till you know if I have broken anything" he bellowed, but I knew he had landed in thickly cushioned grass and tried to splutter my explanation, thru' gusts of laughter when the ignominy of his plight, finally struck him as funny too, and we both howled in unison. Two of us bent two double, still in the throes, howling with mirth. Billy the goat and both horses eyeing us in total puzzlement, stood patiently by, until a semblance of sanity was restored and we could resume the ride, still hiccupping the odd chuckle, or two, on the way.

The cottage lay in a hollow at the bottom of the lane, protected from the wind. Any car found it a tight squeeze travelling down this bumpy surface and in winter, mud made it impossible. The cottage had a little more than an acre of land under cultivation and was called the Nutshell. Surrounding it, were fields and meadows, all located in Richard's Castle, a place too small to be called a village. Not even a pub!, And that's small indeed.

The castle of Richard III, what was left of it, was in the woods near the Old Church, built somewhere in the 14th century. Not much of the castle remained but the outline, and a few sections of walls, bordering on the ancient cemetery, which in spring and summer was lavishly awash with violets and primroses. Up the hill lay the church with separate belfry, both edifices were fun to explore, with a panoramic view of the surrounding countryside from the top of the belfry. On the landing at the top of the stairs right up close, were the two giant copper bells. I didn't quite dare to pull the bell rope, but I was sorely tempted though knew I'd be banned for life if I did.

Due to the advanced age of the church and belfry, these beauties only rang out twice a year when they pealed, to announce each service.

The grey haired lady caretaker's, vine-covered cottage was nearby and you could borrow the enormous iron keys, if she thought you looked reliable, and of course I had already established my reliability, always on my best behavior during my frequent comings and goings. This ancient place and the area around it, always fascinated me. The iron keys were about ten inches long, each one, to unlock a specific door, since the church and the belfry were separate buildings.

Inside the church a wonderful musty smell of age permeated the air sending you back to another time, long ago. The ancient bible with gossamer pages was almost a foot deep, still on the lectern and open to the last lesson. Climbing up and standing behind it, I ranted away, with a will thoroughly enjoying my chance to mime the somewhat theatrical, visiting vicar. I was intent on delivering a sermon, just for the pleasure of hearing the eerie echoes all around me, sometimes alarming my audience of one, my friend and neighbor called Mona, who huddled in the front pew, looking worried. She said nervously, that the roof might fall in if I continued at that rate. I wondered afterwards, if she meant because of God's wrath or whether the safety of the roof was in question? The church was used only twice a year for services because it was so old and so remote. No doubt in need of repairs. Reluctantly climbing down from my lofty perch, we made our way to the ancient oak doors and turning the heavy key in the lock using both hands, I sealed off the atmosphere of centuries until the next time we could step back in history and directed my attention instead to the view facing Mona and me.

Steep slopes opposite were covered in bluebells, in season, creating a blue carpet, and always, there was gorse. The locals said "when gorse is out of season, kissing's out of season" meaning, never. At other times, it was thick with primroses and wild violets and at the bottom of vee-shaped slopes, was a brook, yielding crisp, icy watercress. A picking person's heaven!

There were two farms about a mile or so away from the Nutshell, located in different directions. One supplied us with milk, cheese, whipping cream, butter and eggs, and the other with ham, bacon and chickens etc, all from their own farm, fortunately for us, as the nearest town was Ludlow, several miles away. This too, was a lovely old town with much Tudor architecture, and was one of the ancient gated towns of yore. One of the arched gates, still in fine condition, was in use as a main approach to the town and no doubt, still is. The considerable remains of an historic castle is still there today and well worth a visit.

Joe our gardener came from his farm beyond where his land bordered the orchard of the Nutshell, and here he wrought his magic, created abundant produce as he tended our garden throughout the year. This involved much planting, digging and weeding in season and we were so lucky to have him. He was a big, burly chap who lit a pipe from time to time, tamping it down as he leaned on his shovel, while giving us the local news. Despite the pipe, he had the whitest teeth I'd ever seen and one day when I ventured to ask him what he did to keep them so, he said he brushed them with soot from the chimney. I still don't know if he was pulling my leg, and wasn't at all tempted to try it. However the good looking man who sold strawberries from his own garden in the village, also with gleaming teeth, said he did the same thing, but I still couldn't imagine travelling around with a bag of soot to clean my teeth, even if I could bear to put it in my mouth. I'm still wondering though.

Joe did a fantastic job of growing all our many vegetables. Potatoes, turnips, parsnips, carrots, cabbage, sprouts, string beans and lettuce to mention a few, all tasting of the sunny outdoors. The orchard yielded apples, both for cooking and eating, also nuts called filberts with a little red skinned kernel inside the shell. Raspberries, loganberries and blackberries flourished and were ideal for making Pavlova by adding the local whipping cream to the meringue. Irresistible!

In the Spring, before the picking season, the orchard was rimmed with snowdrops first and later a host of daffodils, narcissus, hyacinths and jonquils appeared. We gathered bunches of these for our relatives, and for ourselves. Aunts, uncles and cousins often came to stay for a week-end or longer if possible. Our family used the cottage on weekends and during various school holidays such as Easter, Whitsuntide and August but at least once a year we went away to the coast together, giving Mom a well deserved cooking respite, while we enjoyed exploring other parts of England, and sometimes Wales, together. Christmas was usually party time, at home with relatives visiting.

Around the Nutshell entrance, flourishing, Albertine roses (peach colour,) climbed it's walls, and the flower garden opposite, bore large fragrant, standard, rose bushes, all available for bouquets in the cottage. Lupins, delphiniums, peonies and many others thrived there, with a little herb garden and lavender planted nearby. We would make potpourri from petals and herbs on a wet day, or lavender bags for the bed linen cupboard. Being tucked in at night amid a soft scent of the garden was worth the effort.

In fact, I could find my way anywhere in our garden, or orchard blindfolded, just by absorbing the heavenly and diverse fragrances assailing my nose.

There was a separate building close to the cottage, built sometime after the cottage, called the End-Room. I was never sure of the original purpose but it was insulated, built in the same stone and came in handy when extra people arrived, also useful for storing apples in winter; the robust aroma lingered long into the summer.

At the white entry gate, stood twin French lilac trees, shedding intricate, perfumed, florets, which fell, confetti-like, to form a soft carpet underfoot, sending up a heavenly perfume, of its own. Winding around those three feet thick stone walls of the cottage, was a slate path leading to a wooden shed, covered in sweet smelling syringa (like orange blossom). This was our outdoor plumbing. The carpenter had taken pride in his work and the nicely grained wood did him credit There was even a second seat in case you wished to entertain a friend? I couldn't imagine the kind of partner one would choose to entertain there, but there it was, waiting. In case. Indoor plumbing consisted of china potties discreetly concealed under beds, decorative and useful if needed at night.

We had our own well, with water pumped into the kitchen sink, very drinkable and crystal clear. Again, great for the hair and skin. Since there was no electricity, we had kerosene or gas lamps augmented by candlelight. Of course, no t.v. or movies, or even a telephone but we made our own entertainment, with many a skit evolving within those walls, often evoking gales of laughter. It was a great place to read, or read aloud from the classics. Dickens being a favourite. The Pickwick Papers was the funniest, I thought.

One of my chores, involved walking up the lane or through two fields, to collect milk and, or, cream, whereupon I was allowed into the farmer's dairy and could watch Mrs Bradley skim the cream from the giant saucer-like containers of farm milk, and at the same time see butter being churned by daughter, Vera. A really slow process.

The Farmer's wife was small and fragile looking with Mikado-mask,-white, alabaster skin, wispy grayish hair caught and held with a clasp at the back. She walked silently, half bent, almost self effacingly, as if excusing herself for being there. I used to worry that she would simply fade away before I saw her again. Hers was a thick country accent. There was a lilting rise in her voice at the end of a sentence as if in question, accenting the last syllable. She used words like "up the goggin," Unlike her husband, she was always gentle, quiet, predictably the same. I marveled as I wondered, how could this tiny person, with such alarming pallor, have borne those three strapping sons and two buxom daughters? She seemed so old, yet her children ranged in age from seventeen to twenty six.

One day in the early Autumn we watched sons Cecil, John and Frank collect a mountain of small apples to make cider. An impressive pile loomed before the crushing apparatus and was fed into the machinery as we watched and patiently monitored the lengthy process of each stage of the operation, until bottling time. Since this took a long time to complete, and to mature enough to be pronounced drinkable, I was allowed a small taste of a properly aged batch instead, in order to appreciate the merits of the finished product A small sip, was indeed all, since it was hard cider and had the kick of the proverbial mule. One taste was enough, and shriveled my tongue, making the swallowed liquid turn into lava, hot from the crater, as it travelled down my aesophagus and I was impressed at the ability of anyone who could swallow a glass full, and survive.

I was sure it could blister paint? Farmer Bradley had no such reaction or restriction and sampled his own wares frequently with enthusiasm, if not downright abandon. Was he lined with asbestos, I wondered? On one of those nights, he decided to give his friend who lived about two miles away, a chance to extol the virtues of his home made brew, so he announced his departure and struck off, on a nearby foot path across the fields, to deliver a large flagon of his best vintage. His big and generous present to his friend!

Not a tall man, but not short either, well muscled from his work on the farm, his big leather belt on the last notch was straining under his natural waistline, as he strode along. He often wore an old tweed jacket with leather elbow patches, shirt open at the neck, and below the waist were wide-wale corduroy pants, tied under the knee with a sort of cord. This outfit didn't vary much summer or winter alike, but he changed headgear from time to time. His florid complexion was a mix of leathery tan with reddish overtones, more red than tan, depending on the quantity of cider imbibed, or, whether he was, or wasn't, too pleased, with life. His moods swung from jovial to bellicose in a flash. But this night he was definitely set on jovial.

Upon arrival, bottle jangling against belt buckle, he found that his friend had made his own cider version, and was equally proud of the finished product. In fact, he was already enthusiastically in the process of trying a sample or two, "just to be sure it was up to snuff, he said." Greetings and toasts ensued and thus began the taste test to beat all taste tests. A contest for their own private, championship cider creation, began, as they alternated bottles, to compare. Endurance was an asset. A lengthy affair with no, quarter given, no respite taken and alas, no decision reached this night. After much rhetoric interspersed with appreciative windy eruptions of great volume, it was decided to defer the final results for another session, another time. Farmer Bradley's friend's eyelids had a decided droop, as he sank lower in his chair, making small snorting sounds as he drifted off, to dreamland. Time to go! Hauling himself up, grunting a bit with effort, Farmer Bradley muttered a goodnight over his shoulder, unnoticed by his host, he navigated his way out of the door, a bit unsteadily, and set off, wobbling and weaving across the fields into a foggy autumn night.

No moon. By now it was late, very late, or rather early a.m. but not yet daylight, with an increasing mist hovering over the landscape, shrouding everything in mystery. Humming a few bars of *'Enery the Eighth* and full of cider, he stumbled on, to find himself in unfamiliar territory and climbing over a steep hill, he fell head first, into what seemed to be, deep hole, so while he was stretched out, reasoned to himself, he might as well take a nap while he was there. He took a last swig from the nearly empty bottle, 'to keep out the damp,' and promptly fell into a sound sleep.

The early morning dawned with milky light, still eerily hazy, and the sound of voices awakened him. Looking up, bewildered, and still dazed with sleep, he saw a disembodied face peering down at him in disbelief. He sat up, groggily, emitting a great blast of a belch, "what time is it?" he asked. The face above him instantly turned white as salt, vanished from view, and with loud unearthly shrieks piercing the ghostly light, the volume growing fainter as he travelled into the distance, and was gone. Mystified, our friend scrambled out of the hole, alone, all others having fled, and found himself near a church, barely visible in the still misty, gloom.

It seems our farmer friend had wandered into a churchyard, fallen over the great mound of earth, to land in a newly dug grave that wasn't quite finished. The shrieker was the grave digger, with his mate, returning to finish the task, and in the half light had not expected to see a ghostly occupant rise up out of the fog shrouded grave, to ask the time. Hard to say who got the biggest fright.

This episode travelled with the speed of a country grapevine, and at first Farmer B. was proud to be the star attraction, smiling and looking clever, until he realized, it portrayed him either as the clown in the story, or the drunken sot, so it quickly became prudent for us all to pretend ignorance of the whole episode. The subject was considered taboo, after that.

Nothing more, was ever heard about the cider contest, at least not at the Bradley farm, but it was just too good a tale to be silenced forever, and away from Bradley ears was always good for a chuckle or two between friends. This was, but one, of several country tales enabling me to say, Norma and I acquired an education in farming, on many levels.

We made lasting, unforgettable memories in those years and I can still smell the heady fragrance of those lilacs, and the roses perfume, mingling with lavender as we walked by.

It soon became apparent as the War made its demands upon us, that it was no longer practical to hang on to the cottage. Availability of petrol was hard to come by, for the drive to Richard's Castle, so the time had come to make changes. The Nutshell was sold early in 1940. It had been ours for seven or eight years and we had loved it. We still had fresh produce to eke out rations for a short while to remind us, but as this experience ended, another began.

This was kind of the last bastion of an era of peace, as we knew it, before the interval preceding the war. A war which involved everyone, from babies to grandparents and all those in between. A war affecting all levels of society from the Royals to the rank and file.

In the interim my parents bought a cabin-cruiser moored on the river Severn, which was not as far away from Oldbury as the cottage and they hoped it might give us a respite from bombing, or perhaps a change of scene, at the very least. There were two bunks across the bow and a convertable seat folding to a double bunk, bathroom with a shower and small galley providing comfy room for four people and a dog on the aft deck. We could use it as a house boat occasionally on a long weekend, until petrol was no longer rationed, after the war. Many good ideas began with, "after the War" I noticed.

2 – Preparing for War

IN SEPTEMBER 1939 changes in Britain were gradual at first, with preparations afoot for reinforcing our cellar, by adding great oak beams supported on heavy pillars, in the main area, which would be used most. Ceilings, were brick built, double groin, vaulted arches giving extra strength. At one end of the room was a separate, steel escape hatch, with steps leading up to the outside world. As I watched it all taking place, technicolour pictures stirred in my head as I visualized the need to use that hatch. If we received a direct hit, how much debris would there be on top of us? How *could* we open it? Three floors extended above the cellar! Better to think about that later. I decided.

Costs for this protection were borne by the Government as the cellar was large enough to provide shelter for many others, if needed. There would be a small sign outside indicating that information.

After the cellar was pronounced safe against air attack, nothing being said about a direct hit, we were then fitted for gas masks. Trying to breathe inside mine felt stifling and weird, the rubber sides snapped and snorted, making rude raspberry noises on my cheeks with every exhalation. "You'll get used to it," they said. We were supposed to wear it every day for half an hour to practice 'getting used to it'. Ha! Cardboard containers housing each respirator were carried at all times, by children and adults alike. A sobering reminder, just the same.

After this, came rationing which grew increasingly limited as time went by. We each had our own I.D. cards and ration books which indicated the amount of any edible item allowed, and every purchase was then stamped by each corresponding merchant. The meat ration was the equivalent of one small lamb chop per week, plus half an ounce of bacon, which was less than half a rasher. Chicken and fish were not rationed but were hard to come by. Eggs were scarce, so one egg a week was usual, and of course, rationed powdered eggs were available but bore little resemblance to the ones in the shell. The fat ration was a total of two ounces per week which included all fats, butter, oil, lard or any other form of fat. Sugar was three ounces a week covering all needs, coffee, tea and baking. Cheese, was a sparse two ounces, for a week. Cake making was the result of pooling rations and saving up for a long time. Forget icing.

Limited orange juice was for expectant mothers and very young children. Sometimes it was possible to buy an orange, one per person, if you were prepared to wait in a queue for as long as it took. Occasionally people would join a queue, any queue in the hopes of something nice to extend the rations, only to find at the end of an hour or so wait, they had queued for birdseed and didn't have a parrot.

Britain was not able to produce enough food to be self supporting, and German U-boats were already at work, sinking our supply ships. Merchant Marines were undeterred in their efforts to keep us fed, risking their lives, dodging mines and U-boats, thereby earning our lasting gratitude and admiration. We also had rationed clothing coupons, and those were severe too. Wedding dress material was out of the question, especially for those in uniform who didn't qualify for coupons, so some people used a soft curtain fabric which didn't require coupons. Silk hosiery became a rarity, and nylons non-existent at this point. It became a matter of some moment to decide which was needed the most, a winter coat, or a sweater and gloves, and very difficult to save coupons when so few were allotted to begin with. Factories, were busily engaged in war work, so manufacturing clothes must take a back seat.

Everyone tried to be creative and use what resources were available. Some diligent knitters would carefully undo old knitted items to re-knit 'new' ones, and dye them afterwards.

Allotments sprang up, providing a variety of vegetables and fruit not readily found elsewhere. These allotments were divided fields, or spare lots, in urban areas, set aside in sections to be rented to food growers, amateur or experienced, thus supplying them with fresher produce than usually seen at the grocers, and no queue involved. Anyone could rent an allotment share and many did.

It was also possible to be licensed to keep a pig to enhance the meager meat ration but you were required to give fifty percent upon maturity, to the local government for general rationing. Pigs were fed table scraps and potato peelings etcetera and of course had to be housed, fenced, sheltered, watered and so forth. Time consuming work: Two friends of ours, an elderly banker and his wife, a more unlikely pair of pig farmers would be hard to find, decided to undertake the challenge, buying two pigs to rear to maturity. A sty had to be erected in their garden and every day they mixed up scraps and fodder, as they braved winter elements, rain, sleet or snow to be sure their animals were properly fed and watered. I had a mental image of a dignified, bowler hatted, banker, in his white shirt and pin striped suit, slopping the pigs in a snowstorm. Or, for that matter, his elegant wife in kid gloves, taking her turn, though I'm sure they found more suitable pig slopping attire, in any case they both gamely persevered until the end.

When the time came, and their carefully nurtured pigs had reached mighty proportions, they notified the authorities and soon, two official looking men appeared with a van to take away the government's share, one plump pig. Their obligations to the government fulfilled, our friends were ready to take the next step and find a humane butcher, and to stock their empty freezer. Visions of a delectable roast, danced before their eyes.

However, within days, two more officials arrived, also in a van, to collect the government 's share, yet another plump pig. Consternation reigned! Flabbergasted, they explained they had already given the required pig to the government representative, only two days earlier, and produced a paper receipt to prove it. A fake they said! In the ensuing discussion it transpired that the second official duo, unfortunately, had the true credentials and alas, the first two men were, shifty eyed, pointy toed, Spivs, catering to the Black Market and were now long gone, leaving no trace. Now what?

Were our nobly named friends, Florence Nightingale (not from the Crimea) and her husband, Ben's efforts, to go unrewarded? Was all that time, cost, effort and dreamy visions of a roast pork dinner for naught? At first it seemed so, but eventually, after yards of paper verification, a sort of justice prevailed and they were able to claim half a pig. A consolation prize was a bit better than the booby prize, they said.

More preparations

Blackout was enforced and sand bags were piled high around all building entrances. People who didn't have cellars bought Anderson shelters. These were do-.it-.yourself. structures with a wood framework, corrugated roof, and when assembled, were then imbedded deep as possible in a hole dug outside, usually in the back garden. Completely encased in sand bags with baffled entry, but these shelters were not entirely successful. They were alright in good weather but in heavy rains the floor became a muddy trench, not very attractive to visit in the middle of the night, especially for the frail or elderly, or small children. No plumbing, of course. In a heavy raid it was not unknown for an Anderson shelter to be totally lifted out of the ground, and deposited elsewhere, by force from the blast. The occupants sometimes, surprisingly, survived. We were still in the preparation phase and this period of inactivity was later referred to as the Phony War but it didn't last very long.

Meantime, I continued to attend Grammar School, in the town about five miles distant, named West Bromwhich. It had a great school, but tough, with long hours and a satchel, heavy with homework, to be lugged home every day. During the five required years attendance we covered many subjects, such as history, English, French, geography, math including algebra, geometry and chemistry, physics, biology, music, scripture and physical training plus, domestic science. Our illustrious teachers, stately in cap and gown, illustrious that is, except for one dreary, bored, and boring old humbug who made a languid stab at teaching us geography, yawning between his reading aloud in a dreary monotone, from the dullest old tomes in existence. He was disinterested himself and uninteresting to us! Looking around the classroom it was not unusual to see heads at rest on folded arms. His deficiencies were all the more obvious when, contrasted with other teachers who set a challenging pace and kept us up to the mark, sometimes even making it all enjoyable.

One very good teacher was professor Pat Caroll who taught us French, and was also endeared to us as father of the famous Madeline Caroll who starred in *The Thirty-nine Steps,* by Alfred Hitchcock. In order to achieve her fame she dared to run away from home to try to find a job in Hollywood we were told, although not by her Father who never spoke of this event.

Our school hours were from nine a.m. to four p.m with an hour for lunch, but added to that were three hours of homework, with a prep book for parents to validate each night, stating hours spent, on each designated subject. Very little time was left for larking about.

Me on RR line at War's onset

I was due to leave the Grammar School after exams, called matriculation, when it was usual to prepare for the next educational step, Uni (University) but my thoughts were already turning towards exchanging school uniform, for another kind of uniform, like enlisting in the forces, to do my bit for the war effort, but not yet. Sixteen was too young for that, so in between school on week-ends, and later a job, I took St. John's Ambulance courses in first aid, which I thought might be useful in an emergency. After that, I followed up by taking Red Cross nursing courses. Here was my chance to be active, to put in some long shifts on ward duty in a hospital about six miles away, after I was a certified as a Nurses Aid, that is. I liked the surgical ward best and thought I looked older in the uniform. Oh good! I didn't feel very old though, when on duty in the men's ward, bringing a patient a urinal, they recognized my green as grass status' and all broke into song, "ain't she sweet" accompanied by whistles resulting in my speedy departure to hide in the nurse's station, blushing from hairline to hemline.

The uniform of a white draped head-covering, blue dress and white apron with a big red cross on the bib, hadn't changed much since the first world-war, for Nurses Aids, and I quite liked the old fashioned aspect.Almost, a Florence Nightingale look. R.N's uniform was different and they also wore RN badges, special caps and a much coveted romantic, navy cape, with brass buttons and red lining.

One evening, after school, I had dinner and left for my volunteer stint of duty at Hallam Hospital, and arrived early after two uneventful bus rides. The eerie drone of the siren hadn't wailed its warning yet, as I entered by the staff gate.

The hospital itself was set inside an iron railing fence, about six feet high, spiked with forbidding spear-like tops, once gilded, but now a worn and gloomy black. One long L-shaped building lay well back from the road, with another similar building, situated behind it, separate in all respects and taller. Its roof loomed over that of the main hospital leaving it in shade, even on the brightest day. The well hidden building at the back was known as the Asylum, which it was.

Both buildings were concealed by a luxuriant wooded copse, completely hiding our back entrance, which was for the staff, nurses and volunteers. There was a narrow, curving, paved path snaking through the mini forest, from the entrance gate to a small clearing before the entry door, taking about ten minutes or so to traverse its length. This was where I went in.

Patients, visitors and doctors had their own entrance. As they turned off the main road they entered a secondary road, leading to the main entrance and beyond that, was the emergency entrance, after which, quite close by, came the car park.

I started down the path, no-one to be seen, or heard, except for the lonely hoot of our resident owl breaking the stillness. A sliver of a moon showed itself occasionally but soon, drifting dark clouds obscured all light, making it necessary to use my blacked out torch to see the path as I picked my way along, when out of the dark a tall figure of a man loomed up and stopped me. He was very upset, and urgently demanded to know where the gate was?. He seemed to think it had been moved, so I thought he had lost his sense of direction. He was so distraught, I turned around and took him back in sight of the entrance, and without another word, he disappeared through it. Evaporating like smoke up a chimney.

I wondered if he had received bad news at the hospital, but if so, what was he doing on this path, not near the visitor's entrance? I quickly forgot about it, as little groups of blue-cloaked nurses accompanied by a few policemen passed me, stepping off the path in order to pass, and obviously in a hurry, all talking at once. Some excitement was afoot.

Once inside the hospital, I heard what all the hubbub was about. A seriously disturbed, potentially dangerous, inmate from the asylum next door, had escaped that night, after hiding the fact that he had omitted to take his medication for some time. They had found his little cache, too late. By the time I related my strange encounter, and inadvertent aiding and abetting, a deranged and lost soul, he was long gone. I never heard the end of the story, or if he got clean away, but where would he go?

Time passed and my departure at night for the hospital became a source of extra worry for my parents and I knew it would have to come to an end, soon.

Before it did, later on in that year when air raids had begun in earnest, neither of my two buses was running, due to an air raid at night. Fire engines tending blazing buildings and rescue workers creating insurmountable barriers on our usual route meant that I must walk the six miles home, in pitch darkness beyond the fire's light, and during the raid alert, alone. Not quite alone, it seemed, as I heard heavy footsteps behind me which speeded up as I hurried to maintain a lead during a lonely stretch, where there were no buildings, but they got closer and closer. I speeded up even more to a trot with my heart doing the same, bent on staying ahead but losing ground, when none too soon, I saw a caped, figure standing in a sand-bagged doorway wearing a tall hat, and a badge, I thought he looked official. Hurrying, out of breath by now, I panted, "someone's following me." The Policeman stepped out of the door and aimed his small ray of light from his blacked out torch into the darkness but my follower had turned tail and was running full tilt, in the opposite direction. All we could see was a long dark coat, topped by dark hair, wearing a dangling scarf. trailing along behind him. Shaken and wobbly with relief, I was most grateful for a police escort home, another mile or so away. That had to be the last late night duty for me at Halam Hospital. It was a bit unnerving, to say the least.

Christmas Day had been quietly spent with aunts, uncles and cousins at our house. Not the usual game-playing, festive celebration of former years, but heartwarming, nevertheless. We speculated on which of us would be involved in military service and what roles we would play. Wynne, a step cousin in her early twenties was married to Harry Green, already serving on active duty in the Army. He kept his sense of humour despite the grimmest

Uncle Walter and son Richard

Richard's dad, mum and Richard, Aunt Muriel, mum's sister, her husband
and their son Jeffrey

Wynne, Aunt Nellie, Joyce and Richard as a new born baby

of battles, managing to evoke laughter in the midst of tears sometimes. A gifted raconteur. Later he fought in El Alamein, was captured and escaped, but that was yet to come.

On Boxing Day we had one last fling of a party on Copthall Rd where my Uncle Walter, Auntie Nellie and cousin Joyce lived. Uncle Walter, was a man of strong convictions, enthusiasms and also a well developed, irresistible sense of fun, never far from the surface. His wife, Auntie Nellie, who really preferred to be called Irene (we tried to remember but old habits die hard) was an ideal match for her spouse, I thought, She, with her delicate pink and white English rose complexion, was the soul of serenity. No matter what problems or irritations she may have endured, I never saw her moody or angry and when she laughed it was as if the mirth just tumbled out of her in helpless ripples. Catching!

I think cousin Joyce inherited some of the tranquility of her mother, and her pretty complexion She was also a very good and lasting friend, always there in a pinch, or readily available for fun. Whatever came along, she was willing to share.

Then, years later another boy cousin was added to the delight of the entire family, Richard Adams. He grew up to successfully run his own business and, using his expertise, spurred me on to write this saga. His help has been invaluable.

At that last party, all kinds of games were played including charades and at the end of the evening when we were all getting ready to leave, at the instigation of my Uncle, we were all directed to form a circle, for a farewell game. We were each given a hat, well, all but one that is. Like musical chairs with hats, I thought in anticipation, and why would that be fun?

Men and women were alternated and each wore appropriate hats. The music started and every person there was to use his right arm and hand only, to remove the hat of the person on his right, snatch it in fact, as the tempo increased, and jam it, on his or her, head. Hats were difficult to grab if you were short, and the person next to you was tall, and each of you only able to use one hand. It was difficult to place a floppy hat firmly on the head. Watching the people opposite, change hats from a man's dressy straw brimmer to a tin helmet, or women's rose trimmed, bonnet concoction on a man's head, or a trilby, or a too big bowler on a woman, covering her eyes, hair on end, hat askew was so comical it was hard to look away. Simultaneously, volatile Uncle Walter was mischievously picking up the tempo while egging on the pianist to do the same. "Faster," he said, "faster," with results funny enough to make a cat laugh. My Mother, whose hair had been coiffed that day before the party, usually was so well groomed, but now her hair resembled that of a frazzled golliwog. But good sport that she was, she played with determination, and vigor, keeping us laughing helplessly throughout. The sight of my uncle's disreputable old garden hat, adorned with old packets of seeds, atop her now wild, hairdo, was a vision to behold. The vision constantly changing as another hastily snatched hat was plopped in place, each funnier than the last. When the music stopped, you were out of the game, if hatless. Not a game to play if you expected to maintain your dignity. We travelled home spent with laughter, and putting any and all stress on hold, agreeing that it had been a night we would always remember.

The New Year was upon us and we wondered where it would lead. The Phony War was rapidly coming to a close.

3 – The Blitz and Beyond

The Real War

I CELEBRATED MY 16th birthday in April, just before the real war began in May.

Dunkirk

On May 10th, 1940 Hitler's Army invaded France. That same day Churchill became Prime Minister. France officially surrendered on May 14th 1940 though some of the French Army fought on after that. The Netherlands, Belgium and Luxembourg also were swallowed up by the German juggernaut on the same dates. At this point, most of Europe, including Poland and Austria were under the swastika. And Hitler fully expected England to come to terms. So sure was he, that he authorized orders for homecoming flags, bunting, and more swastika signs to be made, ready for a big celebration of total victory in Europe. All this to take place in Paris! Britain, however, had other plans.

Right on the heels of the French capitulation came the Battle of Dunkirk. The drama of the battle of Dunkirk began on May 26th. Not about to surrender to invading Germans, the British Army and Allies from France, Poland, Belgium, Austria and Netherlands were caught in a maneuver called the sickle cut, meaning they were trapped in a corridor to the sea, sixty miles deep' and forty miles wide, flanked on both sides by two massive German

Armies. Driven back as far as the Channel with no way out!

Those ships were not to be left to struggle alone, however. Churchill responded with destroyers and whatever shipping he could muster. The appeal went out over the air, and on the radio, for help rescuing the stranded soldiers and the response was at once, overwhelming and moving. Anyone on, or near the coast with a boat, went if they could possibly get there, some from as far away as Glasgow, which luckily was on the right coast for travelling south. Dad, was itching to go, but frustrated by his boat being on a river and as far inland as it could be, on the river Severn in Stourport with no way to transport a boat over land in time. Truly aggravated he followed wireless news with a faraway look in his eyes. In his mind, he was there, helping. A time of high drama!. All those unable to go were firmly glued to the wireless, eagerly following this turbulent, dramatic exodus.

The docks at Dunkirk harbour were badly damaged, but the strong east and west moles (sea walls) protecting the harbor could be used for landing some small craft. Bigger ships, not able to enter the shallows, were aided by flat bottomed boats and other small craft, ferrying back and forth. When there were not enough small boats to do this, there were long queues of men standing shoulder deep in ice cold water, waiting for hours to be picked up and transferred to bigger ships. Small craft were invaluable in this situation and some of them managed the round trip across the Channel more than once or twice.

Royal Navy Destroyers, French destroyers and other sizable craft were sent at once. In answer to the broadcast for help in Britain, the response was whole hearted from all those who owned any kind of craft.

There were civilians from all walks of life, eager, willing and ready to cross the Channel and rescue as many men as possible, heedless of strafing enemy aircraft overhead.

There were, fishing boats, pleasure cruisers, commercial boats, ferries, nineteen lifeboats from the Royal Navy Institute and The Merchant Marine, even the Isle of Man steam packet was there. In fact, almost anything that floated and could take passengers went, of course, there was the occasional refusal, It was a very dangerous mission and took guts. The smallest boat recorded was fourteen and a half feet. These intrepid volunteers made many round trips under fire, strafing, and threat of high explosive shells. Dutch flat bottomed coasters were ideal for ferrying men to or from the beach to the big ships lying offshore. On June 3rd It was decided by Captain Tennant in charge of evacuation that Operation Dynamo was complete, since the Germans were now a mere two miles away from Dunkirk. Too close for comfort.

Churchill was aware that under General Molinié, the remains of the once formidable French First Army of about 40,000 men were still there. It was they who fought on so heroically at the Siege of Lille, holding back seven divisions of the German Army, staving off an added assault on Dunkirk by the German Army, for four crucial days, during the evacuation. They were not to be forgotten so after that, another rescue took place. The Royal Navy ships were sent back on June 4th to rescue as many stoics in the rear guard as possible, resulting in a further lift off of 26,000 men.

Sadly, there were between 30,000 to 40,000 left to surrender, many from the British Expeditionary Force (B.E.F.) were taken prisoners of war, but still the rescue wasn't finished,but this was kept rather quiet. The Miracle of Dunkirk was officially over, but the spirit of Dunkirk will live on in many hearts. This Churchill dubbed to be "our finest hour." Not a victory but not a total rout either.

Ten days later the German's entered Paris on June 14th and Britain, despite the odds, again began withdrawing B.E.F. forces still left in France. Unfortunately, enormous quantities of machinery and arms had to be left behind but more important was the news that by June 25th 192,000 Allied personnel (144,000 British) were safely evacuated from French ports.

It was to take Britain and France six long years, of war together with Canadians, Poles Dutch, and other Allies to end it all. The first three years Britain and volunteers were virtually alone until 1943 when the United States thankfully added their considerable might in 1943 making a huge difference, but this was still in the future. The French though captured in May 1940 still fought on, in the Underground, known as the French Maquis, both sexes included. They commanded great respect from all who knew of their effectiveness, sheer visceral courage and heroism, and they kept up their dangerous and vital work until war's end. A few who were betrayed suffered terrible torture by the Gestapo or the SS.

Meanwhile, Hitler was being kept busy on the eastern front, however not too busy to begin what was soon known as the Battle of Britain, and on its heels came the Blitz, short for Blitzkrieg.

Translated, the Lightning War! Brittain now stood alone, holding the fort.

Battle for the sky: Spitfires and Hurricanes

This was the time Hitler chose to try to establish air supremacy, and this was the time the RAF, headed by Sir Hugh Dowding, decided not to let him. Our pilots were joined by Allies from France, Czechoslovakia, Poland, Canada, etcetera. Fierce fighting began in the SE of England and sometimes, desperate and dramatic dog fights were seen and heard by those below, as relentless waves of German bombers, accompanied by fighters, swarmed over in droves. Valiant young men, flying Hurricanes and Spitfires were called upon to "scramble" again and again, whether rested or not, usually not, often after spending long hours in the air, snatching short naps when, where and if, at all possible. Danger spots were everywhere, but the SE corner was notorious, becoming known as 'Hell's corner."Here some of the bloodiest battles for survival took place in the air, generally over the ocean.

Details of note will follow about the development of two of the most used, and relied upon, flying machines, the Hurricane and the Spitfire, which ultimately played a role in the survival of Britain. Radar was vitally important here, in engaging the enemy early, before they reached their target, and was then comparatively new to the Allies. Air supremacy was the goal of Hitler before launching an invasion, but Britain 's RAF was not going to relinquish that title, despite the ongoing struggle to maintain it.

Flying Hurricanes bore a bigger share of the burden against the Luftwaffe, but Spitfires designed to be short range interceptor fighters, were also a high performance machine, had a lower attrition rate and higher, victory to loss ratio, than Hurricanes. Pilots loved this single seater aeroplane. It was originally designed to have a Rolls Royce Merlin engine, but was deemed sturdy enough to use the Rolls Royce Griffin instead. Changes were made under the wing structure as production increased. RJ Mitchell designed a thinner, more elliptical wing, giving it a higher top speed. He continued to refine and modify the Spitfire until his death in 1937 and Joseph Smith continued after that when more Spitfire modifications were made until war's end, and afterwards. The largest Spitfire factory was in Birmingham and was responsible for producing 12,129 of them, at the rate of 320 per month, contributing more than half of the overall total of 20,000 final count. Obviously, one good reason for targeting Birmingham during the Blitz!

Various versions of the Hurricane were produced, and a model modified for use aboard ship was known as the Sea Hawk, then another, the Hurri-Cat was a catapult launched machine, which in turn was followed by the MK2a providing better speed. In 1939 a constant speed rotor 1 propeller was developed for even greater speed. During the Battle of Britain, Hurricanes were credited with 60% of the air victories, and also served in all theatres of the war.

In the beginning the RAF had only thirteen squadrons, but by 1944 over 14,583 Hurricanes were built, 1,400 of which, were built in Canada. Pilots liked it for its simple, easy handling, reliability and stable gun platform. It became a good plane for night flying, due to its superior visibility.

Those who flew either of these great planes against formidable odds, overcoming relentless and continuous battering, those who barely escaped, with hideous burns, twisted, broken limbs, those who were shot down in water, and those who didn't come back at all were specially recognized and thanked by Mr Churchill in his famous speech. "Never, in the field of human endeavour have so many owed so much, to so few." He spoke for us all. The drama of life and death was played out so rapidly in the air and those beneath had a ringside seat. Over the ocean away from the shore, only other flyers bore witness. The Battle of Britain, as such, lasted from July to October 1940, but bombing continued on and on long after that. In London bombing didn't cease till war's end was declared in 1945.

Not having established his goal of air supremacy, Hitler decided to delay Operation Sea Lion, code name for his invasion plans, until he managed to do so, and he did continue to try, but never quite made it.

It was during this period that my parents responded to Lord Beaverbrook's appeal to start a Spitfire fund. It was entitled the "Women of Oldbury Spitfire Fund" but men were also huge supporters. Dad was appointed Treasurer, and did a fine job we were told.

My Mother tirelessly raided all closets for items to be sold for the cause, inveigling us "to give till it hurt", soon to be followed by whist drives, lotteries, concerts, anything to raise money.

Items in my closet had to be labeled "don't touch" or they might vanish, only to re appear on some stranger before I had time to miss them. She got away with a major haul before I caught her red-handed, and declared a ban. She became very active on the Board and helped design the small silver pin resembling the Spitfire which could be worn on the lapel. Of course, there was a minimum sum required, amounting to two shillings, but that was quite reasonable, for sterling. The pin itself became a proud emblem, almost a status symbol. It was an elegant understatement and could be worn by either a male or female equally well, which made it appealing.

There was a big dinner dance at the Town Hall when at last the target was reached. Our Mother was specially honoured, along with two others, for their extraordinary contributions to the cause.

It was fun to watch her dress for the event. She wore a striking pre-war golden brown silk velvet sheath, ankle length and beautifully cut. She wore it well, and had the figure for it. The bodice had a hand-made French lace appliqué, creating a vee neckline, and a single strand of pearls added the final touch. Just seeing her so dressed reminded us all of a time, when there was no war and we all went to parties, where long gowns weren't unusual. She looked so lovely and young. Well she was!

Since London had been bombed earlier in 1939, a fate which was to continue until the end of the war, plans for evacuating children in danger zones were already under way, yet it wasn't until August 9th 1940 that the siren sounded in Oldbury for real. The bombing of nearby Birmingham started then, and didn't end until April 23 1943. Spitfires were being made there, among other war necessities, so it was a prime target. Almost three years of pounding ensued.

Hitler was still determined to achieve the air superiority he felt he needed to win this war and with that in mind the Battle of Britain began in earnest. We found ourselves in the thick of things.

Deep asleep, one night, in early August I was jolted awake by the determined tweaking of my big toe, forcing reluctant wakefulness. In a quiet voice competing with the wail of the siren, on it's second wail now, my Mother was saying, " time to put on something warm and go down to the cellar" Norma, already in dressing gown and slippers was at the door with book and flashlight. Thinking quickly, "could I wear my siren suit?" "Yes, but hurry up. Come on." All decked out in my new suit sneaking a look in the mirror, I trooped down behind the others feeling grateful for carpet underfoot on both stair flights. It was cold down there even with blankets and tiny electric fire, but we made tea and listened for bombs till the "all clear."Dad was on duty as chief Air Raid Warden, already out in the streets where his duties included directing people into air raid cellars, if they were caught in a raid, also helping with rescue work after an explosion, or supervising Spotters. Spotters were brave souls of both sexes who went up on roof tops during a raid to watch for incendiaries, and deal with them when they landed. A guaranteed fire starter, if left to burn unhindered.

Volunteers were equipped with stirrup pumps, a bit like a bicycle pump, but containing chemicals effective in putting out fires, often used in connection with sandbags. Needless to say, dangerous work especially if flares dropped in multiples, then it was advisable to move."faster than forked lightning," said one worker."

No bombs that night so an hour or two later we trudged back up the 'wooden hill' to try and get some sleep before the new day began. After a few nights of repeat performances, loss of sleep began to make itself felt, so it was decided that beds would be transferred to the cellar along with some comfortable chairs, twin beds for Norma and me, and a double for Mom and Dad. A dividing curtain creating two separate sections gave us some privacy. We planned to go to bed at the regular time, and whether the siren went or not we were in a position to sleep through, if we could. At this time, the brick ledge on the far wall was stocked with items such as a tea kettle, china cups and saucers, plates and supplies included tea cocoa biscuits, plus a few cans of soup.

One night we barely noticed the sirens wavering blast, since it had become a nightly occurence but we did notice the incredible roar of a never ending stream of bombers overhead, vibrating in our ears. A reporter commented next day that it looked as if the sky was lined with aluminium. The determined heavy thrum, thrumming of aircraft much closer, lower and more ominous, assaulted our senses, interspersed with the blast and vibration of explosions all around us. Bombs were falling in continuous concussive thuds. We heard the pounding boom and crack of the ack-ack, as if it were happening outside in the street. We found out later, it wasn't very far from it. Those who were outside saw ribbons of tracer shells slicing through the air overhead. Enveloping noise continued to surround us, swallowing us in sound, drowning out everything else. Incessant repetition followed by palpable vibration. A noise heard deep inside your head, but felt deep inside your gut, and through the soles of your feet. Bombs dropping, some close, others not so close, Birmingham, probably. An un-rhythmic beat of heavy thuds, grinding into the earth, then the booming explosions, assaulted the ears. It went on and on throughout the night and just before dawn, the sound of empty planes meant that enemy planes were finally on their way home, engines droning evenly, almost purring, back to base.

We soon realized German bombers sounded heavily laden on their incoming journey over Britain, creating a sombre, steady, throbbing beat to those of us down below. On return the engines sound lightened up as they dropped their missiles, changing the tone altogether when they turned for home. We knew immediately whether the danger was over or not, and became experts in sound detection. When bombs were headed in our direction we learned to count to ten, as each began dropping, just so that we knew whether to hold our breath for more, or if that was the last one for that particular plane. Then we knew they were headed back to base. Time to breathe, turn over and sleep a bit more, or have a cup of tea if sleep was elusive.

In a massive raid like this one, we just waited for the volume of sound to stop, but merciful silence had been a long time in coming. This was one of the three worst bombing raids to affect us in Oldbury, even though Birmingham was the main target. The other two raids followed on the next two consecutive nights.

Our town was five miles from Coventry where munitions and aircraft were being manufactured. In the other direction lay Birmingham, also barely five miles away and another city making war materiel. Both cities produced significant supplies of munitions vital to the war effort so they were primary targets, and since we were on their path we got the overflow. We were also producing war materials in Oldbury, of course.

It was a frightening time but we bolstered our spirits by using humour as a weapon against fear and the general morale was impressive. People in the street, in queues, in shops on the train and in school, vied to tell the most harrowing tales, about eating dinner in a cupboard under the stairs, when they saw an incendiary, zap down the chimney. Luckily, with sand bags standing by it was possible to put it out, then back under the stairs to finish dinner. These tragic-comic stories of flying muddy Anderson shelters or whatever, were all told in a strange mix of jollity and horror, each trying to outdo the other. Not a bit deluded by the ever present dangers, but somehow assuming this was just a phase to be waited out with as much equanimity as possible. When houses vanished in smoke, neighbours appeared out of the rubble to help whoever was left.

Birmingham is the second largest city in the U.K. and the third most heavily bombed during the war. The first being London, and it received the relentless pounding of all missiles, then next in severity, was Liverpool. War materials of all kinds were being manufactured in Birmingham. Fisher and Ludlow made wings for Lancasters also shell casing and bombs, Reynolds made tubings and Spitfires, and other companies were responsible for carburetors, plastic components and small arms, like rifles and Sten guns. 100% of all Sten guns were made in Birmingham.

After Coventry was bombed so drastically on November 14, 1940 there was another major raid by bombers on November 19 who attacked Birmingham with high explosives, parachute mines and incendiaries, resulting in heavily damaged factories, trapping hundreds of workers. Heroic rescues abounded, resulting in medals for at least one member of the Home Guard and an outstanding electrician also received an award for bravery. Other services did their magnificent work without the recognition of a medal but acts of ordinary bravery were quite common, and unsung. Naturally production at the factories was delayed, after being hit until repairs could be made. In that one night 1,852 tons of bombs were dropped and 800 people killed with over 2,300 injured. But there was more to come.

Next night the bombers were back, starting 600 or so fires and more damage. Once more the sirens went heralding another wave on the third consecutive night. This time 3/5 of the city's main water supply was lost, forcing the fire department to draw water from city canals. Brigades from nearby towns also helped get fires under control. Utilities like, electricity and gas were also badly impaired and were a great disruption.

There was no raid on the fourth night which thankfully gave engineers time to repair the water mains and tend to other most urgent needs.

A period of nightly bombing began with daytime raids interspersed and this became an increasing reality and then spasmodically ongoing until April 1943. Schools were disrupted when school buses couldn't get through the streets. Fires were often still raging from the night before and cordoned off. If a raid was in progress while you were en route, you could either head for the nearest shelter or continue on at your own risk. In a very bad raid the wardon would insist on getting people off the streets and school children would be herded to shelter first, until the all clear sounded. Getting to school and home again was getting to be a bit of a bother I thought. Every day, a different route! The longest of all the raids occurred on December 11th when 278 bombers blasted away until dawn. They left France, reached the target then returned in relays to drop 25,000 incendiaries causing widespread damage industrially and residentially. This lasted thirteen hours and when they left in the early morning, they left behind many buildings in ashes. Far too many became homeless.

On one of those follow up raids, they hit the wrong nearby town by mistake. As raids continued the BBC never once mentioned Birmingham by name, merely referring to it as a city in the Midlands. It is estimated that, 302 factories and 239 businesses, plus hundreds of homes were destroyed as well as other buildings, and many more were heavily damaged. Later, between November 19 and 28 a further 20,000 lost their homes. And this was the city where my new job lay!

Children under twelve were asked to consult their parents about the possibility of being evacuated from our area. Some to America, where there were many willing hosts, or instead to outlying country areas in Britain. Norma was not keen to be shipped out, but didn't like the nightly vigil either, so reluctantly took her shots in preparation for a big move to safety.

It was an opportune time for her to join her friends who were ready to be evacuated to a country house near Kinver, in a different county. Such a pretty area with many unusually lovely views to be enjoyed. Kinver Edge itself, a beauty spot of note. It provided the onlooker with an overview of a deep valley with miles of open country. A vista of grassy slopes, abundant with wild flowers, sprinkled with all season gorse, broadcasting bright gold florets like rays of sunshine over its neighbours, met the eye. The village was sparsely populated with a small school available nearby, and it all seemed ideal. Promising a coveted sanctuary for the children far away from the noise and ever present danger of the Blitz!

Norma completed her shots (inoculations), packed her clothes, small treasures, necessary ration card, and suddenly, she was ready, albeit protesting that she was old enough to stay at home really, but that discussion was old, and it was time to go. Gas mask strap on her shoulder, suitcase in hand, and she was off amid teary farewells. She looked so little as we watched her slowly mount the bus steps, dragging her school satchel. The small jitney, soon loaded with its precious cargo, wasted no time chugging away from the curb, as we waved, and it was soon gone. Boom, out of sight in a flash: it all seemed to happen in the time it took to blink, as we still stood there, eyes glazed, looking into space. Only three of us now to hold sway! I wasn't prepared for the big void feeling that night, as we descended into the cellar. Three of us, quickly dwindling to two as Dad donned his tin helmet, in response to the familiar wail of the siren, and was on his way.

Two weeks later, petrol saved for the occasion, we set off to visit Norma in her new home and to take her out to tea. It was about 40 miles away, so not too far for the round trip, if we weren't caught in a raid on the journey home.

The house was located in a pretty spot and finding it was easy. Squarish, well proportioned, a pinky beige, brick built structure sat upon a small knoll, with a curved driveway winding around the front. Here the attractive landscaping, having taken years to grow in harmony with the building, mellowing through the years, had become a part of it. Today it, was adorned by rays of sunlight, shimmering through the leaves as we approached. Nearby, a meadow fresh and sparkling after last night's rain, became a backdrop of bright green, pin pointing the handful of wild red campian and blue chicory, scattered like punctuation marks here and there, all in vibrant colour.

Most of all we drew sighs of relief realizing we were here in this village devoid of any signs of the Blitz, no gaping holes with piles of rubble to be navigated, like those we had left behind just hours earlier. Another world.

We were greeted at the door by the retired Colonel and spouse, Mrs Broome. Childless themselves, they had daringly undertaken the care of three children, Norma, her friend Denie, and one other little boy. A rather shy Scottish lad, unimaginatively called Scotty, with a strong lilting accent and rolling r's. Denie on the other hand was outgoing, long legged and a blue eyed bundle of mischief, with straight shoulder length, toffee coloured hair, at present shining like burnished copper. Then Norma, her brunette hair pixie cut, quite capable of her share of mischief, usually revealed twinkly, hazel eyes, but not to-day! To-day was serious, and definitely not a time to twinkle. Being evacuated was all very well but she missed her family mightily, she said, leaving us in no doubt, about her feelings, and indeed we got it!

Inside the reception hall, we saw a graceful staircase disappearing into the upper regions and there was only time to exchange a few words with the Broomes, before the children, anxious to show us their rooms, escorted us aloft, Norma in the lead. Walking behind her, I noticed how skinny her legs looked in her brown tights and wondered when she got so thin, as I swallowed a lump in my throat.

The house was large with two upstairs wings, each of them housing bedrooms and bathrooms, and each wing positioned at either end of the house was connected by one long hall, running the width of the house. The children occupied one end, and the Broomes, the other.

In the children's wing, two girls shared a twin bedded room, and Scotty had his own bedroom close by, with a shared bathroom between the three. They were glad to have each other's company and got along well, so that was a plus we agreed.

We left Denie and Scotty to await their parents arrival, while we took Norma sight seeing. Driving along the lanes we found the countryside as lovely as we remembered it pre-war and headed for Kinver Edge, an old favourite of ours, then we parked and walked along the rim.

Looking down over the edge, we saw the beautiful canyon that we knew, carpeted with familiar wild flowers, opening at our feet. A tree, noisy with sparrows, interspersed with the cackle of a crow, reminded us that we didn't hear any birds any more in Oldbury. Where had they all gone? We went from the Edge to the top of an imposing hill known as Barr Beacon to take in the view, where three surrounding counties, spreading out beneath us, met the eye. Beneath us lay steep daisy covered slopes, and suddenly, wordlessly, we were all overcome with the spontaneous urge to breathlessly race each other to the bottom, so over the top we went hurtling down., at breakneck speed. Laughing and panting, feeling more alive, as we rolled among the daisies at the bottom, the war seemed a long way away at that moment. Both parents, flushed by the sun and exercise looked less careworn than I had seen them since the bombing began. Our short time together was all too brief. With reluctance we drove Norma back to her sanctuary, and afterwards left for our home in the cellar, feeling much improved by our short escape in the free from sirens, country air.

"On the other hand, back at the ranch", sometime later, long after the parents had left, the children in Kinver were feeling a bit flat and far from sleepy, so decided it would be a good idea to perk themselves up a bit, and create some entertainment. A game of hide and seek would be the very thing, they thought. Norma's turn to hide, she climbed into the free standing oak wardrobe among the winter coats, but after a while, when no seekers appeared it began to get a bit airless in there, so wrestling with the lock to get out, with no result, she leaned heavily against the door. Well, the shifting balance of weight tipped the wardrobe forward, door still closed, and it fell with a mighty crash onto the bed nearby. The loud bang, accompanied by Norma's frantic cries for help got the attention of her chums who rushed in kicking over a used potty as they came, and full tilt down the hall came the Broomes. The Colonel, hair awry in floppy nightshirt, and dressing gown bursting open, followed by his hand wringing wife, her face creamed for the night and slipperless, sliding on the sticky floor, they skidded to a stop and took in the situation at a glance.

It was "all hands to the pump" to achieve a rescue. Huffing and puffing the motley crew pushed and shoved, slipping and sliding trying for traction until finally the recalcitrant wardrobe was vertical again. At last, a disheveled little girl with skinny legs fell out, stifling her sobs of relief, trying for a smile but not quite making it.

Order was restored, sheets changed, floor mopped with no major reprimands, greatly to the credit of the Colonel and his wife, and everyone glad to go back to bed, the three culprits looking a bit subdued, included. The Broomes, hopefully, wished them goodnight again before departing to the peace of their own quarters. As the door closed behind them, the funny side suddenly hit Norma. She started to chuckle, then burst into side splitting belly laughter, holding her sides, fit to burst, until between splutters she could explain that the ridiculous aspect had suddenly hit her. The thought of their usually, dignified hosts, in their dishabille sliding around on a suspiciously wet, stinky floor, in their nightclothes, hair on end, followed by the inelegant pushing and shoving bottoms in the air, to get the wardrobe upright again, would stay with her long after life returned to normal.

Picturing the scene again, the others began to remember more details and the slapstick quality of the entire proceedings, convulsed them all anew. A fit of the giggles ensued that resulted in side aching howls of gleeful laughter as they recalled someone's foot landing in the chamber pot, as the struggle progressed. Hours later, having had the best laugh since their evacuation, finally, finally, they slept.

The Broomes had coped nobly, but alas, they weren't Mom and Dad. Two more weeks elapsed and time to revisit Kinver again. On arrival we didn't have to wait at all. Norma popped out of the front door, like a shell from a cannon, talking as she came and when she was within range she wasted no time pleading her case, but straight away announced that she wanted to come home, "right now, bombs or not", she said adding that she needed to be with her family and would rather take her chances with us than try to sleep, miles away, wondering all the while what was happening to us in the danger zone. Our parents were not taken completely by surprise as they had heard similar statements before she left home and on the whole decided that a month's trial was enough for now. The decision having been made we made our way back to the Broomes to express our gratitude for all their kindnesses, scooped up Norma and her belongings, said our goodbyes adding a little thank-you gift, and were on our way to whatever lay ahea, for us all.

Once, long ago this town of Oldbury that we lived in, had been a small rural village, predating Saxon times in the early 800's, with farms all around. The Tame valley and areas north remained part of the Abbey and included Halesowen also Halesowen Abbey. Later in the reign of Henry VIII in 1538, came the dissolution of the monasteries, making it a separate entity,. Plain Halesowen now, with no other attachments. As time passed, an important coach road ran through it, starting in the Black Country and proceeding on its way to Birmingham, via Oldbury and travelling westward, whereupon it became a turnpike, with a brick built toll-house. This became the Birmingham Road, the road upon which we lived. Up the same road, stood the Talbot Inn, an old coaching house, used by all travelers and standing firmly alone, still in use but looking a bit the worse for wear these days.

The Black Country, so named for the sooty smoke filled air, in an area where heavy industry occurred, but this did not include Oldbury or West Bromwich where the air was luckily, free of taint.

In the 18th century canals were built all over the Country, plying their different cargoes from place to place. Oldbury's canal transported steel and coal etcetera. Coal from the Black Country, of course! This was in a time when Oldbury was considered very desirable, as it had good housing, good schools, piped water, deep sewerage and a municipal gas supply. It was also, most attractive, with tree lined streets and a park. It still had all of these attributes, including fresh air, but alas did not continue to grow.

Gradually the boat people began to disappear. After the canals were filled in, the town went from a population of approximately 30,000 to less than 500 but that was yet to come, in the 70s. Right now, we were still highly desirable.

The family premises were situated on a hill where there was a bridge, once known as Bustle Bridge, spanning the canal beneath. Still in existence was a link to the so-called Black Country where coal mining continued to thrive, to be transported on long skinny wood barges, later known as the long boats. They did possess some engine power but were often towed by a rope, along the banks of the canal, courtesy of a donkey, or boatman, travelling through towns and rural areas, to their destination. They passed through some beautiful scenery, and at the locks, some exceedingly fine inns sprang up where boat people could meet other boat people and dining was a pleasure. People living on barges, especially the women, wore a kaleidoscope of colours, usually bright patterned voluminous skirts, tightly nipped in at the waist achieved with the help of a sturdy laced up corset. With everything thus propelled towards the top, they wore a kind of Hungarian embroidered blouse with low neckline and pretty sleeves. Quite a memorable look! A tiny waist, décolletage, and bright colours caught the eye.

Not to be outdone, the men wore colourful shirts with a belt or sash at the waist, looking quite dashing but spoiling the effect somewhat with a variety of old hats, perched atop dark curly hair, usually. They reminded me of the Romany gypsies we used to see sometimes, and like them, they always stayed with their own people. As the bombing became more severe they seemed to disappear. I don't remember seeing any boat people after the 1940 bombing began. Many canals were drained and filled later on in the 1970's, thus ending an era in Oldbury, leaving the town rather forlorn, I thought. My brief visit after the war was little more than a drive through, I had no desire to extend it. Everything seemed so run down, and completely changed.

Norma, was back with the family in 1940 where we reverted to being "in residence" in the cellar once more. It was business as usual, the sirens having signaled an air raid in progress, we were awaiting developments while listening to explosions.

One night in particular, from my little hidey hole in bed peering out from under the eiderdown, my eyes focused on the tea tray, opposite, on the far wall, with the canned assortment alongside it. I watched it all rattling away, sounding as ferocious and repetitive as a machine gun. I had begun using that brick ledge and its contents as a reliable barometer to indicate the severity of a raid, and when it clattered the loudest sometimes in accompaniment with the steel lid on the escape hatch, I knew things didn't look rosy. This was one of those nights.

Tonight looked anything but rosy. The ledge's contents continued to emit a cacophony of sound and at the height of it all, joining the symphony, came the surprising sound of a piano trilling the length of the key board. My mother, unaware that no human hand had touched those keys, asked irritably, "who would even think of playing a piano on a night like this? Of course it was caused by the blast of bombs as they dropped. She got a weak chuckle from both of us.

We lay listening to all the conflicting sounds, feeling the blast ourselves now and then, silently thinking anxious thoughts. Stretched out in bed, stiff as a whalebone corset, toes curled, fingers crossed, my eye settled on the escape hatch, waiting and wondering, posing questions I probably did'nt want answered. Wondering if we would be able to get it open in a pinch? How could we, if the house fell on it first? All three stories of it!

My fearful thoughts were interrupted with a brief respite, of sorts, as we heard Dad returning unexpectedly, followed by men's voices, asking if he could "manage to stand up now", and to" just rest."A bit alarming, but we didn't have long to let our imagination run riot, imagining the worst in the few seconds it took, for two wardens to escort him downstairs. It was a relief to see him, alive and breathing, though wan and hobbling, but in one piece and ready to tell his story. The blast of a nearby bomb had hurled him off his feet, landing him in a covered brick passageway, either breaking, or spraining, his rapidly swelling ankle. We didn't know which yet, and it had inflicted a few bloody facial bruises as he hit the surface. He looked a mess, and as pale as candle wax. Mom, ever calm in a crisis, decreed a nice cup of tea and a tot of whiskey in it, was definitely indicated. It didn't fix it, but it helped bring back his colour and restored his twinkle.

I decided, here was an ideal opportunity to practice my St John's Ambulance training, but strangely enough Dad opted to have someone with experience diagnose him first. A bit disappointed, I thought he was missing a good bet, but consoled myself with the thought of being allowed out of the cellar during a night raid, to summon help. It was after midnight by now and still dark. No moon, but no rain either, just the deep blackness of night. Black as tar in fact.

Adrenaline flowing, delighted to be let loose, I emerged from the gloom and couldn't see a thing. My small blacked out torch was of little help, allowing a mere whisper of light through the slit so I resorted to feeling my way along the walls and eerily across someone's face. Oops! Flummoxed, I apologized, and discovered the owner of the face was an embarassed young Spotter whose dark clothes made him a part of the night. He said he was waiting his turn to climb up to the roof above ready for incendiaries. Continuing on, without feeling any more faces, I reached a sandbagged area which I took to be an entrance so poking away I managed to locate a concealed doorway. The building I sought was only three doors away but felt like three miles. The baffled entry was built so that no light would be apparent from above. No keen eyed bomb dropper would ever spy a chink of light from this doorway, I thought, as I mastered my complex ingress.

Once inside, a discreet sign proclaiming "St John's First Aid Post" was displayed at the head of a flight of stairs with an arrow pointing down to the cellar beneath. Descending quickly, my eyes first fell upon a large Wagnerian lady, with bust to match, stationed behind a desk exuding a powerful presence of officialdom, so she topped my list and I headed straight to her. Sure enough, she was the lady in charge, and as my tale unfolded, she took copious notes while I fidgeted impatiently, anxious to fulfill my mission. Consulting her log, she announced that she could come at once, then picking up a little black bag at her feet, we were suddenly upstanding and on our way. Weaving through a cluster of air Raid wardens and a nurse or two, all relaying or receiving information, I followed the leader, who strode Brunhilde-like through the baffle, and over the sandbags, flinging aside any obstacles in her path in order to reach my father in jig time.

Apparently they knew each other quite well as they were on the same Civilian Defence (C.D.) post together. She was Lillie-Annie to Dad, Doctor Smith to me. Dad, after she left, gave me an account of her remorseless strapping of his painfully sprained ankle as he gritted his teeth in silent agony, I nobly refrained from any comment about my gentle hands and undoubted skill, an opportunity missed etc.

After delivering Dr Smith on her errand of mercy, I retraced my steps taking my time to absorb the scene before me. I was astounded! A dramatic change had taken place in the short interval and where there had been impenetrable inky, gloom merely half an hour earlier, the sky was now bright with light, almost blinding, in contrast to the total black out only a short while ago. Was it daylight already?

Above us, the sky was now filled with small bundles of flickering white flames festooning the air like small snowflakes, slowly descending to earth. No wind that night disturbed their progress. It was alight with all the drama of an opera in progress. Navy or black silhouettes were the human figures seemingly floating in harmony as excitement mounted, all against a backdrop of this sensational sky. It was memorable and I was never to see anything like it again.

How pretty it was I said, aloud but a nearby ARP warden left no doubt about his sentiments. 'Goehring's Bread Baskets, you mean," he said. They were of course, the "pretty" but flaming incendiaries which were dangerously dropping en masse. He shouted orders as the air soon filled with similar cries, for "more Spotters on the roof, FAST! "Need more stirrup pumps here!" "Get sandbags over there, straight away! Quick!" "Up on the roof FAST!." Searchlights criss-crossed looking for planes, the ack-ack, was sounding off, and I longed to be helping to do something more active to help in this busy scene, not to go back to skulking in the cellar. But I had no choice in the matter! Unwillingly, it was back to the cellar for me, just in time to hear a strange raid story about an A.R.P. warden. It seemed this man was reluctant to fasten the chin strap on his tin helmet during an air raid since he had a stiff neck and was uncomfortable, but his cohorts persuaded him it was in his own best interests to fasten it anyway, so at the last minute he complied. When the blast hit him from a bomb at close quarters, he was flung sideways along with his partner, but was killed instantly and his partner next to him survived with just a few bruises. Apparently, the chin strap snapped his neck when he fell. A phrase coined specially for quirks like this is "his number was on it." Not much comfort, I suppose, but perhaps it helped alleviate the guilt felt by the do-gooders who had talked him into fastening it.

Odd stories abounded and another such was a tale told by a rescue worker we knew. He told us that sometimes, complete sections of a bombed building would be left standing, virtually intact and one night he saw a perfect example of that. A strange cubelike structure, part of a building with chimney still attached, stood alone virtually unscathed, as it stood in the wasteland where other buildings had vanished like rabbits from a conjuror's top hat, leaving only a hole and rubble behind in its emptiness. A forgotten edifice, the roof covered in glass fragments sparkling in the sun, was almost pretty, an isolated example of desolation standing in the crater where a group of houses had been just a few hours ago. It was a sentinel, left to stand in mute protest–a solitary structure in a now deserted patch of damaged, useless land on what was once there was a neighbourhood street, teeming with life.

Now, a pile of rubble covered the entrance, blocking what might have been a doorway. Thinking that there might still be casualties inside or even a body, the rescue worker took his fire axe and chopped his way in. Right there in front of him was an astonishing sight. An old couple sat at ease in their rocking chairs, rocking placidly back and forth in unison, only mildly surprised to see rescuers. One ancient, knitting, and the other, dozing, both very deaf. They were aware that there had been an air raid but thought it must be over by now and they were ready to go to bed but "thank-you for dropping in," they said. They couldn't believe their ears to learn that there was no more house. No more stairs to take them to their bedroom. A closed door at the bottom of the stairs had concealed the evidence of dust and debris. This account was written up in the newspapers, much to the empathetic amusement of all of us who spent time in air raid shelters. In fact, I wondered about it enough to go and see the site for myself, as it wasn't too far removed from us, and found it exactly as described, without the inmates.

As our lives continued in much the same pattern, it struck me then that the abnormal becomes the norm if repeated often enough. How strange to become used to wailing sirens, sleeping in a cellar despite the noise, living on a restricted diet, hearing the ack-ack and watching searchlights etc., it all became routine.

Norma, at an early age, aced the entrance exam to my former Grammar School and had already begun her first term in the Junior School all business like in her school uniform, while I, on the other hand had just finished training at the Comptometer School in Birmingham. I hoped this would enhance my math skills and be useful to me when applying to join the Forces. My secret plan!.

I was offered a choice of jobs at the comptometer school, including a teaching post which gave my ego a lift, but decided instead to accept the offer of a big fashion company in the city centre to work in their offices and was due to start in November. However, as it transpired Birmingham was under siege just then, so the date was postponed till early in 1941.

After Coventry was bombed so drastically, on November 14 1940, just two days later, Birmingham was again re-visited, and this was a major raid, using high explosives, parachute mines and incendiaries, resulting in heavily damaged factories trapping hundreds of workers in the debris. Heroic rescues were made by ordinary mortals, "just doing their jobs," they said. Medals were given to at least one member of the Home Guard also one electrician, and a few others received awards for bravery. Many services did magnificent work, without medals or recognition, but acts of every day bravery were quite common then, and often went unsung, except by one or two witnesses nearby, or perhaps those on the receiving end of an unreported rescue. This became another norm.

In that one night alone, 1,852 tons of bombs were dropped on Birmingham and 800 people were killed with 2,300 injured. But there was more to come.

Next night they were back, starting 600 or more fires, and inflicting further damage. Once more the mournful drone of the siren blared its warning heralding another wave on the third consecutive night. This time more than half of Birmingham city's main, water supply was lost, forcing the fire department to withdraw water from the canals. Brigades from nearby towns helped get fires under control, working all hours, without sleep. Utilities like electricity and gas were badly impaired, causing a great disruption to industries, schools and families, alike. Then, at last, a breather, when there was no raid forthcoming on the fourth night, thankfully allowing engineers a chance to repair the water mains and tend to other urgent needs. By then there were many, homeless needing to be rehoused

Further raids followed at intervals throughout the year and onwards till April 1943. The lengthiest raid occurred on December 11th 1940 when a total of 278 bombers blasted away, targeting battle scarred Birmingham until dawn. Bombers left France, did their worst then returned in relays giving no respite, and dropping 25,000 incendiaries causing widespread damage both industrially and residentially. This lasted a total of thirteen hours. When finally they left in the early morning, leaving behind countless buildings in ashes, again great numbers of people were suddenly homeless. It is estimated that 302 factories were destroyed, hundreds of houses, and 239 miscellaneous structures badly damaged. Sometime later in November between the 19th and 28th a further 20,000 lost their homes. Unimaginable! And this was to be the city where my new job lay! At this rate it would mean I would be home in the cellar at night and even in a worse plight, in daylight. Who in his right mind would choose to work in Birmingham, I wondered? On the other hand, surely now there was nothing left to bomb?

As raids continued the BBC never mentioned Birmingham by name, merely referring to it as a town in the Midlands, so as not to confirm the target to the enemy. On one of those raids they had made a mistake and hit a wrong town close by.

Christmas had come and gone in a blur and we were still there. Daytime bombing had dwindled, so, daring fate, I proceeded to my new job finding it very interesting and I liked it. Although there were some daytime raids, nights were much worse but I had left the city by then, as a rule. Usually the journey by bus or car into the city on a straight run took less than half an hour but after a raid, the roads were fraught with problems and it took more than double that amount of time, due to unexploded bombs, fires etc so it was necessary to leave before eight in the morning.

One bright morning, sun shining for a change, I took my seat upstairs as usual on the double decker bus, and off we set to navigate diversions and obstacles along the way. Each day, a different route. Today being no exception we dodged fire hoses snaking across our path as firemen were still endeavouring to put out the last smoldering embers left from the previous night's fires. Rescue workers working in the rubble were making sure there was no-one still alive and needing help, looking carefully through the rubble to be sure no bodies or parts thereof were hidden there. Ambulances were on the scene 'in case.'

Bomb sites were taped off where possible and often we had to drive up onto the verge of a taped area, circumventing still functioning fire hoses and other rescue paraphernalia. Watching the devastation left behind after the last night's raid from my vantage point on the bus, was a sobering experience at best.

Our bus completed another circuitous turn and was back on the road again when we were halted by police and rescue workers, all covered in dust, and helmets spattered with lumps of white plaster. Some workers appeared to be dripping wet, from top to toe. Odd! We sat in our seats quietly still, waiting, and our driver turned off the engine. All eyes swiveled to focus on happenings outside, to find out what was holding us up. Looking across the road and beyond we could see a great crater in the ground between two, three story buildings, and realized a house must have stood there. It had been removed as neatly as a pulled tooth, with little damage to either side. Dust motes were still floating upwards, On one wall were fixtures of some kind still hanging drunkenly from the side walls, held by a handful of pipes and wires, pictures atilt and washed by rain with hooks for clothes, helter skelter here and there, while an old earless Teddy surveyed the scene dubiously with his unblinking glass eye. A little person somewhere must be waiting to be re-united, I thought.

My attention shifted to two huddled figures, a young couple, heads down and clinging to each other, standing like stone effigies as if waiting for something. Then two stretchers appeared, blankets draped over two small lumps, emerged from down in the hole and were carried silently out into the waiting ambulance. As they all left, with no blast of sirens from the departing ambulance, the barrier was removed and our driver cranked his engine and we were waved on, wondering what we had just witnessed. Our driver haltingly told the sad sequence of events gleaned from workers on site.

Two young couples lived side by side in two of the houses and like us, slept in their reinforced cellar at night. Both had young children who fell asleep early, and that night the parents in one house decided to slip next door for a nightcap with their friends, thinking their children would be quite safe in the cellar. They had barely arrived when their house took a direct hit, trapping both children in the cellar. The water main was severed, pouring water into the cellar in floods and thus drowning the children, who could be glimpsed but not reached in time. Silence descended on the bus as we took in the horror of it. How does one forget that?

It was unimaginable to contemplate, staying in my thoughts for a long time. There really wasn't any for-sure safe place in a raid. Norma's school in West Bromwich, about ten miles away from Birmingham, had been blitzed, rather badly in places and the town suffered about 80 deaths though we didn't know the tally at the time. Norma told us that trips to the shelter during the day included dragging along school work-"a complete swindle," she said, as they planned to play cards. This was her way of letting us know morale was high, with no regrets about her evacuation. Coventry lay on the far side of Birmingham, creating one point in three cornered triangle, the other points being Birmingham and Oldbury, so we were equidistant between both. Only five miles away from each, which was very little distance in air miles, making us the recipient of any stray missiles from either city. On November 14 all hell broke loose in Coventry as German bombers, 515 of them, together with 100 Pathfinders, bombed industries and factories. Marker flares were dropped to ensure targets were well lit and easy to spot. Electric supply depots, water mains, telephones and gas mains were hit. Craters yawning in the roads made huge problems for fire engines and ambulances everywhere when they struggled to find a way through to help victims. Everything came to a standstill temporarily and the raid continued until next day ending at 6 a.m.

The beautiful Coventry cathedral a lovely medieval building was reduced to a skeleton. Long after the piles of rubble were gone, the badly burned cross was left. stained and charred in the nave. It still stands there to remind us of war's devastation. The historic stained glass windows, once a filter for the silvery and gold rays of afternoon sunshine, beautiful Monk's carvings, sculpture, all of them gone, in one stroke. Hundreds of years old, treasures vanished that night. Cleaning up, a monumental task, leaving only partial walls open to the sky, empty-eyed windows now letting in subdued light, to shine on an ancient grave marker here and there, the ruins remain standing bearing unspoken testimony, to waste and violence. In one night 43,000 homes were gone. Two thirds of the city buildings were seriously damaged also hospitals, churches and the Police Station. This meant a third of the factories were destroyed and a third badly damaged, the remainder just damaged. Essential war production was moved to shadow factories on the outskirts and a few in what was left in the city, restored, if and where, possible. On average it would take about three months to be fully functional again.

After so very many homes had been destroyed, a number of workers fled the city at night and some went to live in smaller communities outside city limits. Air raid shelters proved their worth at this time. Out of seventy nine public shelters housing a possible 33,000 people, very few were hit but even one was bad enough.

Mass graves for 808 souls were interred, leaving a general feeling that England's Green and Pleasant Land had somehow become Chariots of Fire.

The following year in September, Churchill visited Coventry to see the ruins for himself. A strange rumour had been heard that he had received word earlier from Bletchley Park before the raid took place, indicating that Germany intended to launch a powerful attack on that date. The speculation was, that Enigma had decoded that message but couldn't reveal it, and act upon it,as they were unwilling for the enemy to be aware that they had cracked their code. This obviously meant that Mr Churchill could not warn and prepare Coventry, ahead of time. This was, in fact, pure speculation and completely without foundation. When told of this, the head of Air section at Ultra, Mr Peter Calvocoressi quickly cleared up this mis-information stating unequivocally that a big raid was expected but there was absolutely no mention regarding the name of the target city ever made. Therefore there was no choice regarding which city Mr Churchill was to visit. In actual fact, it was assumed that it would involve London, so Mr Churchill headed there especially to be on hand, to face the onslaught. He had no idea whatsoever, where the target lay.

My job kept me busy in working hours, and in between, I went out to lunch or tea with a friend in her early twenties, the sophisticated, glamorous, and beautiful Brenda. She wore a black velvet pill box with an face veil when she met me for tea at the the Grand Hotel, near the main railway station, just off New Street, where an orchestra clad in evening attire, regaled us with their music, raid or no raid. We pretended it was peacetime, as we sipped our tea or danced, on occasion.

In the city craters were everywhere, yet even so, stage plays continued to be shown. The Kardoma still peddled it's dreadful coffee accompanied by three musicians playing chamber music. A strange trio they were, comprised of one very plump lady, and two older men, one with a large wart on his ear, barely escaping the bow on his violin as he scraped it back and forth, I did my best not to stare at his affliction, but I couldn't look away and stared in fixed fascination, feeling quite relieved when the piece ended and he had miraculously escaped again, with wart intact.

There were two main theatres in the city, although I was not allowed to stay for an evening performance, I did manage a matinee at the weekend and much admired those who stayed to fulfill their roles and those who lingered to watch, in the evening, as explosives dropped outside. When raids intensified theatres were forced to close for a while, yet despite this, there remained an unspoken effort to maintain a feeling of business as usual, to continue to make order out of chaos.

Rarely, but sometimes, if I had saved enough coupons to shop, it was also possible to shop for items not on coupons, like hats. One or two other items could be bought without them and this was one small pleasant outlet in the scheme of things, before returning to the dungeon, sorry cellar, at home.

To vary the routine, I visited relatives with some regularity, taking my meat ration with me, such as it was. They joked about wrapping it in a bus ticked and not letting it escape through the punch hole. Bus tickets were two inches by one inch and were an indication of our daily meat expectations-only a slight exaggeration we thought.

There were nine cousins in my family, aunts, uncles and a few good friends but otherwise no-one was special in my life, to share my leisure hours, except perhaps a rather dashing young man I knew, who aspired to be a lawyer. He was twenty one and I seventeen, when we met on a train taking me to comp. school and him to legal studies. Once when the train entered a tunnel he stole a kiss, thus beginning a short romance. A few dates followed, and we went to one or two movies together after that, whereupon I became truly smitten. Alas, he was just having fun. It took me a long time to recognize the difference and I suffered in pure misery, until the day arrived when he disappeared to join the RAF bidding me farewell with a lighthearted peck on the cheek and a carefree wave of the hand. Then he was gone. He had a certain style, I'll give him that.

I thought I'd never survive and moped around for what seemed like an eternity in miserable despair, until one day I woke up and noticed the sun was still shining, and I began to slowly recover. Now, although there was no one in particular in my life, I enjoyed dating boys nearer my own age. Mr Dashing had been my first experience with un requited love so I trod much more carefully these days, not risking a repeat performance.

One of my friends was a cousin's cousin, in other words a shirt tail relative, who was older than I, at twenty four, married and with a husband in the Army. Wynne, always well groomed, not pretty in the chocolate box sense of the word, yet undeniably attractive and more sophisticated than I. In a room full of people she could stand back, observing, until she decided which group she might like to join. She chose her fate, whereas I tended to let things happen to me. Whatever aplomb is, she had it in spades and I was intrigued by it.

Sometime later when we were both in Covent Garden attending a dance, Wynne somehow picked a person that she liked the look of, out of the throng and allowed him to guide her to the dance floor and patiently wait upon her afterwards There was a mysterious air about her and like Scarlett, she never wanted to be poor, she said. She fascinated me and though we were nothing alike, we enjoyed being together and were good friends. She was a secretary to a business executive in Birmingham, and enjoyed the work. Wynne and I agreed however, that it was frustrating to be stuck, like sitting ducks, spending every night in a air raid cellar when we really wanted to enlist in one of the Services to feel we were striking back at the enemy ourselves. I was still too young to do so as eighteen was the minimum age to enter and I could hardly wait for the months to pass. Wynne decided to wait for me to age so that we could join together, so that helped a little.

Emerging from the cellar on my way to work one cloudless morning, and subsequently waiting on the station platform for my train to Birmingham, I became aware that a peculiar thing was happening to the legendary British reserve. It seemed to be melting.! Waiting for a bus, or in a food queue, wherever groups gathered, there was conversation, In peacetime, any cluster of self respecting people who were strangers would stand silently immersed in their own thoughts, but not now. The latest news would be ardently discussed by those same little groups and present happenings, interspersed with smiles, sometimes even a tear ot two, would be shared

Like most big cities, Birmingham was impersonal, bent on business, and certainly not encouraging to a strange individual starting a conversation with persons unfamiliar to them, but change was in the air. It was as if the ever present danger united all of us, in a common cause. On a bus, or train everywhere there were people, as if by mutual consent small items of information were exchanged. Details of a raid, humorous episodes recounted and friendly chats ensued. When commuting on a train, no more hiding behind a newspaper, rattling pages in protest at interruptions. A new spirit was abroad, was it esprit de corps?

Considering multiple raids and major destruction that Birmingham underwent, it was remarkable to note how little grumbling was heard, and even then not about food shortages but about queuing for the extras not on ration. Waiting in a long line for one orange, for instance, was aggravating. It didn't seem fair to complain about rations though, when we thought about our Merchant Marine braving all hazards, sometimes losing lives to get supplies to us, so we plodded on and managed. We communicated our dissatisfaction and chose our grumbles in other areas.

Churchill's upbeat spirit pervaded the air and we felt he had our backs. His straight-forward messages helped, not pulling any punches and giving gratitude to the well deserving heroes in our midst like the RAF, Dunkirk survivors, and all those in navy or khaki fighting on other fronts, also remembering those fighting the battle of the blitz. He had the knack of inspiration and gave himself unstintingly to winning this war of the underdog.

Towards the end of the year, in September 1942 when I was feeling very mature, Wynne and I decided that the time had come to take some positive action, leave our comfortable jobs and sign up. Which of the armed forces needed us most? Not having the answer to that, after due thought we felt we needed to consider the colour of the uniform since we'd be in it day, and some, nights, til' the end of the war. Besides we may as well look as attractive as possible while doing our bit, so away we went to the recruiting centre to try on hats and see which looked best. Well, khaki wasn't Wynne's best colour, so that was out. Off we went this time to the WRNS to look at the navy sailor hats. We both liked navy and those hats were definitely an improvement, but navy! Thinking about it now, we realized that it might be too much of a job to keep it looking fresh, as lint and other airborne fluff has a propensity to be attracted to navy, Rather a handicap we thought. That left the WAAF Of course, definitely the answer! And it suited us both. A great colour to inspire our finest efforts towards winning the war, The hat style left something to be desired, but we couldn't have everything. Most important of all to us, was the fact that the Royal Air Force was constantly battling the odds in the air above us and this is what we knew most about from waiting it out down below. This made it up close and personal, to us and was the clincher if we needed one, which we didn't! This was the right choice for us.

Satisfied with our decision, we asked a few questions like the one about being sent to the same station together after our training. "Oh yes" said the recruiting officer, looking us both in the eye. Oh sure!

Wynne was easily placed as she had shorthand and typing skills, and had much experience as a private secretary and would readily be in demand.

I asked to be placed where the action was, and that was a little harder to pin-point. The officer and her aide liked the Grammar School background, and mentioned a real opportunity that might be possible, then she asked if I could pass a geometry test and I said I probably could, though it was not my favourite subject. Then she told me about a new category having opened up for women with the right credentials. It was vaguely known as Special Duties. This would place me in either the Operations Room or Flying Control, and you couldn't be more active than that, she said. That was it, for me, and Wynne and I gladly signed immediately.

The geometry test for me, and the physical for us both, would take place within the month, we were assured. Well, now all I had to do was tell my parents. Hmm!

There was a consent form to be signed by my parents, since I was not yet twenty-one, or even close, but how could they refuse?

At home over the tea-cups, I made my little speech about having joined the WAAF Pow! It was is if I had dropped a burming incendiary under Dad's very nose. He exploded. "Are you crazy? Sign for you? Don't be silly!"

Phrases like "over my dead body" cropped up and Mom joined in with her own objections, both of them expounding in turn, giving me reasons why I wouldn't like it and mentioned the many menial jobs I would be called upon to do, like latrines, scrubbing floors and so forth. Days passed without any further mention of my plans, and I had an idea. They agreed to listen quietly to what I had to say so I told them about feelings of restlessness and my need to do something useful in this war and then explained about the new Special Duties category having opened up, which really appealed to me. It would mean using my education to advantage I said, and finished with a question. "Dad, how old were you when you signed up in WWI?"

A fleeting smile, smothered before it spread, told me he had taken it in. When he started to say something to the effect that it was 'different for a man' I knew I had my mother on my side and in all fairness they signed.

In preparation for my geometry exam I prevailed upon my cousin Douglas to help me as he was a math whiz, who contrived to make sense of it all for me. He was a talented teacher and I sailed through, managing to pass the test when the time came and afterwards aced the physical, so all I had to do was, wait. It was a bit like waiting for a fingernail to grow. My eighteenth birthday had come and gone! Our lives continued as usual punctuated by siren 'alerts' and all 'clears,' until the long awaited call up papers finally came through the letter box in October and as promised Wynne received the same instructions along with a warrant for train fare. There was time to have a small celebration before we were due to leave on November 4th 1942. On this day, we were instructed to report for duty in the north of England, in the Lancashire town of Morecombe. A cold, flat, windy seaside resort on the northeast coast of England, during November. Oh Joy!

This was where we were to do our training, commonly known in the service as 'square bashing' otherwise translated meant marching and more marching. In between we attended lectures, had inoculations and were outfitted for uniforms. It was several weeks before we would be sent to a posting on a Squadron where we could expect to settle in to do some serious work. Little did we know that Morecombe was the only time we would be posted to the same place.

November 4th morning came, shedding pale sunlight into the room, an auspicious start for a new venture and the long day ahead. No rain.

Breakfast over, small suitcase in hand, gasmask and travel orders at the ready, I waited with an eye on the clock for my parents and Norma to tend to last minute details, like making a sandwich lunch for the train journey. At last, we were on our way to the car. Instructions for keeping in touch repeated once more, plus admonishments for taking care of myself, and we were on our way to New Street Station. The traffic as we approached the entrance was heavy and small car queues were forming to wait their turn for access to the curb, taxis jockeying for position, small commuter buses in the mix and eventually it was our turn. We unloaded my luggage, exchanged last minute hugs and kisses and as I watched Dad pull away, it struck me as ironical that I was leaving them to spend their nights in the cellar, dodging bombs, while I headed for a safe area by the seaside. And they were worried about me!!!.

4 – On Parade

NEW STREET STATION was busy disgorging the last trainload of passengers, threading their way through the new arrivals. It looked like an impenetrable mass of humanity from where I was perched.

I stood on the step near the curb, taking a survey, as Dad left, and looking over all the heads, I saw a waving hand, beckoning. It was Wynne, cleverly poised next to a major pillar, smiling amid the melee, hair freshly coiffed, short bangs on a high forehead' beneath a perky hat. I fought my way closer, noticing that she wore a little make up, manicured long nails, brown eyes glinting in amusement as if this was all some big lark. I suppose fleeing the Birmingham drama and going to the sea side to march along the peaceful sea front might qualify as a lark.

Both of us had independently opted to wear suits, hers black, mine bottle green, and carrying rain coats we headed for the platform. Once there, we didn't have long to wait, as the train chugged along, hissing its way towards us with puffs of steam, belching small clouds, obscuring, and painlessly beheading passengers waiting nearby. As the vapours vanished giving back their heads, we saw carriage doors banging open, their occupants disembarking, in haste to be gone.

My travels had been mainly by car, though an overnight trip to Scotland had stirred my imagination as a child. A small group of us from school, the average age about twelve, had travelled on a wagon lit to see the annual Tattoo, famous in Edinburgh, and I hadn't forgotten the feeling of adventure.

A steam train conjured up visions of the famed Orient Express, where long coated ladies with ivory cigarette holders, and veiled hats shadowed mysterious eyes, as they swept aboard. They were usually accompanied by glamorous men, trench-coated, with collar up, of course. This train was not a sleeper, nor visiting foreign lands with exotic passengers, yet still it had a certain aura, spelling possibilities and excitement, I thought, hopefully.

Back to earth with a jolt, half hearing Wynne's comment on wartime ugly 'utility' clothes, as she watched passengers boarding, making even the young and beautiful, take on the drab appearance of old time, blue-stocking, maiden aunts. Utility clothes were produced during wartime to serve a function, and cover the body, but not to delight the eye. There were no extra ruffles, lace or ribbon on anything labeled 'utility.' Underpants were hideous and even these were strictly rationed. Pre-war clothes, began to look pretty good by comparison.

We found corner seats opposite one another and settled in for a good chat. Conversation flowed as we pondered the forthcoming training, wondering how long it might take before we would be transferred to a real station and be of some use. There were no signs announcing the names of towns or the railway stations we passed through, as this fell under the guise of letting the enemy know too much, should they set foot on land. Perish the thought! There weren't even sign posts on the roads. We knew that Morecombe was the termination for this train so it didn't present a problem to us, but we realized that difficulty would arise when travelling at night, with no lights, no station names and the need to change trains, and we wondered then, how we could tell where we were? Perhaps the conductor would come and whisper to us if the need arose.

Pulling into the Morecome station, head out of the window, I spotted a burly WAAF Sgt. holding up a sign with just two letters, "MT", which we already knew meant motor transport. Most services were referred to, only by letters we discovered, and there many of these.

Picking up our overnight luggage we presented ourselves to the Sgt. whose terse response, was to tell us to "wait here," so we "waited here." Five others soon caught up with us, chattering away like magpies, and still no sign of a "glad you're here" or "welcome" or "my name is—" Just a brisk "follow me" gesture, as she led us to a parked van with instructions to "get in."

On our arrival at our new quarters we received a belated, no nonsense, "welcome to your Nissen Hut, choose a bed and I will be back to take you to the mess at 1745 hrs sharp. Dinner at 1800 hrs!" Not exactly a barrel of laughs, our Sergeant, we decided. Wynne and I chose a corner with beds side by side, and the others quickly followed suit and chose theirs.

Nissen Huts were constructed, first by bending sheet metal into a semi circle, the ends then planted into the ground, stabilized afterwards, with concrete footings. The arch was then reinforced by bending sheets of corrugated steel, and adding that to the arch. The entire structure used fifty-four plates overall, creating a sturdy building, quick to assemble and ready to use. The floor could be either painted concrete, or wood strips joined by tongue and groove. Huts varied in size the smallest was sixteen feet long, the next, twenty four feet and the biggest was thirty feet, so it was possible to tailor the size to fit the purpose. There were some other variations, differences in size and type of windows, was one, but whatever size, they were all, leaky and draughty. Anyone with the lingering idea that the sound of rain on a tin (or steel) roof was romantic, soon got over it, while living in a Nissen Hut. It also spelled miserable marching conditions next day, besides providing us with a few extra unwanted drips inside. Ours was the largest size, with windows, and four beds ranged along each long wall, with the latrines conveniently located at the far end. Beds were stacked according to a diagram, but we weren't allowed to make the bed ready for use, until evening. Everything had to be done in the manner so prescribed, every day. In the morning the bed was to stacked in a certain order, bedclothes, folded a particular way and piled against the iron head board, as before and then one could think about breakfast. Our beds had no mattress per se, instead there were three so-called biscuits measuring three feet by three feet and about four or five inches deep, resilient as concrete. At the appointed time, in reverse order, the bed was made by placing the biscuits end to end and then binding them together with a barely adequate white bottom sheet, always remembering to do hospital corners, or the whole caboodle quickly fell apart. One more similar sheet, three blankets and an un-submissive pillow comprised a completely made up bed. This was to be made up each night, every night. Not before. No fooling!

The Sergeant was back to take us to the Mess. Contrary to its nomenclature, it was anything but a mess. A neatly organized, long buffet with food mounted on hot trays and flanking it, were long wooden tables with chairs or benches alongside. Orderly as could be. We passed along the line extending a dinner tray, a great dollop of something was plopped on it with such force it almost bounced. As a dollop came Wynne's way, spattering her manicured nails and sleeve she said, "oh thanks too much" rather sarcastically and the server thought she said, "oh that's too much," and whisked half of it away, saying impatiently, "next." The look on Wynne's face caused a ripple of mirth all down the line.

Next day breakfast, procedure was the same, only with dried eggs causing no untoward ripple, before being taken to the MO (Medical Officer) for physicals and vaccinations for smallpox, followed by two other inoculations for unstated ailments. Just for practice, perhaps? The physical was at best very perfunctory, but jabs with the needle, frequent, and carefully noted, by a WAAF nurse, so that you were sure to get them all. Heaven forbid you should miss one! Most of the time it seemed our arms were swollen and sore, resembling well used pin cushions, and in ten days time those with vaccinations had all the symptoms of flu", but sick or not, rain or shine, we marched, had lunch, then marched some more. We were to find out that the weather would become all important to us, and every day upon rising, we peered anxiously skyward, hoping to see some blue and if we were truly lucky, a little sun. If it had just rained, the pavement would be wet and puddled, splashing our legs and very slippery in spots. If it was just about to rain, moments stretched like years, till we were finished and could escape the wind that usually preceded the relentless downpour. However, at 1300 hours on this, our first full day, we were comparatively un-sore and the weather surprisingly kind. All was well.

Back in the billet, after lunch, we were summoned to our feet to be greeted by a corporal accompanied by a WAAF officer, the latter then proceeded to shower us with verbal and written information, paying special attention to KR's, short for King's Regulations. Whenever the phrase, 'going by the book' was used, this was the book they meant. It covered every situation from induction to demobilization, including court martial, describing enormously varied ways to qualify for the latter. Thoroughly chastened, after that, we were escorted to the Quarter Master's store for uniforms.

The QM with a knowledgeable eye, took one look at me and handed over a size eight tunic, I couldn't believe she could do that so quickly. Luckily she was spot on, and the rest followed accordingly. Two brass buttoned tunics, two skirts, regulation length, one and a half inches below the knee, could have been tailored for me and I liked the fitted greatcoat which was heavy wool and lined. It had two tapered rows of brass buttons and a nice big collar for foul weather. Quite glamorous, we decided.

There were three good quality blue shirts, three pairs of pretty ghastly lisle hose, and most of the rest came in pairs, like gloves. Next we found the very basic, basics, quickly agreeing, that no self respecting person could be expected to fight a war in 'that underwear,' so it was hastily stowed out of sight in the bottom of the white canvas kit bag where it stayed for the 'duration.' We would have to part with some carefully saved civvy coupons for replacements, but well worth it for our morale.

I must admit the flannel pajamas came in handy in the ice cold weather that followed. The hat with brass WAAF emblem, black ties and black, leather, flat heeled. lace up shoes, completed the list. The heavy leather shoes would take a bit of getting used to after the soft, leather, heeled, court shoes that we were accustomed to wearing.

One last item which had to be tried on was the service sized gas mask, a more business like affair than our civilian one, and in its own case. Since we were not allowed to carry a purse, the case was important. Sometimes a few substitutions were made, like a lipstick, comb, wallet etc, but not to be thought of, if you ran the risk of being inspected. Definitely, not approved by KR's.!

Completely attired in our new uniforms, the sun glinting on our newly polished brass, we thought we looked pretty sharp and were ready for whatever came next, except for the feet. Not used to the weight and unforgiving quality of the leather in our shoes, I felt like a hob goblin in them. How would I ever dance? Still they made a nice sound when on the march, if my toes survived the pressure.

Day two, found us all breakfasted, beds stacked and already on the parade ground attended by our sergeant at 0800 hours. The watery sunshine was not strong enough to turn muddy sludge, back into the green grass patches of earlier days, but better than rain, by far. Other recruits from huts near ours also joined us, until we were about sixty in all, while several groups similar to ours were assembling elsewhere, usually along the front.

Our Sergeant, rather pugnacious looking, with yellowy bleached hair, a bit overweight, busty and possessed of a voice capable of drowning out an amplified brass band, literally. In moments of exasperation however, it flew up a register from a threatening growl, to the head-splitting screech of a peacock. Usually she just roared her commands with ear-popping intensity. We never saw her smile. Instead, she wore a scowl of such ferocity, it frightened the birds, perched on overhead wires, who all took flight when she bellowed. Dogs were terrified. One dog in particular a pitiful, stray ginger mutt, neck stretched, always set up a piercing, high pitched, wavering, howl, whenever he saw her coming along the sea front, where we often drilled. She tried to order him quiet but he only wailed louder, creating a most comical duet. We didn't dare laugh, but as Wynne rolled her eyes, I nearly ruptured something trying not to. Tough as hob nailed boots she was!

Standing at attention for inspection, lined up in rows, woe betide the person whose shoes didn't glow, buttons didn't shine, tie was askew, or whose hair touched her collar. Deadly sins! The guilty were loudly berated and threatened with dire consequences, should they repeat the offense. One shudders to think.

Marching technique was demonstrated, arms swinging shoulder high, never mind about those aching from inoculations. Each pair of feet keeping exact time, and in step, goes without saying, coming to a halt precisely at the same moment, upon the command to "halt."

We marched twice daily, often in blustery north Atlantic winds sweeping over a gunmetal sea, reflecting a glowering sky in deepest shades of grey, threatening more frequent squalls as we reached December. When our toes ached from the cold in unyielding shoes and our poor fingers froze in their inadequate gloves, I began to think Dad was right. What was I doing in this mess?

Inspections, while standing at attention were the worst, sometimes in a heavy drizzle, I could feel the ice-cold blood in my spine congeal. At least, our circulation was switched back on, when we were on the move.

Back in the barracks, the draughty windows were bearable and we were all so glad to stretch out after a hot meal. Those biscuits on the bed could have been made of stone and we would have slept on without stirring, given the chance, but instead, were rudely awakened by the klaxon, all too early. 0600 hours was not my usual rising time, back in the war zone, and here it seemed to come in the middle of the night. It was still dark outside then.

Some WAAF had chilblains which developed in very cold weather. They were ugly little red lumps attacking fingers or toes and were very painful, I'm told. Some had sore heels and toes from the unaccustomed footwear and all of us felt the aftermath of frequent shots in the arm (or elsewhere) I counted nine, in four weeks and we had two more weeks to go, to tempt needle-happy medics when they had a few hours to spare, out came the needles.

We marched in all sorts of intricate patterns, sometimes forming fours, changing direction often, saluting, 'eyes right,' on the march. In fact, in marching forwards, sideways and every way but backwards, we became expert, even in a downpour and sodden in our dripping greatcoats. If the driving rain continued to pelt down, hitting us from the side as it came, sleeting and blustering over the sea wall, we were then taken to the nearest available shelter to try to wait it out. But those days in England, no-one had central heating and tiny fireplaces, or small cala-gas stoves gave little heat, so it wasn't much more comfortable inside, than out, while wearing wet clothes.

Days turned into weeks. The blisters were better, no inoculations lately and we were in our sixth week, heading towards Christmas. The day of reckoning had arrived, and our skills were to be tested in the very near future.

By contrast to the usual rain or mist, the day finally dawned, crisp, cold and clear with a spasmodic sun smiling down on our carefully shined brass, already to welcome us to the parade ground along the sea front, for our passing out parade.

There stood the grandstand, bunting waving, and a sizable group of dignitaries assembled, imposingly attired, many decorated with assorted ribbons in place, scrambled egg caps denoting rank, and all brasses shining. Dazzling, in the sunshine! There were several heavily braided RAF officers of both sexes, also the Lord Mayor, complete with robe and chain, and others of some status I supposed, and right next to the elevated dais, was a section for the large brass band.

Well this was more like it! Why didn't they give us the brass band when we arrived? Much more pleasant and far easier to march, I even enjoyed it.

Our turn next, and all eyes were focused on us as we swept past the grandstand, in the lead. 'Eyes right,' in perfect step, in flawless unity, with other passing out groups following on behind:

Complicated formations gave us no problems and we moved as a unit, the salute exactly right and as we looked sideways I could see the lines were dead straight. Not even the smallest flaw. We sailed through our commands, which we heard quite clearly over the amplified brass band, thanks to our sergeant's well developed vocal chords, and it's only fair to add, and her ability. She had trained us well, if mercilessly. Flags waved, while our salutes were returned and as the band played, upping the volume, we moved as one.

We could see a large gathering of civilians on the pier beyond, watching, some with binoculars, and when we left to march back to quarters there was a lot of clapping and stomping going on in appreciation. Wolf calls aplenty. They were expert watchers, having been there many times before, while countless parades had passed before them, and most received restrained, polite clapping, but for us they upped the ante. We felt suitably rewarded and just a bit pleased with ourselves.

Our Sgt B. congratulated us and while there was no sign of a smile forthcoming, there was, a decided glimmer apparent in her eyes. We had to be content with that.

Postings were due next day. In the meantime, a few of us felt we were due for a small celebration, so after a better than usual dinner in the Mess, we slid out to the local pub to find several other groups had had the same idea. I ordered my usual shandy and we gathered around exchanging little snippets of information about our hopes for the future. Some, exchanged home addresses, planning to keep in touch, and the evening ended on a high note, A few hugs and good wishes for safety, success and happiness were made, as we parted ways before heading for bed.

Breakfast over we waited for our postings, each with our own private hopes, and so ready for the next step.

On the day of departure Wynne was first to receive all her papers and travel info, along with her ticket, handed to her, with directions for her posting to a station in the south of England. Not to be kept in suspense long, I soon received my orders discovering that mine were for South Wales. Only a Country apart, no less! Whatever happened to, "yes, of course, you will be stationed together?" So much for the assurances of recruiting officers, we grumbled.

It was some consolation to realize that we would be home on leave at regular intervals in the forthcoming year and could swap notes then. In the meantime we would not be out in the elements, in all weathers, as we had here. Off at last, to a real job, to help win the war.

Morning came. The day of departure, the sun gave us its blessing, and came out in all it's wintry splendor, to see us depart. Kit bags packed, railway vouchers, posting papers and gas masks collected, out we went, in small groups, to a waiting MT. Wynne belonged to a little unit, all going together, to a Fighter station, lucky Wynne. She already knew some of the girls, which made the transition easier. We hugged in parting, wondering when next we might hope to meet. Alone in my departure, I had the MT driver all to myself. He was chipper, and helpful, sensing my disappointment, having seen all manner of departees come and go, and was knowledgeable. He, himself, had been in the RAF for eighteen months, with many stories to relate. I began to have a little insight into how varied the same job could be, depending on the station one was sent to, and it proved to be true in my own case as well. He helped broaden my thinking, realizing that this was just the beginning and could easily change, but when?

On the station, waiting for my train I had time to think, about my not going to a Fighter or Bomber station, which I had expected. Instead, and still I was not very elated to find myself headed for "balloons." My thinking wasn't that broad yet, and I felt a bit let down. Once a balloon was up, what else would there be to do, I pondered? How little I knew! "I did not sign up to fly a balloon" was my first thought, and I was truly mortified the more I thought about it.

Already, it was two weeks before Christmas and I would be spending it somewhere in Wales where I didn't know a soul. Not only that, but I didn't know how to find my way there, to Swansea, when confronted by a train change. All stations had no names, this was an unknown route for me, and I had to connect with two different trains to get there. Consulting with the guard, his flag temporarily at rest, it seemed as if the best route would be to change in Birmingham, then another change in Bath and then, on to Swansea and he kindly volunteered to get the ticket collector to give me a heads up, warning, two stops before I reached my destination. What a relief!

Now I could relax. As if in approval, the sun burst through the clouds, taking some of the bite out of the frosty morning, not quite reaching my toes or fingers. Uplifting the spirits and making my prospective move, and everything around me, brighter as I waited patiently, sitting on a bench, at peace with my world.

5 – Secrets in Wales

THE PLATFORM BEGAN to fill and incoming passengers surged towards the edge vying to be first to board and choose a seat. Surprising me, out of the crowd the Guard appeared, waving me over as the train steamed into the station. Without a word, he took my kit bag and hoisted it high into the luggage rack in the first carriage. I could have hugged him, instead, with a grateful smile I sank into the seat, instantly brighter. He turned at the door, smiled and was gone before I could wave. I was so touched by his gesture and would like to have had a chance to thank him, at least, but there was barely time to settle in, before he waved his flag mid train, and we were off.

Off, on the long journey to Birmingham, only five miles from home, but alas, just passing through. At least I would recognize it when we got there and wouldn't need a prompt.

My gaze was diverted to check out the other passengers. A mother with two small chattering children opening their sandwiches, three army buddies in serious conversation, drinking out of paper cups, a parson sitting quietly, lost in thought, and a sailor reading.

Outside the glass door, were standees in the corridor, some of them, squirming on luggage, hardly adequate as seating, but a little better than standing for hours. Corridors ran the length of the train with connecting links between each carriage. Mostly serviceman here, the RAF well represented, some sharing newspapers, and some talking. A busy train. Once again, I was grateful to the Guard for my seat.

Picking up speed the train developed its own rhythm, da,da,da, daaaa, da,da,da, daaaa like a snatch of a tune as it went over the links on the rails. The sun, warm on the window, the low hum of conversation coupled with the early hour of rising, caused my eyelids to droop and finally close. Soon I was deeply asleep, head pillowed, in the niche by the window.

The screeching of brakes as the train approached a stop, together with departing sounds of the little family all waving goodbye, brought me hastily back to the surface, to realize that in another hour, we would be in Birmingham. Possibly, enough time to get a sandwich and phone home.

Time flew, and once on the platform it was easy to find a red phone box. I was able to speak to every member of my family in turn, each so happy to hear from me with up to date news, instead of a censored letter, but so sorry that Christmas, just two weeks away would be spent apart, for the first time ever. Maybe next year, we said.

Birmingham Station abuzz as usual, with Army, Navy, and Air force thronging the platforms hauling kit bags to and fro. This time after watching me struggle briefly with luggage, I was helped by a tall, dark haired sailor, a serious looking fellow with long graceful hands, who was also going to Swansea and was familiar with the route.

Once aboard the train, eating our sandwiches, he told me roughly where his base was, although unable to reveal specifics about his location, or navy work, we still found plenty to talk about. He was a concert pianist in peacetime and seemed dedicated to music. It was enjoyable to listen to his ideas for the future and his past experiences, as we watched the city vanish from view.

First, the big industrial buildings, warehouses and the like, then long lines of identical houses, row upon row, their roofs marching up the slope, like tiers on a wedding cake, leaving the city and the smoke behind. Further on, England's green and gold fields began to slowly unfold, defined by hedges and the boundaries creating odd triangles, squares, and assorted shapes not seen much in geometry The entire panorama all stitched neatly together, to emulate the 'patchwork quilt,' our landscape is known for. Interspersed, were small clusters of houses, no longer in rows, but becoming a village, or a small town, with a pub in the offing.

A pub, served many functions. Always a centre for the community, often with wood tables scattered in a garden, sometimes with animals, some penned, others loose, and all friendly allowing children to pet them. The 'local' served as a club providing a pleasant place for a family outing on a summer evening, the last of the sun's splintered rays showering the heads of those beneath The slow, drinking-dining crowd, formed their own small groups, accompanied by the steady hum of chatter and punctuated by the occasional peal of mirth, while off in the background, a darts contest was under way.

The "local", so much more than a pub, fulfills a social need, becoming the village hub for some of its leisure hours. A small oasis in a hungry, thirsty, or just a lonely moment; As the day wanes, the call for, "last round please" goes out, soon followed, thirty minutes later, by "time, gentlemen please," on the tick of ten p.m. Some areas vary the time frame, and are open till 10.30 p.m. or even 11 p.m. but then are required to open later. Licensing hours are considered a bit strange by those from other Countries, but the British Publican knows where he stands, how to plan his day, and stringently conforms to opening and closing hours, to avoid the loss of his license.

Rattling along in tune with the rails beneath, we soon approached Bath, presenting no problems in changing trains. Donald's know-how, eased the switch. We located the right platform quickly for our next train, which was just about to leave, barely in time for us to board for the final leg of the journey. Conversation resumed, and on we sped, anxious now to reach the end of the trail. It had been a long day.

Pausing in the act of applying a lipstick refresher, I noticed the hour, and it seemed no time at all before the train slowed, once again, and finally, we had arrived to find Swansea was bustling.

Donald briefly described the layout of the city, or what was left of it, after a massive raid the year before, and I was already planning to explore further on foot, but not quite yet.

Moving towards the exit we saw the MT in the usual place, waiting to take me to Sketty, and my new billet. Donald hoisted my kit bag into the van and we said, goodbye after a pleasant journey shared, so glad to have met, both of us having enjoyed the company.

Sketty, a little village, about five miles from Swansea was the home of 958 Squadron. The Balloon Squadron, where a whole new, un-thought and unsought, experience lay ahead. Gazing out the window as we drove, I saw a totally different terrain from the endless flatness of Morecombe, this was the antithesis. Hills everywhere! Some streets were so steep it was unimaginable to expect a car to travel such a perpendicular line, up or down them. From the bottom it seemed equally impossible to climb up, on foot or otherwise, and from the top looking down, it felt as if you could just plummet in free fall, as off a cliff. Two, such streets, seemed frighteningly vertical, in Swansea but as we approached Sketty the more moderate, rolling, country thereabouts, seemed far more manageable, but still hilly.

The first stop was HQ. Once a gracious house, Green Willows was now adapted to RAF use, as the main activity centre. It sat on top of a small hill, overlooking the formal garden, and backed up to a thick cluster of trees known as 'the woods,' effectively screening it from any neighbours on that side. The front entrance and both sides were also shielded by high leafy hedges, abundant with sweet smelling blooms in Spring-time, so it was completely private, on all sides.

Entering through the front door we made our way to the Orderly room where I was checked in, introduced to some of the busy clerks, then promptly taken upstairs to Operations Room (Ops) where it seemed I was badly needed. They had been waiting a long time for two replacements and I was first to arrive and heartily welcomed. Unfortunately, the other WAAF wasn't expected to put in her appearance until later in January, in the New Year, when another body would greatly shorten the long hours we needed to put in at present.

Ronnie (Veronica) a lively Welsh girl, the only other girl besides me, who had been working there, was just finishing her shift, and handing over the log to a male corporal. Both told me how delighted they were to see me, and introduced themselves. We three comprised our entire special duties, staff.

Ronnie was about to go off watch, but offered to show me to my new billet and join me for dinner in the Mess, thankfully, giving me an opportunity to get my bearings, before going on duty next day.

The other occupant in Ops, was the officer on watch. There were three of them who rotated in shifts, so that there was always one on duty and one "special duties" person as well. My first session was scheduled for 0800 hrs next day, when I would be shown the ropes by corporal, Kevin.

Ready to leave and exchanging salutes with the duty officer, Ronnie and I left together, setting off down the hill, walking about a mile, or so, to my new billet. On arrival strangely, we turned into an unprepossessing opening in a fallow field, growing nothing in particular, and looking a bit neglected. The dangling entrance gate, hanging wildly askew, also looked rather dilapidated, and was totally dysfunctional. There was an apron-like, patch of pock-marked concrete attached to the front of what appeared to be, a tumble-down old church, of no recognizable architecture and this derelict proved to be the chapel. Bethel chapel, in fact! This was it? My new home? This was, indeed, IT.

Trying not to have any preconceived ideas about it being a dump, I followed Ronnie inside, to be confronted by a great cavernous space with a raised dais at one end, host to a lone sacrificial bed on the 'altar,' so to speak. I secretly hoped that wasn't to be my bed. Blackout curtains were billowing into the empty room, propelled by gusts of wind blowing forcefully through long broken windows. There were about five of these, tall and double paned, each about ten feet in height on either side of the wall, in the body of the chapel. When I asked about the strange hiss and the funny smell, pervading the air, I was told, quite matter of factly, that it came from the leaky gaslight, suspended from a high arced ceiling bracket above us, audibly sizzling away as we listened. It cast an eerie pulsating light on everything beneath, projecting moving shadows on walls and ceiling in the dim and gloomy room, giving it a haunted look. But not to worry about being gassed she said, cheerfully, we have air conditioning, and pointed to the broken windows.

The only furniture in this large room were two lonely beds ranged along one long wall and three others along the opposite side, plus the one on the raised dais. One little table, bearing a few personal items, was Ronnie's, so I chose a bed on that side, as far from the escaping gas as possible. "Fear naught," I had my broken window above, leaking any gas to the outside world, handily placed, next to my headboard, as I silently said a prayer for no rain. Only one other bed would be occupied so when, one of us was on night duty, there would only be two inhabitants to share this creepy place. I was reminded of an old Ingrid Bergman movie entitled Gaslight, in which the villain attempts to drive the heroine mad, by monkeying with the gaslight. Ours needed no monkeying. It was already creepy!

Completing the tour, we came to the ablutions (Air Force for bathrooms) which revealed a row of washbasins parallel to the wall and behind the wall to the right, were three enclosed toilets. To the left, through another rickety door was a room off this one, leading to the tub. An enormous, ancient porcelain affair, with a red tide-line, painted inside, to indicate how much warm water we were allowed per bath. (a meagre four inches), a bit like sitting in a shallow puddle, without your clothes. Faucets worked with a reluctant creak, followed by an odd sort of deep, bass groaning sound, as if it was all too much to bear.

The tub was placed on a dais, under the glass skylight overhead, a dubious asset since it leaked, providing a very cold, bonus shower when it rained. Occasionally there were snow flurries in January, so you might find yourself sandwiched between four inches of warmish water and a layer of sleet. Rather like a Christmas pudding without the holly sprig. No plug, but a penny wrapped in a handkerchief, worked, since no rubber was to be found for a proper plug. A broken lock on the entrance to our palatial residence completed the picture. I was right first time. It was a dump!

At lunch, in the Mess, all was revealed. The men on our station had protested strenuously, to the MO when they were lodged in Bethel Chapel on the grounds that it endangered their health, was inadequate and unsafe, and as a result, it had then been condemned for their use. We got it by default. Not fit for the men, but quite O.K. for the weaker sex.

Coming off night duty next day after breakfast, wearily wending my way down the hill, bed beckoned. Even in the ghostly chapel, a bed, any bed would be welcome. At least it would be quiet. Little did I know!

Sleep was almost instantaneous, when suddenly out of the drifting waves of deep sleep, I began to be aware of a male voice, coming closer and closer to my bed, raucously bawling out "knees bend, stre-e-etch, breathe, repeating over and over. Nothing dream-like about those vigorous commands.

Coming to, in a hurry I sat up, now wide awake, outraged, at the sight of briefly clad men, beads of perspiration glistening, bobbing up and down like Jacks-in-the-box, and demanded an explanation for the invasion of my bedroom. This was just a bit over the top! Peace had been shattered, and when sleep was interrupted, it always became elusive, particularly in daylight. Apparently no-one had notified the gym instructor Sergeant, that the chapel was occupied, so since it was raining, it was logical to him, to bring in his troop of twenty men, he said.

Logical or not, time to voice a few complaints. Three of us like-minded inhabitants, banded together to make our objections known to the authorities, via the Adjutant. By then, we were all steamed up in righteous indignation, and set off to confront him in his office, but his guilty, apologetic welcome, rather took the starch out of our collars. He seemed to be expecting us and assured us that our habitat would be off limits to all personnel but the occupants, and happily gave us the best of all news, that a new billet, in a house not far from HQ, would soon be forthcoming. He was probably embarrassed that the men on the station were housed much more comfortably, than three hard working WAAF shift workers. With good cause, we thought.

We left feeling relieved, and appeased, but somehow there was something, ridiculously, absurd, if not hilarious, about the whole situation and we laughed our way home at the farcical aspect of the physical training scene. In retrospect, it would have made a good comic strip, all of us in some state of undress, in an old, tumbledown, spook chapel, rain pouring down and gaslight hissing as curtains billowed like shrouds in a nightmare.

The other good news was that our food was especially good, seasoned with skill, expertly cooked, and quite delicious. The reason for our outstanding luck, was, that our Chef had been in charge of the Royal kitchens in Buckingham Palace, before she volunteered for the WAAF. She, of wondrous skill, had cooked for the King and Queen, no less. Her name was Mary, slim, rather reserved, chestnut brown hair, attractive and in her twenties. She made all the difference, and was much appreciated by us all. She well deserved the rousing cheers that greeted her comings and goings, always responding with modest smiles and a little wave.

Seated next day at my desk, with Kevin alongside enlightening me about my job, stressing the importance of recording all pertinent information in the log, I learned the ropes. Every order, weather report, given or taken, and details concerning balloon sites were dutifully inserted, in the required book. Consulting the log from the shift before, to get updated was necessary each time we reported for duty and signing it, indicated that you had done so, all part of routine. This part was simple.

The officer on duty was a man about my Father's age, who had served in the first World War, in aircrew. I was yet to meet the others during the week following. There were two more officers on rotation including an Australian Flight Lieut. who joined the trio later. He was the only Australian I ever met, whom I didn't like, however the third person became a favorite of us all, younger than the other two, with a natural dignity and grace. He was a gentle man, unfussily efficient and liked by all. We got to know each other well, as time passed.

It became apparent during the day that gaps in my knowledge concerning balloons and meteorology needed some further study. The latter was easy to fix, and I was soon signed up for a short course, given by a meteorology officer, in another part of the building. It was an enjoyable course with several lists of signs and symbols to be committed to memory and a test at the end of it all This took about two weeks of my spare time, but worthwhile, the test having covered what I had just learned, so it was easy to pass written requirements.

As part of my job, weather bulletins were transcribed, and kept updated at regular intervals by me, on the office blackboard, then relayed to the balloon sites. Orders for changing heights, due to weather, or possible approaching enemy aircraft, were also issued by me, after receiving directives from the officer on watch. It seemed there was a bit more to it all, than leaving the balloon up there to take care of itself, but I was soon to be better informed and the gap in my knowledge attended to, as I was being sent to a balloon site for a week to learn what it was all about. What on earth could all those people in the crew be doing all day? I was about to find out, in the not too distant future.

There were mysterious "starfish" sites, which from time to time were given the order to "shine" These exercises were planned and organized by the officer present, then passed verbally to me to pass on, to those on site. The sites represented, deeply secret decoy areas, made to simulate a big town or city nearby, when seen from the air. There were areas to be set on fire, representing the result of an incendiary, direct hit, often combined with other fake fires, which could also be simulated. Very hush hush! I never heard anyone mention these outside Ops then, or at any time since. Balloon sites placed in the area enhanced and maintained the hoax.

Christmas was less than a week away, so after the new year was deemed soon enough, to visit the balloon site. Weather reports became of vital importance to me, as I would be spending a lot of time in the open air in January. Winter conditions in Wales, especially South Wales were much milder than in the north, or even elsewhere in England, but still, it turned frosty in the morning or evening, and near the ocean we felt the blast of wintry winds and a fair share of rain. Christmas day would be spent among veritable strangers. Rather a dismal prospect.

Ronnie's family lived in Swansea, so a twenty four hours pass combined with time not scheduled for duty, meant she could go home. Many of the clerks in the orderly room were inclined to be a little clannish, so it was a bit difficult to find people who shared my interests.

At first, there were only two of us WAAF in Ops and the rest of the women were either cooks, secretaries or ACHGD's meaning aircraft hand, general duties, indicating any job which had no category. Kind of a dogsbody, or a person who might be called upon to do a variety of tasks, just lending a hand wherever needed. They worked regular hours so our paths didn't cross often. Many were local, and spoke Welsh almost entirely when off duty, making it a bit difficult to socialize. Much later I enjoyed. learning a Welsh song or two and once, on top of a small bus in Llanelly I joined the crowd in singing one, but at this point I was still a stranger and felt rather isolated.

The Welsh Eisteddfods were famous for their for wonderful choir voices, and concert tickets for their performances were well sought after, in Peacetime, but now in Wartime the best place to hear beautiful Welsh voices singing, was in church, pubs or at a private concert. Not readily available on Christmas day, however.

Mary, Queen of the Mess, made a truly memorable dinner and I was not due in Ops until twenty two hundred hours, but what to do in between on the 25th? Bethel Chapel stuck in a lonely field, oozing gas and dimly lit, didn't exactly present an appealing picture.

Aimlessly wandering down the road after dinner, feeling a bit lost, I turned a corner and there stood a Services club I had heard mentioned. The Georgian brick building, a former manor, nicely kept up, evergreen ivy trailing the walls, properly blacked out, and open, judging by the sound of piano music. It looked inviting. This seemed a good time to investigate, perhaps even to see a familiar face, though that seemed unlikely.

Inside, coloured paper chains criss-crossed the room. Christmas lights on a big tree, and sweet smelling pine branches adorned the stair banister, as it gracefully curved into the reception hall, all conveyed an immediate welcome.

A tall, groomed, fortyish WAAF detached herself from a small group of WRNS to ask me if I'd like to have tea with her. I would indeed. On better acquaintance, she proved to be an educated person from Oxford Women's College. Dignified, spare of frame, with glowing hazel, brown flecked eyes, her economical gestures wasted neither time nor energy and were a delightful part of her personality. We liked each other immediately. Her name was Mac and this is where our friendship began, on Christmas day 1942. She worked days, and was secretary to the CO. and liked her job,' most of the time,' she said.

Leading the way into the adjoining room where a piano was being most energetically and skillfully, pounded, expertly playing a Beethoven Concerto. Amazingly, the pianist was someone I knew. I couldn't believe it! Here was Donald, my recent train journey companion, putting those slender hands to good use at our local club. With a final flourish, receiving much applause, he sat down, amid foot stamping, and calls for an encore, he made the V-sign in response, and sat at our table to be introduced to Mac. Then, turning to me, he said, rather whimsically, " I knew you'd show up sooner or later, but I was getting a bit weary of waiting, besides I've read all the books lining these walls, at least twice."

He didn't know how else to reach me, as I hadn't an address to give him, when we met, so he had frequented the place regularly in his off time, hoping I would be there. Finally here I was.

Now I had two familiar faces, friends to share a cup of tea with, at the very least. As twilight approached, a giant punch bowl appeared, in time to toast each other, the new friendship, and the swift, successful outcome of the war. This had been an unexpectedly, happy occasion. Not so bad after all, for what had started as a doubtful, lonely Christmas day.

Twenty-two hundred hours, my deadline rapidly approached, and I was escorted up the hill by my new friends, to Green Willows in time for the nightshift. Dates having been set for future meetings, we three parted company, until next time.

Inspecting Swansea with Mac a few days later, we found the city centre had been gutted, and many business premises devastated, but still there was life in the city, even in half-restored premises, a small shop or two clung on, in defiance of all future threats, open, and operating, anyway. An upbeat spirit of determination to make the best of a bad job, prevailed, along with the expectation of the successful end of the war, if we just hang in there, together, and of course, we would!

Dylan Thomas, who wrote *Under Milkwood*, was born in the Uplands which lies between Sketty and Swansea, had once described Swansea as an "ugly, lovely, town." Somehow, it rang a bell.

Before I entered the picture, in 1941, for three nights in February, 19, 20, & 21, German bombers had given Swansea their full attention, after having first devastated the town of Cardiff nearby just one year before my arrival.)

There were 30,000 bombs dropped on Swansea alone, in that period, turning night into day with fires visible for miles around, taking radar stations by surprise, damaging ships, railways, a power station and a munitions factory.

Some of the shelters, civilians used, were Anderson, and sometimes, Morrison, but this last option was not a favourite, as it was basically just a steel table to hide under, inside the house. Some people preferred to spend the night in camouflaged tents, in cars, vans, or even on the beach.

Although those three nights didn't compare in intensity, or duration, to London, or even Birmingham, they created great havoc and homelessness, just the same. A decimated city was left behind to testify. Industries involving smelting, and mining were targeted and the docks, nearby were not overlooked. It was severe while it lasted.

In the midst of one of those heavy air raids, a woman in a crowded, concrete shelter, was asked, where her husband was. As she draped blankets around her two children, the terse reply came through gritted teeth, "in the Army, the coward."

Emerging from the remnants of a particularly damaged street we noticed a little Odeon Cinema tucked away in an unlikely corner, and looking closer we saw there was an Alec Guinness movie playing, so in complete agreement, we decided a little comedy would be a welcome relief at this point, and was just what we needed. We were not disappointed.

On my next free evening, I met Don, who had discovered a surviving old hotel in Swansea where he planned to take me for dinner. A solid square of a building, doing its level best to emulate peacetime elegance and quality, limited supplies, notwithstanding. The menu was extended when possible, by serving local fish, laver bread, cockles etc. The laver bread was a kind of seaweed, tasting a bit like spinach but more richly flavoured. The owner also kept chickens, which helped extend the menu.

Dinner was served in the first floor dining room, enhanced by soft lights, fresh flowers adorning the tables, then after dinner coffee, (ersatz) in the lounge upstairs, was served to us. We sat in easy chairs around low tables, where a tiny cherry brandy was often served, to counteract the taste of chicory coffee, Don said.

Operation Balloons

Instructions for my sojourn on site, came as promised on the heels of the festive season, in January, and departure for my balloon experience, two days later, found me en route to the docks. Our approach heralded by the plaintive cries of sea gulls wheeling, soaring, and swooping low, over a deep grey and pewter highlighted ocean, brought us to a bleak looking spot, exposed to the elements on all sides. Not far away stood two Nissen huts, one, of which, contained my bed, thankfully, with windows intact and no accompanying leaky, gas light. The other smaller version, housed three men, so the full crew consisted of eight WAAF and three RAF. Eleven in all, if no-one was away on leave, or in Sick Bay.

Across the street, once stood a row of warehouses but now, almost in dead center, there was just a big hole in the ground, surrounded by leftover debris, and an area of flattish waste land (an aftermath of the series of air raids in February 1941). Local children found it curiously inviting, for games like hide and seek, and swarmed all over, completely ignoring all posted warning signs of the dangers lurking there, should those precarious piles of rubble start to slide. No-one policed the area, it seemed.

Approaching the balloon for the first time, I saw how surprisingly large it was, measuring sixty-two feet, by twenty-five feet. This was the average size.

It was, at present, on the ground secured by many tail guy ropes holding it in place, with the cable attached to the winch. This position was known as tail guy mooring. Out came the notebook to record the forthcoming avalanche of facts I would be expected to know on my return to civilization.

The top half of the balloon was filled with hydrogen, topped up daily, leaving the lower half empty, allowing air to enter as it rose in height. The main cable was attached either to the ground or to a lorry, in order to be winched up or down, as orders came from Ops to change height. The entire surface was covered with three heavy coats of silver paint preventing hydrogen from escaping, and should there be need for a patch, the patch would have to be treated the same way, with another three coats of paint.

The main purpose of barrage balloons was to keep enemy aircraft high enough to avoid low level target-bombing or strafing. The ROH, ruling operational height, was five thousand feet.

An aircraft in collision with a balloon itself would result in an explosion, destroying both. If it should hit a cable, a riplink would deploy, releasing a parachute which would create enough drag on the wing of an aircraft to bring it down. If it presumably, dropped on the site, I never got a good answer about the risk for those beneath.

Handling a balloon in difficult and dangerous conditions, was a revelation to me, arousing admiration for the way this crew seemed to cheerily handle this heavy, risky, work, in all weathers. They were so matter of fact about it all, and so few of us on the outside had any idea of the risks they took, or the skill they exhibited. Mental images of balloons in Dover, in a high wind during an air raid, crossed my mind, where ack-ack, bombs, and tracer bullets were all elements in the picture and on top of that, there were strong coastal winds, or other uncertainties of weather. These heroes, and heroines, were truly under rated.

Early one evening an order came from Ops to fly to 3,500 ft" from our present height of 500ft, so everyone, obeying instructions from the Sgt, got into position, while I tried to stay close enough to see the procedure without getting underfoot. The wind was forecast as a light chop, but as the balloon was released and being winched up, it seemed to be bouncing all over the sky making it tough to secure. Just to hang on to it was a challenge. Much later in a light, to moderate wind, I was allowed to add my hands to the winch, but the resistance was so great, it almost backfired, and for a second, I lost my grip on the handle, as it lashed back at me, hard. With a smile, the RAF operator, Jim, still holding on, said that in a real storm, it becomes a battle to maintain control, needing more than one person's hands to keep a grip, despite the use of motor power. A good spot to sustain injury if you were inexperienced;

Barrage balloons were used everywhere there was heavy bombing. Some were struck by lightning and sometimes they were shot down. During the heavy bombing of Dover, the Germans, frustrated by the barrier they presented, shot down fifty balloons in one day, however they paid dearly for their efforts and lost several bombers in so doing. This was some indication of the high esteem enemy aviators had for our barrage balloons. Next day when the bombers returned, expecting clear sailing, thirty two new balloons had popped up in their place. The balloon teams had to work harder than one legged tap dancers to make this happen overnight, but there they were, back on the job, defiantly keeping the enemy at bay.

A version of the barrage balloon was used to good effect on some ships, in order to deter low flying aircraft from sowing land mines.

On my last night, I was able to witness the high drama of a balloon being brought down to TGM, tail guy mooring, in the cold, pouring rain, while the wind made soughing noises as if we were aboard a ship.

The whole experience made me grateful once more, for the kind of job I held inside a building in comparative comfort. It also broadened my thinking about the very serious work done by such a stalwart crew. I was glad to have had the time here, and delighted not to have to do it again.

I left knowing that I would have a healthy regard for those on site every time it fell to my lot to pass on orders to alter the balloon height, especially in bad weather.

Back in Sketty, my circle of friends had increased considerably. There now were several clubs within walking distance, though the first one I visited, on Christmas Day, remained my favorite. It seemed, there were always several young men eager for company and happy to have someone to chat with. The clubs provided a genial meeting place, for both sexes, perhaps over a ping pong game, followed by tea, coffee, cookies and now then a cake of dubious origins. No one had any fat to spare or sugar either, so cake was often a mixture of strange substitutes, but we ate it with cheerful abandon. Was it mineral oil I tasted? Often it was.

The volunteers made us welcome and there was usually a piano, darts as well as ping-pong, with plenty of willing players. Americans stationed on the coast trickled in, and seemed to enjoy the home like atmosphere. At night though, many preferred the pubs.

One man, handsome as a young Errol Flynn, who was in training to become a Commando in a tough impressive battalion, somehow managed to combine his love of the arts with a challenging, hazardous, life in the Army. A strange mix I thought. He had a special fondness for opera and was himself gifted with a beautiful voice. I enjoyed talking to him, about life in general, though we barely knew each other. Like so many young men who were about to be shipped out, never sure of the future, he wanted an anchor, he said, someone to come back to. I went out with him twice and we discussed the pre-war peacetime movies, also Opera, and anything and everything that occurred to us as interesting. Nothing of a very personal nature, though. One evening on our third date he revealed that he thought I was just the person he had been looking for, to permanently share his life. He already had a ring and would like me to wear it. Was he serious? I was totally flabbergasted.

How could he come to such a conclusion practically overnight? We had known each other so briefly, and then only superficially. We knew very little about each other's lives outside of wartime. No build up, or serious conversation concerning ourselves, or a shared future, had ever been mentioned, so it was an absolutely unexpected question. A rather chaste goodnight kiss on our second date was the only mild expression of personal warmth and hardly rated as an intimate gesture of love. We were little more than acquaintances. The whole idea was preposterous but it seemed best to be a little gentler conveying this on the eve of his departure.

Pointing this out and adding other thoughts that might be un-hurtful, and helpful, I repeated my observation on wartime mis-alliances, that so many marriages were made under stress of imminent parting, between people who were almost strangers, that it's no wonder they often didn't last. Besides I was eighteen, a bit young to make that kind of commitment I said, and suggested that we might write as friends.

This seemed to inflame him even more and he stormed off into the wetness of the night, leaving me guilt ridden, though I had done nothing to encourage such a devastating proposal.

Later that night on duty in Ops seated at my desk where absolutely no personal calls were allowed, breaking all rules there was a personal phone call for me at about 0100 hrs, to the very obvious displeasure of the 'old school' Flight lieutenant sitting at his desk nearby. Not having given my unlisted phone number to anyone, I was totally mystified, especially at such an hour.

With nervous horror, I answered the phone to hear my erstwhile friend

Eric, who had left me at the entrance to HQ to go and bog down at the local pub, with the sole intention of getting 'polluted', which he was, by now. And ready to voice his sorrow, but not to weep in his beer, more's the pity. Instead, he broke into song, his powerful voice pouring out his anguish in my ear, singing the crying clown aria from Pagliacci. My desk adjoined the one occupied by the Flight Lieutenant on duty, and my struggles to muffle the escaping sound must have been ludicrous. I squirmed every which-way, to shield the sound, wishing I could hide under the desk, like the ostrich with head in the sand, rear end in the air. Although, I had the receiver pressed excruciatingly close to my ear, all the time, Paliacci's ringing tones clearly penetrated the quiet in this room, until the laughing, crying, finale, reached its climax.

Impossible to conceal, and by now, another officer friend had stopped by to talk with the Flight Lt. on duty, and was suddenly silenced by the fervent clamorous aria, both faces expressed total disbelief at this unsolicited, operatic solo assaulting their ears in the middle of the night while on watch. Their watch! Eyebrows were up in the hairline.

I felt compelled to listen, because I knew Eric would call back if I simply hung up the phone, which I desperately wanted to do so I nervously, waited it out, said a hasty goodnight and warned him never to do it again. Please.!

It was so upsetting, my face was obviously deep, peony coloured, leaving me completely speechless, while I was reprimanded for my breach of security, even though the resourceful Commando was the culprit. It was with a certain amount of sympathy and perhaps a touch of humour that I was scolded. No retribution for Eric, as I heard he was shipped out next day, and no doubt with a king of hangovers. That was the end of it. I silently hoped he would return safely to a slower paced world one day and find the right person with whom he could be happy. Perhaps his proclivity to opera, had him casting me as the usual unrealistic, reluctant heroine role? I'll never know.

What was in that room on the ground floor of GHQ? Every time I passed it, I wondered. I knew the rest of the building quite well and knew the CO's room was under Ops, and the room next door, allocated to his adjutant, but had never been in this particular room, or seen anyone coming in, or going or out of it. The door was hardly noticeable, as the paneling, included the doorway, which was always closed. I dared to poke my head inside, simmering in expectation, and was admonished, "quick, close the door and come in." The sole occupant was busy at a large switchboard, plugging and unplugging phone calls. I had stumbled on our communications centre, and the person in charge that day, was a Welsh girl, with hair the colour of ripe wheat, named Joan Nicholls. This room was off limits to all personnel, with very few exceptions (like the dispatch rider) but in this forbidden space, we began a friendship. Talking, between busy announcements and phone interchanges, we planned to meet on our next mutual half day.

From there, the friendship bloomed, and I became a regular visitor at her home. She was able to live at home while stationed in Sketty, which as an only child, pleased her parents mightily. They doted on Joan, and it's a wonder she was so un-spoiled. Emily and Frank soon treated me as part of their family and included me in their lavish, caring attention. Occasionally staying overnight on a sleeping out pass, I found a hot water bottle in my bed and a mug of hot milk on my nightstand. Creature comforts were lovingly administered, by Mother Emily.

Both parents were unself-consciously funny, highly entertaining without apparent effort, and possessed of a delicious sense of humour. It was so easy to become fond of them and I did.

Joan had a fascination for theatre, movies, and music and possessed a vibrant personality, underscored by a melodic Welsh accent. She became my best friend and confidante. Later on during my stay in Sketty, she came home with me on leave, where we stayed up, till all hours with my parents, telling stories, often about our encounters in wartime, reciting limericks, generally howling with mirth at the ridiculous. It was a good friendship that was to last long after the war ended.

Swansea area was inundated with troops, many English and now, Americans, too, flocked, in full force, in and around town, or in the local pubs. Manoeuvres, were taking place all up and down the coast and we were constantly reminded of the need for secrecy. Of course we knew a big push was coming, so no leading questions were asked, concerning anything to do with the war effort. Emphasis was placed on ruthlessly, censored mail, warnings against careless talk were everywhere, broadcast on air, or on reminder posters displayed in public places, and limited leave granted, only in emergency. It all built up to an aura of expectant pressure, and suspense, which we concluded meant that the big day wasn't far off.

In the meantime, some English and Welsh girls were falling in love with American men wherever they were stationed, though it seemed a bit disloyal to some of our men who needed female support and attention just as much. Friendships were a different matter and sprang up everywhere.

My letters from home told me that my parents had taken in an American officer from the Medical Corps and how much they enjoyed each other. We never met, but I saw photos on my leave afterwards. They exchanged correspondence throughout the war.

I had been dating one of the officers I worked with and since this was frowned upon, I disguised myself in civvies, even more frowned upon, but worth the risk I thought. Officers and non-coms were not allowed to date, unless married to each other, so we decided a little subterfuge was in order.

We went to a coastal dance in a hotel nestled in beautiful Caswell Bay on the Gower coast. I had begun to smoke by now, although I never inhaled, and since I didn't much like the taste of ordinary cigarettes, I smoked Balkan Sobranies instead, which were Turkish, usually flat, black with a gold tip, sometimes pastel coloured. I used a long cigarette holder, hoping it made me look older, besides, the aroma was appealing. Guilo, (a nickname) used to get the cigarettes for me, and once, an ivory cigarette holder with a red tip appeared in my desk drawer one morning whilst on duty, along with a note from him. All very secret and exciting, and I enjoyed the intrigue.

One evening we took a train to the next town to have dinner at the Angel in Cardiff. It was important to catch the train on time or there wouldn't be enough time to eat, and return in time for my curfew. On that particular day there was every interruption possible, delaying me. Would I make that train in time? It was a race. Despite all, we finally, met at the station and had seconds in which to board, and close the carriage door.

He was older than I, by fifteen years, rather elegant, and very informed about the history of England, political structures, and the arts. I learned all sorts of fascinating things while painlessly acquiring an increased sense of curiosity about life, from his vast store of knowledge. He helped me grow, and stimulated my mind, making me feel more alive. We spent a happy time having dinner, followed by a languid dessert, coffee and a small liqueur, and all too soon it was over.

Time to leave for the last train; Three hours had disappeared, fast as a whip crack, but G. kept a sharp eye on the clock and under cover of blackout escorted me back to the billet minutes, before my curfew at 2230 hours. We said goodnight, expecting to meet on duty together, two days hence.

That was the last time I was to see him alive. During the night he suffered a severe headache, and other symptoms, which rapidly developed into meningitis. He died within twenty four hours. Only close friends, and my parents knew we were dating, so it was an enormous shock to find out so casually, in Ops when I went on duty next day, expecting to see him there.

No letter in my drawer awaited me that day.

I was shaken to the core. Wartime casualties were expected but not something like this. My feelings were muddled, with a pervading sense of loss. I had developed a feeling of deep friendship for this man, not 'in love,' though he may have been with me, but I didn't think so. His presence had meant something good and valued, in my life. He would be much missed.

This was a good time to take my seven days leave. Once home, it was good to be immersed in the reorganizing of my new bedroom. My parents had moved their place of residence, but still maintained two shops in Oldbury. We now lived in a little village called West Hagley, about twenty five miles away from their business. Our house had three bedrooms, and bathroom and the enclosed garage attached to the house was large, with a half bath, and an enclosed cubicle for fuel for the fireplaces. The kitchen overlooked a pretty garden, and boasted a fireplace and the living room had a similar view of the garden, then next to that was the den. Both rooms with fireplaces. There was also a large pantry on the ground floor which proved very useful, and a powder room adjoining.

They were so happy to see me and most sympathetic to hear about Guilo, (short for Guildford) who had apparently written them to introduce himself, as he hoped to meet them soon. Both parents commuted for their work, back and forth to Oldbury, so I only saw them in snatches, until the week end. They were at home every evening, but gone during daytime, for several days during the week, on buying trips, tending paper work, and overseeing two store managers. This left me with some useful free time on my hands, and peace and quiet for resting.

Kidderminster was within a few miles and so was Stourport, where the boat was moored, The Dalmation. No petrol available for taking it out for a ride, of course, but lunch on deck and rowing the dinghy downriver were happy events, if the weather held. On the week end, we decided to do just that. It was a shot in the arm for all four of us and the pooch, a beautiful brindle bull dog, named Judy, who energetically, wagged her tailless bottom, overcome with joy and approval, at the sight of the boat, and being out with family. It was a perfect day and we all returned, feeling better for the sun, fresh air-soaked, pleasantly weary, and happy to rest. No threatening noises interrupted our peace.

The countryside around Hagley was quite beautiful, and the house we lived in had a garden stocked with all the old fashioned plants one expects, to find in an English garden, so both parents could indulge their hobbies.

Dad said, he did the digging, and Mom did the picking. She just smiled and went on picking.

Visiting relatives as usual while on leave, I travelled on two long bus rides, raids being less frequent, but still occurring at night in the Midlands. Trying to rotate my visits between families, I first headed for a little suburb called Hill Top, hoping to see some of my cousins there.

Cousin Douglas, my geometry teacher, was medically unfit for the Services, so he was doing some kind of office war work, as a draughtsman, but his wife Lily, was in the ATS. She was an anti-aircraft gunner on the coast and attached to the Royal Artillery (proper title).

I was in luck, both, came home shortly after I arrived, luckily for me. Lily was on leave, and Douglas had taken a short break from work to be with her. After a hugging welcome we sat down to tea, and Lily said she had a remarkable story to tell, and we sat back to listen.

Stationed on the southeast coast in a heavily bombarded area near Dover, Lily was one of a team of people protecting the town, from her position on an ack-ack site, right on the outskirts of the city. Her team had become a close knit unit, as often happens when a group shares imminent danger and in this case, nightly air raids dominated the scene. In moments of stress and after a tough night, they sometimes speculated on how long they could expect to be lucky enough to escape the overhead death threats? The hours were long, the menace showed no sign of slacking off, and too often they were all truly weary.

Then, coming through the night unharmed, and watching the rosy dawn, they proceeded to get on with the job at hand renewed, and talking animatedly about the night's events, when they could be heard above the noise, that is. Life seemed good and possibilities endless, and last night's worries receded into forgotten memories. The crew relied heavily on each other, for moral support, both on the job and off, functioning well as a unit. They spent much of their spare time in small groups together off duty, and on duty, depending on each other, and finding relief in fun where ever possible.

Leave for each member of their team became essential, but sparing only one at a time, was the rule, so as not to leave too big a strain on the others, and it was Lily's turn to go. This was the leave before the present one. Gladly she departed, with promises to bring back something good to eat, as their Mess food was pathetic, she said.

She and her husband, Douglas, made the most of their short time together and time vanished, brief as a shooting star, or so it seemed, until it was time to return to work. Armed with home-made, shepherds pies for her chums, Lily reached her base only to discover strange faces at her position. Looking around, still no familiar faces. It was as if she had come to the wrong place. Odd! Could they have been moved on, and forgotten to notify her? Where were they all? Was this her new unit, and if so where were her chums? Bewildered, she went to the Orderly room to find some answers. On further enquiry, by now worried and upset, she discovered the terrible truth. In her absence, while she was enjoying her leave, the battery had received a direct hit and the entire crew was no more. Wiped out! Everyone gone in one hit! Lily was the only survivor. Sick with disbelief, the dreadful truth finally sank in, as she tried to absorb the shock. She felt suddenly old, beyond counting, she said afterwards, and we could barely imagine the jolt it had been.

We agreed that she was incredibly lucky to have been spared. In itself, a reminder for me to get back on track, happy to be alive, enjoying each day.

My leave was over and time to return to Swansea, grateful to be back in balloon command again, instead of on site, however, I was a bit discombobulated, to find Bethel Chapel a thing of the past. Suddenly, we had moved, in my absence, a major accomplishment had taken place while I was away. We now lived in a house and I was told that my few possessions left in the chapel had been taken to our new billet, by my co-workers, hopefully, without breakage. Would we have a real bathroom? And real closets to hang things in? The long awaited house! At last!

For now, my bed was designated to occupy the front room on the ground floor, but later, a few of us on shift work, would be given a large room on the top floor, out of the daily hubbub, escaping the noise of those coming, and going, loudly ringing phones, radios and the like, all the usual noises of daytime activity, silenced so we could rest. After our long wait, we were to be rewarded with a room where we could blot out the world and sleep, real sleep. Yes, to the closets, bathrooms, plural, and other present day, amenities. It was all good news.

Relieving our new Ops member, Eunice, sharp at twelve noon, our long overdue Special Duties Person (SDP), had recently arrived, and we decided to eat dinner together, providing me with the opportunity to get to know her a little. We talked at length and I got the impression that she was a volatile, mercurial, very likeable WAAF with whom I could share a few adventures. First impressions are often good ones for me and she became a good friend, during our time in Wales. Brown sparkling eyes with unbelievable lashes, rather small, about five feet and a fraction, and 'well' endowed, as I heard one of the men say. Her husband was in the desert, and they had last seen each other four years ago. When we got to know each other better, she confided, that it was a hasty marriage, made under pressure of wartime parting, and they hardly knew each other, she said. Now, through their letters sent back and forth, they were trying to remedy that.

Next day, was spent on duty at 0800hrs until noon, due back again, in Ops. at 2200 hrs. Usually the latter shift began at 1700 hrs but the hours had been adjusted to accommodate a WAAF house warming party to take place at our new house, that very evening, all news to me.

After lunch, I returned to take a siesta before night duty, but 'fat chance.' Preparations were already afoot for the big party and my shared bed-room was to serve as cloakroom, so I may as well abandon any hope of a nap, go to the party and be a hostess, a totally unexpected turn of events. Giving in with good grace, I shared the chores, and pitched in, enjoying the novelty of the upcoming surprise party.

People began to come, invitation in hand bringing wine, beer and sometimes scotch or gin. We had our own little supply, along with soft drinks, but contributions were helpful, particularly as those invited, brought guests. Hard to know how many guests would come, so we just had to 'wing' it and enjoy the celebration. One small gin and lots of soda, was about my capacity in those days. Either that, or a shandy. Some of the girls drank beer or gin and 'It' (Italian vermouth) but there were no big drinkers among us residents, so our supplies should last.

It proved to be in fact, a rare event, as there weren't many such parties possible under the prevailing circumstances. One of a kind, we were told enthusiastically by our guests.

'Magic Mary' from the Mess had supplied us with tempting arrays of edibles conjured out of vegetables, bread, potatoes, nuts and anything not rationed. No cheeses, meat or cakes, but it didn't seem to matter. The food all vanished by evening's end, and most of the booze.

I recognized many of the RAF, (some pilots came all the way from Fairwood, in Wales) and most of the WAAF, but there were lots of new faces too. How did they all know? There were Australians, Americans and one or two other nationalities, new to several of us and so welcome. Looking around, at the various uniform insignias, the international aspect, struck me as heart-warming. Our own version of the United Nations was assembled here tonight. The word must have spread further than we expected

People wandered through the ground floor as the crowd got bigger, more voluble, and conversations were rolling right along, when some gung ho person began organizing party games. Without warning, one of the organizers grabbed my arm, thrusting me into the centre of activity while a circle formed around us, completely cutting off an escape route, and I was directed to choose a man as partner. Surveying what seemed to be a multitude of faces, my eyes fell on a tall, slender, American soldier with a nice face, obviously amused by the proceedings, so I pointed to him. He was given a black beribboned garter and told to place it on my ankle, someone simultaneously doused the lights. In the dark I received an over familiar pinch in a personal place, and then the room was flooded with light. I was supposed to be outraged and react accordingly, but I realized that the pincher was female and except for a loud "ouch", there was no retaliated violence on my part. However, I was known to be a blusher, much to my discomfort, and as often happened, colour flooded my face from hairline to neckline which satisfied the perpetrators, as they enjoyed my painful, technicolour display.

'Tall and slender,' about six feet, proved to be a person named Frank, who proceeded to capture my attention for much of the evening after that; not leaving my side unless he must. He had a naturally light complexion, hair dark blonde, curly, despite his determined efforts in plastering it down with water, sensitive, triangular, face, and greenish hazel eyes alive with amusement as if sharing a private joke. Somehow, overlooked was a determined chin, which came to my attention much later. In general, his appearance, was not at all the dark haired, Brylcream, fly-boy type I was apt to gravitate towards.

He was very intelligent, far from dull, most articulate and had a witty sense of humour, I discovered, in our brief exchanges. Distracted by attending to our other guests, interrupting us, only briefly, until it was time to grab my coat and go on watch, Frank did not move an inch away from my side, instead he helped me on with my coat before leaving, and asked for a date, but looking at the calendar, showing my free times off duty, I could only give him one in about three weeks. Before he left, coat in hand, out came the little pocket calendar to record the event along with my telephone number so that he could use it to remind me the day before, he said and be sure there were no slip ups. Discouraged? No, determined!

Catching up with Joan, both of us on night duty, she told me about someone new she had been dating in my absence. His name was George, also an American, who seemed to like all the same things she did, and she was looking forward to seeing him again soon.

Almost three weeks later, the day before my date with Frank, I was assigned to fire picket duty, an extra duty entailing, watching for roof fires, so when he phoned to be sure we were still on, I explained the circumstances. with apologies. He sounded very disappointed, after waiting so long, it was understandable, but we rearranged to meet the next night, instead, which helped.

Shortly after that, news came that I had passed all trade exams with flying colours, even the technical balloon parts. There was some discussion then, about whether or not I might like to apply for a commission and I was promised good recommendations, if I did. Asking, if I could still be in Operations or Flying control as an officer, it seemed that wasn't possible. Only commissioned males, were appointed to this special field. Women weren't quite, equal yet, it seems. The nearest thing to this job would be working as a Code and Cipher officer. This sounded like paperwork and more paperwork to me, before computers of course, so I said it would be best to think it over, thank you. I liked this job too much, and the variety it entailed.

My colleagues thought we should celebrate my exam passing, and because they had known about it before I did, they had already persuaded a willing WAAF to do my fire picket duty, so that they could take me out to dinner at the Metropole hotel. I felt very honoured to find the surprise all planned ahead, fait accompli. The whole thing decided for me was unusual, and most unexpected.

We took the little red, chugging bus, with its neoprene bag strapped on top to save fuel, and we clambered upstairs in a little group, finding seats together, and headed for Swansea. It was one of those evenings that was so congenial, from the very start, when everyone had a chance to talk about what our lives might be like at the end of the war, and about reasons for entering the war, and soon we were telling funny war stories, and laughing our socks off.

On arrival we were shown to a reserved table in the dining room where, with decorum restored, we were served a surprisingly good meal. Not all potatoes. Afterwards, following the usual procedure we left the dining room and went upstairs to the lounge for coffee, some of us, having after dinner drinks around softly lit, low, round tables. Tugging on my sleeve as we sat, I turned to see a beshawled Welsh woman, holding a big basket of flowers, and from it she offered me a pretty little bouquet saying" from the gentleman over there." Not seeing any gentleman over there, I regretfully said I didn't like to accept presents from someone I didn't know. "Oh, he says he knows you, bach" (dear, in Welsh). So I followed her pointing finger and to my utter consternation, there leaning in the doorway, stood Franklin Smith from the "night of the garter". My date! My cancelled date! As I looked, he touched his hat and turned away. This was the man I had had to stand up, after he had patiently waited three weeks to see me. I sank down into the leather armchair in pure mortification, knowing how it must have appeared to him. Before I could recover my wits, he had melted into the shadows and was gone, but not before I saw a look of hurt, mingled with disgust, cross his features.

That was the end of that, I thought. But not so! He was just marshalling his thoughts. Next day I got a hand delivered letter, really an outraged missive, to the effect that, why, if I didn't want to go out with him had I not had the guts, and civility to say so, in the first place? Well, who could blame him?

Still I didn't know what to do about it. No return address. No phone number. While I was thinking it over the following day, an even more, angry letter arrived. To this, I vigorously responded right away, asking in my turn whether he always condemned the accused without providing a chance for an explanation, and sent it back with the soldier who delivered it. The morning after that, he followed up with a phone call, calling for a truce and asking for a new start, so we set a date, and both kept it punctually, with considerable success. Explanations were made and no further blunders ensued. Frustration and vexation behind us, that, was the beginning. It occurred to me at the time that, here was a man who didn't give up easily. Still I didn't remember the chin!

After this, we spent a great deal of our mutual spare time together, exploring the beautiful countryside along the Gower coast from Swansea, travelling on a sort of tram known as the Mumbles train, to the Mumbles and beyond. The weather was lovely with the sun glinting on the waves, bees humming around the wild flowers and the new growth of grass, springy under our feet, next to the beach.

It was quite a long walk from Mumbles to Langland Bay, and then on to Caswell Bay to reach the hotel on the bluff looking out to sea. The hotel, the Osborne, was a most enviable spot, seeming almost to be perched on the wave tops themselves. A small enticing citadel!

Inside, looking down over the water below, it seemed as if one was under sail on the deck of a boat. A quiet spot in the daytime as a rule, so that the gulls climbing and diving down to water's edge, could clearly be heard making their own comments in a shrill, two noted wail. At night, dinner

Frank in a happy moment

was served with a flourish and a small group of good musicians provided the irresistible dance music. This was the setting for our first real date.

The spectacular beauty of the coastline beckoned us back again and again, luring us around its curves. We strolled along the cliff tops, sometimes venturing down below into the sandy coves and once, we stretched out in the sun on the short grass on a small knoll, lying on our backs, in the lee of the wind, taking time to study the clouds. Puffy, cauliflower clouds, whiter than whipped cream against a sky of hyacinth blue, were forming peaks and valleys, gently changing shape as we watched. Slipping, sliding and moulding into faces, bewhiskered, and jutting jawed, full of character. As the scene changed, long tressed waifs, floated past, hovering like lost mermaids. No reminders up there of the bitter struggle for survival, a fight for freedom of beliefs, and the threat to an entire human race. But down below us on the beaches were reminders of all of it. Menacing, heavy barricades, and barbed wire to guard against invaders, with barriers extending out from the shore, also discouraging beach combers. Most of it was off limits to the public.

Anywhere near to Swansea it wasn't safe to venture on the beach anyway, because of land mines. We revisited this area many times, talking all the way, swapping ideas, relating stories about family members and challenging each other's convictions. Then, returning, going back the way we came, on the famed Mumbles train, clanging our way along the rails in the open air and watching the sea beat its foamy path, trailing the shore. In the moonlight it was quite a sight, with no electric lights to compete with the reflection of the full moon mirrored in the water. Truly memorable!.

Mumbles had earned some notoriety for having the only murderer in the area in forty years. He, the murderer, was said to be a doctor who had lived there peacefully for many years, until one day, in a fit of rage he chopped up his wife sitting in the bathtub, and stuffed her remains in a trunk. The reason was not known, and the locals didn't much like being reminded of such unheard of Welsh behavior, so we didn't ask questions.

Strolling through Singleton Park, half way between Swansea and Sketty one sunny day, enjoying the flourishing palm trees and surrounding flora, with Frank, I was jolted out of my reverie to become aware of a shift in conversation. Half realizing then, that the time was coming when I would be asked to make a decision. Though Frank had not asked me to marry him in so many words, I could sense we were getting into deeper water. He was, at the moment, telling me, that his Mother would be writing to me and that he would like to meet my parents. Gently, I explained once again that proximity to my family was very important to me and though I looked forward to travelling in peacetime, perhaps around the world, or to the States, I would not wish to live abroad, permanently. I could not contemplate leaving behind family and life-long friends. I was nineteen and he was twenty seven, which left a gap in our experiences. Besides we didn't know how long the

Me in uniform, age 18, in Singleton Park

war would last, or what was ahead of us, or how we might change during that time. That being the case I thought a platonic friendship was all I could offer. Silence reigned.

Sitting on a bench under a sweet smelling tree now in bloom, Frank, picking the petals from a daisy one by one, glancing at me now and again, stayed very still. He was obviously far from enchanted at the prospect of that offer. Finally, 'better this, than nothing," he said. "In the meantime we should make the most of the time we have." Agreeing on that as our plan,

I relaxed secure in the knowledge that cards were on the table and I had been entirely honest with him and was understood. Marrying an American was as likely for this girl as flying to the moon which nobody in his right mind considered as the remotest possibility then. In hind sight, the simile was apropos.

On the other hand, Joan and George seemed to be contemplating a future together, and George had evinced a great fondness for her parents, Emily and Frank, which fortuitously, seemed to be mutual. They spent many hours debating the possibilities of being together after the war and both seemed very happy in each others' company. I was there for dinner with all of them, when they made a commitment to marry, as soon as it was feasible, celebrating the occasion with a rare bottle of champagne and many toasts. Both glowed with anticipation and joy.

Not long after my heart to heart with Frank, I was given three days notice for a course in North East of London, lasting almost two weeks. Not much information was forthcoming as to the topic, and I was intrigued by the mystery.

Frank was sad to see me go but offered to drive me to the station, or rather to have a driver and his CO's flag car take us to the station, but it would be more of a novelty for me to have my first ride in a jeep I thought, which he found amusing, but felt it could be arranged. His CO was someone he knew well at home. Frank was a Technical Sgt by choice, it seemed, in the corps of engineers. Before that, a Harvard graduate, tho' he didn't mention that for quite some time. He had refused a commission, feeling that he didn't want the responsibility of ordering men into mortal danger. In the meantime most of his friends were officers who looked out for him when they could, hence the vehicle.

Frank gave me his APO address. He was stationed a long way out on the Gower peninsular, about forty miles, as the crow flies, but as the road twisted and turned, who knew how many? It took over an hour for him to reach Sketty, in favourable conditions. I had already seen amphibious jeeps, ducks and LST's on our coast, and as preparations intensified, they became a familiar sight.

The general atmosphere everywhere, was permeated with a strange feeling of suspended animation, everyone a bit on the edge, and on the brink, waiting for a big move of some sort. Under this threatening cloud, we said goodbye at the railway station maintaining stiff composure. Well, more or less, under the circumstances.

It wasn't a long journey compared to most, but viewing the crowded platform queues, vanishing slowly into the carriage doorways, I wondered how the train would hold us all. Only at the last minute did a seat appear in the middle of a row of passengers. Kit bag outside the door, we travelled almost nonstop, except for brief pauses in Bath, Swindon and Reading, major links to other destinations. Hardly noticing my neighbours, my thoughts flew backwards to Frank and my hurried departure. I began writing a quick note, hesitating mid stroke, wondering, was it fair? Was I leading him on? Should I try being more casual? Should I just not write? What was the right thing? On and on questions persisted. No answers ensued, so I did nothing, but think, think and re think. I was haunted by indecision, caught between the desire to see as much of him as possible while I still could, and the need not to be in a position of a heart-aching decision to leave my home after the war.

Time passed as the rails chanted their rhythmic beat and sooner than expected, I realized we were there, coming into Paddington. All change. Finding the right Underground, on the big wall map, showed me the best option was the Bakerloo line to Kenton. Downing my kit bag at the gate, showing my pass, a pair of hands hoisted the kit bag and a voice said, "Which platform?" Hurrying along behind the owner of the voice, an airman wearing the half wing of AG denoting air gunner, plopped the kit bag at my feet, I just had time to thank him as the train drew in, before he disappeared upwards, on the escalator to catch his own train, two steps at a time. No words exchanged.

At Kenton, the waiting MT took me on a fairly short ride, to a spot just outside the little town. Entering an enclosure, attended by a guard in a small hut, we saw several assorted buildings on our left, with a small paved road leading around the back. Following it, we were led to a three story building, once an old house, and there was my new billet. Just a hop, skip and jump from the Mess in the usual, by now familiar, Nissen Hut, just a few doors away.

In one of those brick built buildings on the opposite side, our lecture began next day at 0900hrs. The subject revealed on the blackboard was 'Identifying Various Gasses.' Notebooks and pens were issued at the door to a small group of about fifteen of us. Both sexes represented, we filed in.

During the next ten days from 0900 hrs to 1700 hrs, with an hour for lunch we were given lectures on about five or more known gases, and procedures for identifying them and hopefully escaping their evil results. Information on the properties, and potential damage caused by inhalation, or touch, with a discussion afterwards, completed the lecture series.

For the final test we were then issued with gas capes, shown how to roll them up so they could be carried behind a tin helmet worn in the nape of the neck, with the rip cord exposed, ready to be released by a single tug, allowing the cape to cover the entire body quickly. Then came the practical part of the test. This involved a visit to the ominous sounding gas chamber. And it was!

We waited in an ante room to go in, and entered one by one, exiting on the far side with no chance to ask what was coming, from the person ahead.

My turn to enter the room, gas cape in position, gloves, gas mask and tin helmet on, I entered the dimly lit space. Walls were covered with a special material to prevent leakage, and windows were sealed. At one end was one small opaque window, with an open funnel like device beneath, directed at me, then, a voice from a nearby speaker told me to jump up and down to test the respirator. I didn't like the next part much.

Next, there was a soft hiss, misting from the funnel thing and "take off the mask and proceed to the door to identify the gas just released", was the next command. Altogether I identified about five gases, after five trips to the gas chamber, mustard gas, smelling of geraniums was one, and the last one was easy as the resulting red eyes and tears told its own tale. Tear gas. Back to the real world, the outdoors never smelled so good.

I was told without further waiting, that I had passed the test and would leave tomorrow, to return to Sketty. There had been no satisfactory answer to my questions about whether or not we could expect to have to use this training, only a vague reference to the fact that we should always be prepared for anything and now we were. Not exactly reassuring!

Next day, feeling a bit silly with gas cape rolled up behind my tin helmet, its little string dangling, I boarded the train for an uneventful journey back to base.

In Sketty, I headed back to the billet to consult the duty roster to find that my first watch would not be until 0800 hrs next day, giving me a rare opportunity for an evening at home to catch up, preceded by one of Mary's good dinners.

During all this time away, I had resisted the many urges to write Frank fearing I had already begun to feel too fond of him for comfort and needing to keep some distance between us.

Suddenly on the slope approaching the Mess, it struck me that a certain corps of Americans and British Army were no longer in evidence, either here, or in Swansea. Could they have moved out in my absence? Was it panic I felt? Of course not!

My question answered, I saw there, at the entrance, leaning towards the Mess, hatless, one arm along the top of the gate, stood one very fed-up looking American soldier. As he heard my footsteps he straightened, feet scraping the gravel, sunlight slanting on his hair in the late afternoon, turning it light blonde, he got right to the point, firing his first salvo, "why didn't you write?" Flummoxed, I said the first thing that came into my head," I didn't have any stationery," provoking him still further. He shot back," it really doesn't become you, to be so blasé." I forgot in the heat of this verbal attack to ask him how he knew I was expected back, but it didn't matter, here he was.

This gave me pause to consider the situation and to tell him in a more reasonable way, how I actually felt. He made his point that even as a friend, it was pretty poor treatment, and if that was how I treated friends, it's a wonder I had any. Ouch! It had left him painfully up in the air, he said, when everything else seemed to be coming to a head, the future, being precarious and his stay coming to an end. Surrounded by uncertainty, shouldn't we hang onto whatever was good and lasting in our relationship? One thing led to the other and we began to explore possibilities. The upshot being a decision to see each other whenever possible, and to write to each other when apart; Otherwise, we would make no binding decision until we could meet again, after the immediate pressure was off. This seemed more realistic and fair to both. We said a very friendly goodbye, wondering if this was "it" for a while.

The Big Push

It was a time when the air was heavy with secrets and the sure knowledge that something big was imminent, and it constantly hung like a pall over everyone. Most Army units were confined to camp. Next day, there was a phone call from Frank telling me that all leave and passes had been cancelled. The Corps of Engineers were among those confined to quarters before shipping out. To my utter amazement in the late afternoon, I heard that he had after all, used his hidden influence to wangle one last pass, best not to enquire how, to see me one last time.

It was a very brief visit and afterwards an emotional, but upbeat parting and we once more renewed our agreement to write, the only commitment was to see each other after it was over. Both of us were strangely sure of this, despite the ominous happenings certain to be ahead.

The parting left a big hole in the fabric of my life, nothing was as much fun, and I was ready and willing, to move on to my next job, which I thought would be happening in the very near future.

During the many months Frank and I had been seeing each other I had been aware of general air of resentment from some of the British men in uniform. They felt ousted by the 'Yanks.' One Australian RAF officer with whom I worked was clearly of that ilk and used every opportunity to regale me with stories illustrating the faithlessness of American men, their lack of history and culture, and on and on. I made my rebuttals to the point of rudeness, avoiding him at all costs. Luckily I didn't encounter him again after Frank left, as my new orders to leave for Plymouth came in, just about a week after my parting with Frank. Not a posting as such, but to another course, also shrouded in mystery. What could be worse than gas, I thought?

It was all so hush hush, giving no clue about what was supposed to be learned from this venture. The day before my departure, I woke early and every radio in the house was blaring the news of our landings in St Lo and Omaha Beach. It was June 6 1944. The Allies had made landings on five Normandy beaches along fifty miles of heavily fortified coastline. Americans on Omaha Beach met with major resistance and sadly sustained the most casualties. The British and Canadian forces landed on St Lo and two other beaches which were slightly less well defended, but still they suffered their share of losses. This attack was the largest ever recorded in military history. The code name for it was "Overlord."

Five thousand ships with troops and supplies, had left for those shores. Eleven thousand aircraft provided air cover and support. Air support also bombed bridges so that the delay affected German troop reinforcements, who had to take the long way around to reach their destinations, thereby losing time and advantage. One week later on June 11th 326,000 troops, 50,000 vehicles and 100,000 tons of equipment had landed on Normandy.

We found out afterwards that the Allies had leaked information that Pas-de-Calais on the Norwegian Coast would be the chosen landing site for the attack and the Germans were expecting them there, so the element of surprise prevailed.

We were over the moon with delight and relief. This was what we had been waiting for all this time, an end to so many nerve wracking uncertainties, except for one. Did those we cared about survive? Pushing all negative thoughts aside, I decided to continue writing as usual to the APO that Frank had given me, and Joan decided to do the same for George, nervously keeping an eye on incoming mail as we waited for word.

On this, my last duty in Ops we were each given a glass of wine to toast this never to be forgotten day in our lives. We felt as if we too were a small part of this historic event.

Next day, found me en route to my next course in Plymouth. Pulsating with activity, the railway station presented a study of life in motion, rather like a piece of music, the "flight of the bumble bee." It was indeed buzzing like a jar full of bees with the lid on. People alighting and departing, meeting and parting, some troops on the move, kit bags everywhere. Lots of two fingered V-signs being waved about, accompanied by smiles in general, as people recognized the successful landing as a major and significant step in the right direction towards a successful end to this war. It was indeed just that!

6 – Buzz Bombs and Rockets: V-1s and V-2s

Plymouth

AS THE TRAIN steamed in, I joined the smallest queue waiting to board but too late to find a seat. Resigned to a long journey in the corridor, I found a spot for my kit bag and a window wall to lean on. Like a restless dog circling his pad, I squirmed around trying to find a way to sit on the kit bag without falling off, when a sympathetic airman offered me his seat in the carriage behind me. Stowing my kitbag in the overhead rack, we spoke through the open door, as he perched on his luggage and generously shared his thermos of hot tea. Blessed with a brief leave, he was on his way to meet his new son, born only two days ago, and was so excited. Like a boiling kettle with the lid jammed on tight, he burbled on, happily expansive, about taking them home from hospital and deciding on a name, trying out suggestions on me, as we travelled.

Before his departure I saw a photo of his pretty, shyly smiling wife, outside their small, well kept, brick home. The entrance was sandwiched between two great clumps of heavenly blue cosmos, at the front door, where she was posed. "She is lovely," I said, giving back the photo, where it was lovingly returned to its home in his wallet, whilst beaming his pleasure at my comment.

Bath came into view, and in minutes he had his luggage in hand, and was on the move, straddling over obstacles, of feet still standing, or sitting, in the corridor, and jumping the doorway step, with a cheery backward glance, he waved, before striding away. Through the station he went, looking buoyant, and eager, disappearing as I watched, bounding up the steps with great leaps, whistling softly to himself as he vanished from view.

Closing my eyes as we pulled out, my thoughts wandered to my own situation. It would be some time before letters would reach me from abroad, with Allied troops constantly on the move after D-Day. Letters to Wales (my last address), would probably be sent to Plymouth first, and then be forwarded to Stanmore. Slow as a goods train, time consuming, and madly frustrating.

Was Frank one of the ones to escape harm, or had he been injured ...or worse? How would I know? Perhaps his Mother would contact me if anything was amiss? We had corresponded in the past two months so I felt we knew each other a little, and I liked her descriptive, warm and friendly, letters.

We all knew the Americans had landed on one of two beaches. Which one, I wondered and how soon would I hear from him? I didn't listen to casualty listings, nor would I, always keeping positive thoughts to the forefront and concentrating instead, on ideas for a reunion, when at all possible.

Looking back I thought of him then, remembering one of our conversations, as we wandered over the Welsh countryside, and through Singleton Park, noted for its palm trees and other semi-tropical plants. It had all seemed so idyllic in retrospect, our conversations never ending and stimulating.

Apropos of the future, Frank had vividly described his academic life at Harvard. Deciding on a major, his first choice had been Business School, but after earning his degree, he suddenly realized that was not how he wanted to spend his life, number crunching. Although it proved useful later on, it did not appeal as a career. Instead, his architectural ambitions surfaced, and fuelled by the presence of the renowned Professor Walter Gropius at Harvard School of Design who was the proponent of contemporary design, he decided that was for him, and Frank became one of his most dedicated students.

Gropius had escaped from Germany and spent some time in England, before coming to the US to become a revered Professor of Architecture at Harvard in Cambridge, Massachusetts. Almost singlehandedly he influenced the shift from repetitious, old styles, copied from earlier times, to new, avant garde, creative ideas. He was well known also for his use of indigenous materials. "Form follows function" was his byword, repeated often by his followers. It was exciting for Frank to be in the vanguard of a new era, and his enthusiasm was infectious. Only one more year of tuition remained before he would have his degree in architecture, and free to find a position.

He could expect a choice of locations when seeking a job and was flexible, and hopefully a promising future beckoned. Right now however, he longed for the bloodshed and tragedies of war to end, so that he could live a life of creativity with me he said, but this was jumping the gun and all pure speculation at this point. That decision to share his future had not yet been made by me, and it produced a mixture of joy and angst in my heart. Too many unknowns! Was I already in too deep? The same old question, over and over.

Forcing my thoughts back to the present and seeking distraction, I looked towards Exeter as we approached, waiting for a glimpse of the ocean. Just a glimpse was all I saw. There it was, in the distance, framed by the window, like a colored slide projected on the screen, now rapidly disappearing, as we chugged along. The scene changed minute by minute, moving on steadily, obscuring the beach as it curved and we didn't, the rails prosaically following a predestined straight path, as railroads do. In the distance, I already knew we would see the ever-present evidence of attempts to ward off marauders. Predictably, the inevitable barricades and barbed wire fences would be visible on the cliffs overlooking the beaches, and we couldn't wait to see them removed since those aforesaid marauders wouldn't be coming now, I thought, heaving a heartfelt sigh of relief that reached right to my toes.

Down below, what did those rippling, innocent looking waves, lapping gently on the shore, conceal? How many land mines lurked silently in their depths, waiting to be provoked into action? Would we be free to swim and children to paddle there, ever again in safety, I wondered? The idea of a worry free swim in the therapeutic briny ocean conjured up happier days, and a longing to do it all again one sunny day.

Leaving the coast, we angled slightly inland, (the beautiful new Tamar bridge had not been built yet) and we were on the last leg of the journey heading for Plymouth, along the old rail path. A city full of history, and I hoped to have an opportunity to explore it in my off time. If I had any! History and archaeology always fascinated me.

Punctuating our arrival with a loud belch of steam, it seemed we had arrived, and walking towards the exit, I saw my transport was there already, the driver leaning on the door enjoying the sunshine, turned as he saw me, smiled and asked how was my train journey? He was a dark haired, tall, capable kind of person, I thought, as I helped him stow my kit bag, tin helmet, gas mask and gas clobber, tidily into the van, and decided to make a bold move and sit in front with the driver, rather to his surprise. Better for conversation, and I was hoping to enlist help in getting my bearings, however after a few basic pointers on the route he was taking, he then fell silent until a familiar Nissen hut hove into view. We quickly dropped off my kit bag and other belongings at the entrance, without pausing, even for a cup of tea. The change of pace made itself felt as people outside seemed to be scurrying along, heads bent, as if late for appointments. We picked up three WAAF waiting at the door, immediately setting off again to be briefed on our forthcoming training. Not a minute to waste, apparently. Thoughts of the Mad Hatter flashed through my head."I'm late, I'm late, for a very important date"

Feeling a bit travel stained, after a long train journey, I hurriedly ran a comb through my hair on the way, added lip gloss, and joined the others for briefing. A bath would have been nice. Fat chance!

It seemed we were to learn the ins and outs of plotting hostile aircraft, among other things, and would be going to Ops at 0800 hrs next day, but not on foot, in a small van. I never got a direct answer when I asked where that was. Just an offhand "oh it's about an hour or so ride away from here."

Roughly an hour later, the sun was low, flashing crimson through the trees, as we tiredly walked to the Mess, spending only enough time to refuel our long suffering bodies, before heading for bed. It was with real relief that I found my neighbor had made up my bed from its biscuit pile, to sleep-able bed, and expressing my grateful appreciation, I wasted little time in preparation before closing my eyes until 0630 hrs and that was all too soon. Another hour would have been heaven, but nobody asked me.

I tried again next day, to find out where we were going as we all assembled to meet the driver, and were hurriedly bundled into the van, but he merely said over his shoulder while putting the van in gear, "It's out in the country. I'll let you know when we get there." Still no wiser when we reached our destination, we climbed out of the back of transport, feeling a bit cramped and crumpled, after a long ride to our mystery destination, but no apparent sign of Ops met the eye. Bewildered, we looked around for enlightenment, but none was forthcoming. In fact there were no buildings to be seen anywhere within walking distance. What sort of destination was this? Was the driver lost? It looked as if we were to be deposited in an empty field, attached to a seldom used, golf course. Little mounds of grassy hillocks and patches of sandy areas dotted the landscape, and it all looked rather neglected. One or two wild flowers flourished on the edges in the long grass, and a sprinkling of ox eyed daisies turning their faces to the sun, greeted us. A few starlings seemed to find some kind of seed in the deep grass areas, occasionally there was a tree or two, but little else to be seen. Bucolic wilderness greeted the eye and not a soul in view. What were we supposed to do out here? There was only a nondescript weathered wood, shed-like structure, with a sort of truncated tower, more or less stuck in the middle, shabbily painted, small, and a bit scruffy looking. Mystified, we trailed along anyway, behind the Sgt, who seemed to be leading us to that unlikely, scruffy, shed, without a word or gesture. Odd!

Astonishingly, through the wooden door he went. We followed, slowly, straggling behind, totally at a loss. Hardly enough room to squeeze in after him.

Strangely, once inside this small enclosure, we saw a lift, which it seemed we were expected to take. It looked reliable, not like a dim, dark coal miner's cage, amazingly spotless inside, and there was room for us all. Nothing was above us, so we had to be going down. The Sgt. pressed the button, we filed in, and it took us down about three or four flights. Where in the bowels of the earth were we going? Imagination ran riot. Once more I was reminded of Mr. Milne, when Alice fell down the rabbit hole, but no tea party awaited us on emerging.

As the gates noiselessly opened, we found ourselves in a wide hallway and looking left and right we could see other corridors branching off this main aisle, and were told these led to toilet facilities and rooms with cubicles for resting, when off duty. Where *was* duty?

In answer to my thought, we came to the main hall at the end of which, there was a door and beyond this on the other side, was a huge Ops table, where plotters were stationed at intervals around the table edge. There was barely enough room to walk around the perimeter, behind them, moving close to the walls to do so. Each WAAF was equipped with a long rod, like a croupier's rake, and wearing earphones, completely absorbed in the task at hand. Doing what? we wondered. The map table itself covered most of England and Europe.

Upstairs was a gallery forming an oval amphitheatre which gave a clear view, from every angle, of the entire proceedings. The oval itself was enclosed by soundproof glass and divided into pie shaped sections, creating separate, wedge shaped, small rooms one for each military Service. One room for the RAF another for Army, and one for Navy. All British.

There were similar sections for the USA and France. Other nations were also represented, each in a separate cubicle around the curving balcony, all displaying their national flags. Scanning the gallery, I observed lots of brass and gold braid in evidence, and realized that this was the upper echelon, of all services. Later on, we concluded that it was one of the Head Quarters for Supreme Headquarters Allied Expeditionary Force (SHAEF) under the command of General Eisenhower, and a meeting place for Mr. Churchill. It was obviously top secret and no doubt an important facility.Information on any occupant seen in this curved circular balcony, was not forthcoming unless it directly concerned one's job responsibilities or security. This location was never mentioned at any time. It was not hard to realize that we were made aware of this place only on a "need to know" basis, and were cautioned later to refrain from answering any questions about our training or its possible location, no matter who asked. The whole experience left me with a feeling of un-reality, and a little like a secret agent.

Journeying to and fro to change shifts and riding in a blacked out van by a circuitous route, gave little clue as to our whereabouts, and any mileage or direction questions pertaining to the route, had been answered in the vaguest of terms. Foiled at every turn and the mystery prevailed. On thinking it over, we decided that it was a privilege to be a part of something so very secret as this hidden location, and we stopped asking questions.

Our journeys back and forth were carefully timed, leaving just enough time to log in and out, before leaving. We were given a small tour around the facility on our initial visit, but there were other areas unaccounted for, that we didn't see. Some passages were wide enough to admit a small car, figuratively speaking, so there was no sense of claustrophobia. Branching off these there were corridors we didn't go down and rooms we didn't go into, which made me endlessly curious. Pity I couldn't be let loose in there, but wondered if so, would I ever have discovered the way out of that labyrinth alone? Unlikely!

Preliminaries over, we returned the way we came, but this time emerging into the real world, newly aware of what lay beneath the surface. We took a closer look at the sandy hillocks outside, noting that they disguised the air ducts servicing the activity below us, as we discovered anew the freshness of the air we breathed. No telegraph poles in sight, so I assumed, all electrical services must be buried. The whole experience had a dream like quality, seeming like pure fantasy, as we blinked owlishly in the bright light of day. The green spongy grass, firm under my feet, and a few buzzing wasps, helped reacquaint me with the real world again, and I saw in the far distance a sturdy oak, its branches of green silhouetted against the cloudless blue of the sky, offering a symbol of enduring solidity and reality. Still, it would not have surprised me to see Auntie Em and Toto with a waggly tail, standing there in the shade of that tree after to-day's experience.

Absorbing our recent adventure in the hidden world lurking beneath the field we walked on, still a tad dazed, our little group quietly mounted the steps of the MT, wondering what other revelations were about to be sprung upon us. We returned to the main Nissen hut, used for lectures or information, a bit subdued after absorbing all the new information garnered that day. Just in time to proceed with a map reading session, and to learn about the function of co-ordinates, followed by updated information on new missiles being directed towards our coastal regions, and London. This then, must be why we were here. No time to be wasted. No time to spare, because trained personnel were now a priority. We were needed in a hurry to deal with these blighters, and this was really all we needed to know.

The missiles were first dubbed "pilotless aircraft", afterwards known as "doodlebugs" and occasionally "buzz bombs", all one and the same. In appearance a little like a spitfire with a red glowing, evil looking, tail light. When it stopped blinking, that was a deadly indication of imminent explosion. We soon found out it was best to keep your eye on it, if you could. But first, you had to be able to see it of course, otherwise in bed, and in the dark, when the red light went out, if the engine stopped then you just held your breath and waited…and waited! We had only seen photographs and diagrams at this point. In Ops the code word for these havoc makers was "diver."

We learned how to process information received via head phones, into factual data, to be shown on the map table, clearly visible to observers above. Each plotter was equipped with a rod, and headphones, accompanied by letters and numerals, these were to use in the indicator placed at the end of the rod. The indicator sign must show the number of hostiles, the direction headed, and the height, using the rod to place the sign on the correct map co-ordinate. As they progressed, information would be adjusted and the present position kept up to date. The rod was just the mechanism to place and adjust indicator signs, because it was important to keep all information current.

Everyone in the gallery could clearly see the progress of each missile, or cluster, as it happened. Plotters listening to information on headphones were only concerned with their own section of the map, and were unaware of other areas being plotted, so even if "divers" were overhead, it was likely that only the person handling that section of the table would know they were there, chugging away above us.

The Operations room was a somewhat silent place, as incoming and outgoing data was transmitted over the air into the plotters ears, and the observation deck was enclosed so emitted no sound. A few hushed tones might be heard at the shift changeover but that was about it. The gallery was in a position to view the whole picture at all times, of course, which we saw demonstrated earlier in the day. Now we understood what we had witnessed on our first visit.

Every plotter had a section of the map and as 'hostiles' progressed to the section end, information was automatically passed to the next plotter, who would take over from there, until detonation occurred, or else passed into the next part of the map until it did. The plots might begin at the launching pads on the other side of the Channel if the location was known, but sometimes missiles were not evident until after that, sometimes mid-flight. In the launching process, V-1s were propelled down chutes leaving Germany or other coastal sites, elsewhere. The map covered all of Britain's areas under attack, including some of the above sites.

Each plotter covered a specific area, tracking single or plural divers, moving the indicators, following their progress over the Channel. It was hectic work at times, to keep up, when a sudden concentrated attack was in progress. "Divers" usually came in clusters, but were detonated separately. In the gallery it was possible to see where the launching sites in Europe were and where the heaviest concentration of hostiles was likely to be targeted.

At last it was time to quit and head for the Mess. By then, I was so tired and hungry, that the frazzled feeling again crept up on me. It had been another long, long, day.

One other weary sufferer from the north, walking homeward alongside me, said she recognized the signs as she too, had been exposed to the non-stop routine, after a long journey only the previous week. She joined me for dinner, where we compared notes on our experiences here, and wondered what other secrets we would be required to keep, in this mysterious place. We walked back to the hut together afterwards, enjoying each other's company.

My toilet was minimal that evening, before flopping, almost instantly, into the unconscious for the night.

Next day, in class, there was more instruction on missile behavior, its construction, and expected damage. I was to learn more specifics first hand at a later date. We also were given a glimpse into the importance of spotters at work on the cliffs. The Observation Corps, those brave souls gave us invaluable information which could not have been supplied from any other source. They were fearless persons who would be out in all weathers with only makeshift, sandbagged shelters, and umbrellas to protect them from the elements. Perched on cliffs or en route, around the rim the brollies would often be blown inside-out in a strong wind, or during a downpour, leaving the person underneath sopping wet, with hours to go before quitting time. A spotter could be a retiree, usually male, but young teens on vacation, also knew their planes very well and made excellent reporters, but a spotter could also be a housewife, or anyone who passed the stringent plane identification test, had binoculars, and enough time to put in some hours, day or night. They needed to be observant, have instant memory recall, accurate, articulate as well as hardy. Their contribution proved to be vital, and was deeply appreciated.

I was put on plotting at first, and found it absorbing but since a broadcaster was urgently needed, I was instead given tuition in handling the mike, and shown what to do. Apparently it was decided I had the right kind of voice that "aired" well, with no discernible accent or dialect, clear delivery (my drama coach at school would have been pleased) and well suited for the task, they said. That became my new job which I quite liked. They didn't have many of us broadcasters then, but expected new trainees as soon as possible.

Relaying plot activity from the balcony, I worked with one male officer present, and both of us were kept busy almost non-stop, from the time I entered the inner sanctum until it was time to leave, longing for tea, but seldom able to take time to help concoct a cup during the long watch. No one else had time to make one either. Being anchored to the mic, scarcely leaving my post, it was a relief when eventually, a general-duties person took over the tea cups, giving us a new lease on life, plugging us in to the tea pipe line, and even a chance to visit the bathroom when necessary.

Once, when on duty for the long night shift, I had developed a sore throat that slowly robbed me of my voice. By the time I was sent to rest after croaking away on the air for many hours, I was by then barely audible. A Medic on the other end phoned in to the officer on watch, to say: "Get that girl to bed." Luckily it wasn't misinterpreted and treatment was promptly forthcoming.

Leaving the amphitheatre on foot, and guided, by a WAAF nurse, we entered a labyrinth of wide passages leading to one of the cubicles, rather like the cabin on a ship, softly lit, and quiet… and there was a bed with blankets.

Bed! Glorious bed! Achy and shivery by this time, blankets were pure bliss. Exhausted, I was so thankful to get my head down, and surprisingly, fell asleep almost instantly. On being awakened, sometime later, I was told to report to Sick Bay immediately on return to HQ The MT was already waiting for me as we surfaced and wasted no time getting me there. Wrapped in blankets, still shivering, I dozed en route.

This took me out of action for many days of enforced rest and medication, incarcerated in Sick Bay, with a diagnosis of strep throat, and high fever. At first I was glad to be in bed to sleep and rest, but later, though miserable, itching with frustration and impatient to recover, I was sorely tempted to get up too soon, but decided not to risk a repeat, reluctantly waiting for the all clear from the MO.

At last, with rubbery legs, and medication in hand completing the course of antibiotics, I was released, in time for my final afternoon duty. Afterwards, I was asked to join a small group going to Plymouth Hoe where one of the girls was meeting a Fleet Air Arm cadet.

There had been no chance before this, to wander around the town of Plymouth, a noted city with a long history and probably no other opportunity, but this one, to go and explore, before being posted. The city dates back to the Bronze Age, still thriving through the Iron Age and continuing on to the exodus date of the Pilgrim Fathers in 1620. Perhaps not very widely known, are the important caves that exist in this area. These are of great archeological significance, containing bones of very early homo sapiens, but unfortunately there is no public access and the caves are not easily located. It would be hard to visit them, without special credentials and a guide, but given these, entirely possible. Perhaps, after the war, I hoped.

Before WW2 the Royal Naval Base was well established here, and a major shipping industry thrived, building anything and everything, from small fishing boats to battleships. Both the base and shipping were heavily bombed in the Blitz and much of the city was reduced to rubble. Afterwards it was reported that about 100,000 people left the area during that time. When a raid was known to be forthcoming, lorries would appear to take people out of Plymouth to the edge of Dartmoor, for the night. Dartmoor is a great expanse of wild, common land, bleak and mysterious. It even has its own wild ponies as well as other wildlife, plus a few human stalwarts who live on the fringes, but otherwise, it is not inhabited.

A great number of children in Plymouth were evacuated to diverse areas in England, and some went to hospitable, welcoming homes in the U.S.A.

where lasting friendships were often formed. Others went to remote country villages in England, where factories were impractical and there was little to attract enemy interest.

Plymouth's two main shopping centres were destroyed, and most civic buildings were gone, plus 26 schools, 8 cinemas, 41 churches and 3,754 houses were all destroyed, and about 18,000 houses were seriously damaged. One public shelter got a direct hit, and 72 people were killed outright, which was so frightening to those depending on that kind of shelter. Happily, not a common occurrence!

One main church called St. Andrews, having been basically destroyed, was left with a small section still standing, alone, amid the rubble, with only one door section intact, but no other walls. A staunch, church lady purposefully, hung a sign over it, expressing her views. It said "Resurgon", Latin for "I shall rise again." This was carved over the door permanently when the time came to restore the church.

Since this evening would be my last chance to go to Plymouth for the foreseeable future, I decided to accompany Linda, who knew the ropes and led us and another friend, to the right bus, immediately, and from there to a Service Club. Judging by the noise, a very popular one! The Navy was overwhelmingly represented. Almost at once, Linda's Fleet Air Arm date, Bill, appeared, looking a lot like Andy Hardy, a lad with snub nose, ginger hair and freckles, a movie character portrayed by Mickey Rooney. He was accompanied by two friends, one of whom immediately sat next to me at a table near the stage. His name was Cliff Anderson, who upon being introduced, shouting to hear above the din, asked if I'd like to dance. I got the point. It was too noisy to talk, so rubber legs, or not, it seemed like a good idea to move away from the clamor. Three dances later, legs improving, we sat at a less noisy table, and I nursed a shandy while we talked, he revealing his nice smile and manners to match, as we chatted. Cliff, was from way up north on the east coast of Scotland in a town called Arbroath. He too, was a cadet, in training to be a pilot, yet he seemed so young (he was a year older than me, actually) but mentioned, he was half way there, towards his goal, and had only had a few months to go before being shipped out, as a newly graduated Ensign.

Linda and Jim had left our table by then, to dance, the other WAAF had acquired a partner, and as time ticked inexorably on, we began to make noises about leaving. Just one more twirl around the floor to this good music, and we were on our way. At the bus stop, Cliff asked me to write to him, explaining that his family was small, no siblings, only a few scattered friends, and he would like a broader view of the news, so if he wrote to me, would I respond? His parents usually, only presented a small version of the world in Arbroath in their letters, plus other news from home, he told me, and would I oblige by enlarging the picture? Mail was so important, so far from home, he added, pressing a small piece of paper in my hand ...his address. He confessed he had obtained mine from my friend. As I stepped aboard the waiting, vibrating bus, the neoprene bag rattling away on the roof, I yelled, "Just a news bulletin? Fine!" he shouted over the chug chug, bang bang, of the buses departing blasts. And so it was, we became pen pals.

After about two weeks or so, working steadily in the bowels of the earth, and watching many high ranking officers of various services, coming and going, reminded me that we were all witnessing a totally new type of device threatening England. I continued to ask more questions, getting few answers because not much was known, just yet. It was history in the making. Soon after, we learned that the new missile was jet powered, looked like a torpedo with small wings, or a bit like a miniature spitfire. Sometimes, they were launched in clusters from chutes resembling ski jumps, or small roller coasters and were aimed from France, Belgium, and Norway and carried 4,740 lbs of explosives each. Included in the construction was an auto pilot which regulated speed. The first of these was launched as recently as one week after D-Day, and we expected more of them, at any time, especially in London and on the SW coast. In the meantime, Allied bombers were trying to stop them at the source. Fighters helped to eliminate them on their path across the ocean.

Three weeks, plus two days, had passed since we arrived and now were considered trained and ready to go. The very next day found me en route for my new post in NW London.

Pulsating with activity, the railway station presented a study of life in motion; reminiscent of a certain piece of music I remembered hearing. Nikolai Rimsky-Korsakov's, "Flight of the bumble bee". It was indeed buzzing like a tightly closed jar full of bee-like people alighting and departing, meeting and parting, some troops on the move, kit bags everywhere. Lots of two fingered V-signs accompanied by smiles going around, as people recognized the successful landing as a significant step in the right direction towards the end of this war.

Orders in hand, I was all set for the journey ahead to my new post in Stanmore, about ten miles outside London, at the other end of the Jubilee line on the Underground. On receipt of my travel documents, I was advised to check that my gas cape was rolled properly, or I might get stopped by the MP's (Hitler was pulling out all the stops since D-Day and who knew what might come next?) That gas cape however, was a source of uneasiness, because of what it implied, besides which, every once in a while some joker, always the opposite sex, would find it greatly amusing to pull the cord behind my neck and of course the cape descended to cover me completely. It was often a ploy to start a conversation and even though the culprit re-rolled it for me, I didn't find it an endearing gambit. This trip, luckily, was not interrupted by such antics, and I reached London intact.

London

Once the train pulled in to Paddington, I descended to the underground to check the route, on the wall map. First stop, Baker Street, change tubes, then, carry on to Stanmore, seemed simple enough. Friendly, helpful, people made the journey easier, especially on and off the tube trains when there wasn't much time to haul things aboard before the doors, snapping at my heels, clanged shut. I noticed that the escalators on stations we passed through seemed to be deeply underground, judging by the pitch and length of the escalators. Some even had two levels of descending escalators. People used these stations as air raid shelters at night and obviously felt well protected, deep below ground.

I was told that a bomb did drop on the entrance to one of the stations, blocking the exit, but people were able to get out via the tunnels. There were some casualties, but I never heard of a repeat performance and it didn't deter people from seeking refuge in Tube stations after that. Street shelters on the surface were more exposed, colder and often damp, so the underground was still considered viable and comparatively safe. Safe as any shelter available, though a bit noisy;

I was the only new arrival at Stanmore, and the MT. gave me a friendly smile, filling me in on local news… warning me ahead, that it would be a brisk pace in Ops, as we were getting doodlebugs frequently now, and were a bit short of personnel. The latter sounded familiar and meant long hours again, but that was nothing new. He left me at the HQ orderly room, where I reported in, and was taken to my new quarters pronto.

A house, quite new, and conveniently located for work and meals, was to be my abode, and already, upstairs, a room had already been set aside for me. What luxury to have space and privacy! Other bedrooms showed signs of dual occupancy. One girl was at home, in bed, in a small room downstairs, catching up on sleep after a busy night shift, but not to worry, she would be available to conduct me to the mess for the evening meal, said my guide. Duty was scheduled for the next day at 0800 hrs.

In Ops all was familiar as it looked much the same as the underground Ops in Plymouth, only smaller. I saw the plotters hard at work around the map table. No time for any verbal exchanges. Moving on, upstairs to the balcony, there was a hurried introduction to the Officer in Charge, and next to him sat the WAAF I was relieving. She whispered quickly: "hello, my name is Charmaigne (pronounced Sharmian) Pittaway, see you later," and handing me the mic, I was ON.

By the time I came off duty at 1200 hrs, whatever was happening in our immediate area was news to me, since my part of the map had been the section approaching London, further south of us, so both eyes and ears had been completely immersed in that part of the world. Was there an "all clear"? Or were we under an "alert"? Not knowing, I met Sally Simons, who had been plotting that morning, and also going off duty, I found she was mentally still in Maidstone. She didn't know either.

Did we have an air raid shelter? Sally said there was a small half cellar in our billet, so we decided to have lunch on the way back and have a look at it.

Yes, an air raid was in progress, so back to the billet to find the cellar. It didn't look very big and not reinforced, but was probably the best spot to be in, if things got hectic, so we sat in the living room next to the stairs, thinking we could duck down a few stairs if the "crumps" sounded too close. We could hear explosions in the distance, but none very near, we thought, so we settled down to talk.

In answer to my queries about what was available in our off duty time, Sally gave me a broad range of events to choose from; all in London, of course. As an afterthought she added that it was off limits to go into the centre of London while there were heavy raids but, well, what did they expect us to do? Was it risky? Definitely! But at nineteen I think we all thought we were surrounded by some sort of natural immunity.

We arranged to go together to the Queensbury Club in Soho, in the East End of London, the following night, to hear Glenn Miller's Band. That ought to take our minds off the war for a while and… what an exciting prospect!

Our shifts coincided from that night at 1700 hrs to 0800 hrs, the next day. This would give us time to rest during the day, before leaving.

It had been a very busy night and I was ready to fold, after breakfast and barely pausing to take off my make-up, I hopped into bed. The siren's eerie warnings kept interrupting my day time efforts to sleep, but I must have dozed enough in between to feel better... eager to go, and I began to get my bath ready.

At 1605 hrs, I was climbing out of my bubble bath when I heard a weird kind of motorbike noise, up in the sky outside, so I peered through the shoulder high window to see what it could be. It did look like a miniature Spitfire, or a torpedo with wings, just as described, flying low, less than 500 feet, over the roof tops opposite our billet. At the rear was the infamous, evil eyed, red tail light, a pulsing, glowing, leering threat. Of course, I knew immediately, what it was but, like a deer caught in headlights, I stood transfixed as it chugged right out of view of my small window. Not four minutes later, the buzzing stopped, and in seconds a loud thrummp announced the destruction of something large.

The house felt the reverberation and so did those in it. From the soles of my feet to my scalp, I felt the shuddering vibration and was surprised that it didn't at least, loosen the plaster, or our teeth.

Emerging from the bathroom, starkers, in my towel, just in time to see Sally and two other WAAF, luckily not in a towel, rushing outside to see what had been hit.

That was my first doodlebug, up close and personal, but by no means my last. Apparently the first such weapon launched on England was exactly one week after D-Day on June 11, just before I began my course in Plymouth, so I was starting from the very beginning.

Getting dressed for the club I decided to stop using my respirator container as a purse. so, dumping the contents on the table, I stuffed my gas mask back in the case, and there was still room for lipstick and a comb. Somehow all the extra gas tackle we had to carry didn't seem quite so onerous now, and though willing to take a few chances, I was not without some caution. Would they really gas us? The question flashed on the screen of my brain, to be firmly squashed before it took hold, but just in case...I'd be ready.

Keeping an eagle eye open for any further overhead interruptions to our plans, we left on foot for the tube station to catch a train to Soho, which was easy to reach. Once there, we exited the tube station at Shaftsbury Avenue across from the Queensbury Club. Inside, we paid a small fee for membership and were given access cards, and upon entering, we found a conversational hum of voices, images were softened under night club lighting, illuminating this busy place. A sea of uniforms of all kinds milled around us... some finding seats, or ordering drinks, and a few chatting in small groups. There were tables for four, comfy looking wooden arm chairs with lightly padded seats, with some of the tables pushed together to accommodate bigger groups. Banquettes lined the walls and at the far end, was a full stage with a dance floor below that, equipped with a mirrored, lighted ball, which slowly revolved playing on the dancers, dispensing little spots of light, reflecting off faces and figures in a strangely intriguing manner. Brass buttons glowed and shadowed eyes were mysterious.

As we took our seats, an appreciative and welcoming audience erupted in a burst of hearty applause, reverberating throughout the club, as Glenn Miller and his band appeared on stage, and began with their signature tune, "In the Mood." What a toe tapping start to the evening. They played all our favorites taking only small breaks between and during off moments. Some of the musicians would join friends among us in the audience, all smiles, seeming glad to be there, despite the overhead menace. The big band era, exemplified by this band, stirred the senses, exciting the psyche to be a part of it all, and to have requests honoured with panache.

Glenn Miller was a tremendous favorite in England. Later in December 1944, when news of his death reached us, with word that he had died on the way to France when his plane crashed, it was a blow! The loss was felt by music lovers everywhere. Not much official news or any details were made known at the time, but rumours were rife for sometime afterwards, and even now, a shroud of mystery is drawn over any questions that pop up from time to time. Speculations abound, but the sad event has yet to be fully explained to his fans.

At the side of the stage, was a small illuminated sign announcing that an air raid was in progress, noting that "anyone wishing to leave for the shelter across the street, should do so quietly." Heaven forbid you should make an unseemly noise by leaving this "jumping" club, in the middle of a clamorous air raid. That same notice board also announced the "all clear," when we had one, if we had one, but in the hours we spent there that night, I didn't ever see even one.

Jitterbugging was an American thing and new to the Brits, but we watched with great interest to see some brave English girls trying it. Every dance I'd ever heard of, and some I hadn't, appeared on the floor that night. Sally and I participated in quite a few until the witching hour of 2200 hrs. and it was hard to tear ourselves away.

Two friendly Americans saw us to the Underground platform, waiting with us till the train came in, before departing in their turn, for their own. We appreciated their consideration on this active night, but didn't take them up on their invitation to dinner, next time we came into town. It was so heartwarming to experience the courtesy and friendliness between various members of the armed forces during this time of siege, and it was evident everywhere.

The Underground came to life at night presenting a different cast of players than the daytime travelers, always in a hurry. A whole new community inhabited those same platforms, as night fell over the city. An ever changing scene, where lovers embraced along its walls, while families settled in for the night, and old men played draughts while sipping their tea, sometimes adding "a wee dram", "to keep the spirits up."

Continuing on to our destination, the train rattled to a stop in Stanmore amid all the metal beds bolted to the wall. Stacked in tiers, sometimes two, sometimes three to a stack, all along the rear wall of the platform, each holding a body, either sleeping, or trying to.

Babies, Moms, teenagers, tots and Grandparents, all there, but no young men! Conspicuous by their absence, they were off doing their bit for King and Country, except for the occasional few, who were medically unfit; Next to the beds sat bundles of cherished possessions, hastily snatched up at the sound of the siren, dumped into a tablecloth, tied by the corners, and placed alongside the owner. Here and there, a portable canvas baby bed, the occupants asleep, by now, used to the nightly ritual, completely oblivious to trains arriving and departing, doors banging and people talking and laughing. It was still better they said, than staying at home, listening for the throb of aircraft overhead and the inevitable explosions, wondering who wouldn't be around tomorrow, and if there would ever be an "all clear."? But as the first silver rays of dawn penetrated the greyness of night, faces seemed to be washed clean of the night's anxieties, relaxed but tired, and hope reawakened, they moved towards the exit and a new day.

Back in the Underground again next night, the scene only slightly changed; trains bearing military personnel travelling till the wee hours, came and went, while those who could, slept through it all. Now and then an elderly person, teeth in a jar, feet in carpet slippers, and Mom in her Churchill-inspired battle dress, called a "siren suit". She did her best to cope, alone, with three generations in her care. Since her husband went away, naturally the load fell heaviest on her.

The lighting in the tunnel gave inhabitants a ghastly pallor but as they made their weary way trudging up the escalators and out into the light of day, some semblance of real skin colour, returned. From there the routine was, home to change, and off to school, or on to work, for the most part. The elders might have a chance to rest, if there were no air raids, and they weren't doing volunteer work, but in general it was business as usual.

I overheard an account of one incident concerning a family during an alert, which, I think, bears repeating.

The warning siren, having sounded, was now increased to full throttle blaring away at deafening volume, while a harassed Mother was trying to round up her family. Two teens, one tot and Mom, were all at the door, waiting to begin the trip to the Air raid shelter, but no Grandfather! He was upstairs looking for his false teeth and flatly refused to leave without them. His daughter patiently called up to him to hurry, because they were all waiting for him. Nothing! No response, though she could hear drawers slamming, doors clanging, and mumbling going on, plus a naughty word or two. Downstairs, toes were tapping, fingers drumming as they all stood clutching pillows, blankets, and trinkets, nervously waiting in the dark by the front door, listening to the mournful, urgent wail of the siren. Once more she tried, then exasperated beyond belief, she yelled from the foot of the stairs, "Oh for Pete"s sake Dad, get a move on, 'itler's dropping bombs, not ruddy sardine sandwiches."

This kind of humour prevailed, unexpectedly popping up at odd moments, and it seemed to restore the equilibrium. In the Underground a decided sense of camaraderie existed, and even flourished. One Grandad was overheard responding to a curious American who asked, why he didn't go to a public air raid shelter, or buy an Anderson shelter for his garden. His answer was, that he thought it was nicer to have all these families around him. There was always a card game going on, and he had a bed, thermos of tea, and sandwiches brought from home, even a nip of Scotch for emergencies. "Like a club," he said, winding up with, "besides, it's safer, ninety feet down and dead cozy." The "dead cozy" bit opened up new vistas of thought that never would have occurred to me to relate to the Underground. Somehow re-assuring.

Arriving at Stanmore, after a twenty minute walk to GHQ from the station, we headed for bed before the midnight curfew. Surprisingly, I was actually able to sleep through all the interruptions. Having danced away the jitters earlier helped, I was happily, completely, physically tired. Sally echoed the feeling, and for a change we just zonked out till morning.

Whether in Ops or off duty, there wasn't much let up! Every third day we were on duty morning, evening, and all night, which allowed us to take two nights off with one afternoon duty sandwiched in between. Sleep, always important to us, was hard to come by. At night, waking up to the familiar Bzzzz Bzzzz Bzzzz, easily heard from a considerable distance away, the shrillness of the siren commandingly, warbling away, we were faced with three choices. We could go into our closet sized room under the stairs, a tiny spot with no room to lie down, or get under the bed giving minimal protection, or just try ignoring it, at our peril. We tried all the options, finally succumbing to the latter. That was pretty much what we did on duty anyway. The trouble was, we knew, when the tail light went out and the buzzing stopped, the doodlebug would either drop down in straight descent, like a plumb line, or in a strong wind, drift like a glider, in silence, for several long minutes while we waited, in agonizing suspense, hardly daring to breathe. Not knowing which to expect, was the miserable part. Just lying there, holding one's breath, waiting. Waiting for those deep concussive crumps, feeling them in ones belly, followed by a sense of shuddering shock after the really close ones; Hoping they would miss this flimsily built little house, we waited. At times, the flash of a searchlight would slide over the blacked out windows and we could hear the ack-ack sounding off in the area.

We wondered why anyone bothered to sound the all clear sometimes, when the next wave would come so soon after. I gave up trying to know, if we were under "alert" or "all clear" most of the time. Just plodding on, longing for a little p and q. We were all rather sleep needy, much of the time.

Bad as the Blitz had been, and was still ongoing, we had known when a plane had finished dropping its bombs, the empty, bomber air plane would head straight back home, after dropping its quota, and that would be that. A bit more predictable! Here, under the new menace, we never knew what to expect. This missile, the doodlebug, created a war of nerves, more so than being bombed had been. In my experience, the V-1s, left us always on edge, waiting, wondering, not knowing when we could relax.

Of course, it all seemed worse at night. The feeling of vulnerability heightened in the dark because there was nothing to distract ones attention.

We kept busy during free evenings so as to be tired enough to sleep through it all, when we could, and sometimes it worked, though often we only dozed fitfully, leaving us just plain weary and unrested. The stress made itself felt so I was glad to know that my leave would soon be forthcoming. We took turns by rotation.

Sleep deprivation plays havoc with a victim, leaving one feeling worn and tattered around the edges. The whole nervous system seems to be rendered threadbare and vulnerable, everything moving in slow motion, after a prolonged bout of it. Decisions and thoughts emerge from a hazy film, fogging the brain, causing clumsy, awkward attempts to be verbally lucid, a bit like recovering from an anaesthetic. The only reality being the promise of sleep, with the vital urge to experience oblivion, soon; Snatches of sleep wouldn't do it. Rather like putting a band aid on a gaping wound.

In the meantime we hung on, doing the best we could to induce the arms of Morpheous to envelope us, in a sleep of some hours. When the possibility eluded us we anxiously waited for our scheduled leave and a chance to sleep uninterrupted, until we woke. Dreamless, please!

Mail had begun to trickle in from France and Normandy to my vast relief, and it was only then that I knew that Frank had made it. He had been in D-Day + 1, and didn't elaborate on the horrors he witnessed. He said nothing about the actual landing, and few details were broadcast. All our mail was heavily censored by eagle eyes anyway, looking for careless talk or anything that might have even hinted at a private code. We didn't have one, of course. I got the message that my letters had not yet reached him, and in his first few epistles he went quickly from grumbling, to frantic. Spurred on, I wrote at once, again. Eventually he got a torrent of them all at once, to his delight and my relief.

At my post on Ops balcony one night, I noticed the Corporal pacing the floor near the map table, looking a bit edgy, abruptly turning away from the table he went back towards a skylight near the entrance to Ops. I sneaked a look at our immediate area on the map (not on my telling section) and saw "diver" activity directly over our heads. It looked like it was right in our bailiwick, but I had to give my sole attention to another area elsewhere and couldn't watch our local section of the map, to see what developed. Below me, Sally was plotting Maidstone area so she wasn't aware either.

Glancing up briefly, I saw the Cpl. had cracked the skylight open a little, enough for me to see the little familiar red light, and then... I couldn't. It had winked out. Someone instructed those on the ground floor, "quick, under the table. Helmets!" No time on our balcony for us to do the same. No sturdy table up here, anyway. Just before the lights went out, I saw plaster falling on Sally's tin helmet then her shoulders, as she looked up, to find me, followed by a huge juddering, thudding, blast. In the dark, I just waited for whatever was next, Feeling helpless with nothing to do, but wait.

Minutes passed, though it could have been longer, as it felt like being in a time warp. Much to my surprise, those of us on the balcony were still there. It was an odd feeling, to be so strangely calm as the buzz bomb fell, but there had been no time for a build-up of fear. There had been no time to be anxious. Just enough time to realize the danger. Our headphones had effectively silenced local sounds. The staccato, throbbing, droning, noise of the pilot-less aircraft overhead, completely obliterated.

We looked at each other by torchlight, in various stages of relief and disbelief, with a nervous laugh or two at our astonishment in having escaped, then someone went to put the kettle on for tea, so that we could continue, and on we went, glad to be active, again. A cigarette lighter came out, then another and another, giving us some measure of light on the map table beneath, and soon emergency lamps were in operation, and so were the rest of us, now that we could see. Back to work as usual.

The attached building behind us took the brunt of the explosion resulting in a large hole in the ground. Debris and a great pall of grey black dust, hovered over all plaster and bits of metal everywhere, a burst water main, gas lines broken and electricity problems greeted the eye and, the nose. A distinct metallic smell of foul air assailed us before the gas mains were capped off, then that helped eliminate some of it.

Sally stood in water over the tops of her shoes, as mops were produced, to take away some of the excess, on the ground floor There was a huge hole in the roof, so we were lucky it wasn't raining. Some of the plaster had lavishly dispersed itself on Sally and she looked as if she had been caught in a snow storm. Soon a tarp was spread over the roof and repairs followed fairly promptly afterwards, keeping us operational.

We finished our shift, and contrary to expectations, on returning to the billet I fell into a deep sleep, swallowing me whole, until hours later, when I was drowsily aware of being prodded back to consciousness by Charmaine offering me a cup of tea before I was quite alive. I was aware of the asthmatic wheeze of the kettle, in the background, as I tried to focus enough to give her my attention. Oh, what a divine sleep I had had at last! She was about to go on watch, had heard about our bomb and wondered what to expect in Ops. and wanted details, so I dazedly sat up, refreshed from a real sleep, and obliged.

That evening, Sally and I thought we deserved a break, and decided to visit the Nuffield Centre, near Oxford Circus, another busy club, called the NAAFI, founded by Lord Nuffield for those in the Services. Feeling lucky to be alive we set off for the familiar Tube station, to take our minds off the war, and into the danger zone, though it barely crossed our minds that we were being a bit quixotic, about our ventures into the very centre of the target zone. Although Sally and I were almost total opposites, both in appearance and in our plans for after the war, we found much to debate about and agree upon, and a good friendship flourished. We looked out for each other, shared a sense of humour, and enjoyed spending time together.

Once inside the Club, we saw refreshments on a buffet, small tables and a stage at the far end. It was packed with every kind of uniform, including the Polish Air Force, who were by repute, fine pilots.

The star attraction was Beatrice Lillie, familiarly known as Bea Lillie, a comedienne of some renown, although her name in real life was Lady Peel. She was known for her performances on both sides of the Atlantic and had performed with other notables such as Jack Haley, Bert Lahr and many others. She was liked for her subtle and witty innuendos on seemingly innocent stretches of prose, conveyed by a lifted eyebrow, a curl of the lip, a flutter of the eyelashes; a shrug. These she used to the utmost, with great effect. "Her parodies were masterpieces of the exquisite sense of the absurd," remarked a New York critic, in his revue.

She appeared looking elegant in a long gown, and began with "there are fairies in the bottom of my garden," and went on from there, keeping us all in her thrall, until several encores had been fulfilled and she left the stage, gracefully waving, to thunderous applause.

Several nights after this event we learned that a telegram had been delivered to her earlier that day, informing her that her only son, Sir Robert Peel had been killed in action on the HMS Tenedos in Colombo Harbour, Ceylon (now Sri Lanka). She had refused to cancel her engagements for the troops, and very few knew of her personal tragedy, until much later.

Mingling with the crowd, Sally and I were asked to join a table of assorted airmen, both English and Americans who were in the process of regaling each other with "narrow squeak" stories. If these tales got too serious they would be parodied by those listening who would come in with a droll, chorus of, "and the wing fell off" followed by, "and then the engine dropped out," "the prop died" and so on, with appropriate gestures, until a horror story was reduced to bathos instead of pathos. Still, some of these stories needed to be told in all simplicity, with fitting impact on listeners, usually these were colleagues, or very old friends. It's called de-stressing. These fliers were stationed near Norwich and around the S.W. coastal areas, often known as "Hell's Corner" to pilots, as it was a major area for hostile confrontations, and sudden deaths.

At that time RAF bombers were responsible for night bombing raids over Germany, while Americans took the day shifts where both met with countless fighter attacks, often outnumbered, witnessing death and injuries on an all too frequent basis. They endured terrible losses, flying through ribbons of flak, and now for a busman's holiday, Americans and RAF in London were dodging "buzz bombs;" their word for doodllebugs. They labeled them, "terrifying." Brave RAF pilots, valiant Eighth Air force chaps, and other expert flyers, had earned our highest esteem, for maintaining crucial air supremacy against a well trained enemy so this comment, made Sally and me feel so much better about our nervous sleeplessness. If those "knights of the air" thought them "terrifying," we were excused for getting edgy, we decided. We were allowed!

London was a remarkable city during it's time of trial. Under constant bombardment throughout the war, and yet maintaining a cheerful air of constant bustle, as it teemed with life, and too often, death. Uniforms, of all types, office workers, salesgirls, bus and taxi drivers, and others who made up the life of the city, all going about their business, as if no dire threat of extinction hung over them. Literally! Churchill's V for Victory signs were apparent everywhere and excerpts from his inspirational speeches posted in tubes or buses such as, "if we shall live for 1,000 years men will say, this was their finest hour," or as Britain stood alone until 1943, "we shall fight them on the beaches, in the ditches etcetera, but we shall never give in."I remember hearing the guttural growl in his voice as he uttered that word, "nevah," with such unequivocal finality. No fooling! He set the pace.

The heart of the city still throbbed to the beat of romantic songs sung by Vera Lynn, and others, twanging at the heartstrings with, "the White Cliffs of Dover" or "Don't sit under the apple tree" and a favorite in all pubs, "You are my sunshine."

Covent Garden, the scene of many famous operas before the war, now held sway with special tea dances, or evening galas, all on a lavish scale. Its palatial hall, interspersed with imposing pillars, was spacious enough, in the era of big bands, to have two of them playing at the same time, one at each end. Each band was famous already, and drew large numbers of patrons, civilians and Service people of all ranks.

Such was the space and the acoustics, that you didn't ever hear a combination of both playing at once. One faded as you danced to the other end, then the other made itself heard. It was a novel experience.

On one occasion when I went to a dance, Ivy Benson and Her All Girls Band was at one end of the hall playing boogie woogie, while at the other end was an American band playing a waltz, enabling a couple to start out at a fast moving tempo, as they moved towards the other end, slowing to the opposite beat required by a waltz. It was great fun and best of all, you couldn't hear any ugly war sounds outside. It was a good place to work off excess adrenalin and become physically depleted enough to sleep…the magic word.

Covent Garden used to be the scene of the great flower market, outside the opera house, as depicted in My Fair Lady, but this was no more, during the Blitz.

Movies were all operating during this time, and you could smoke or drink tea without leaving your seat, as it was served to you, leaving the china cup and saucer underneath the seat, when finished. Ice cream was served the same way, in peacetime. The best seats were, in the balcony and the similar little notice about air raid warnings would appear in a small illuminated sign, always with the reminder that if you left, it should be done quietly, inferring that it would be" rude to disturb your neighbours, while being bombed." These signs always seemed amusing and I enjoyed them all, seeking them out for a smile. In typical British fashion they revealed an innate desire to think about ones neighbor, polite as always, but laughable in some instances.

Despite the upbeat quality of those working with, and around us, our routine took its toll. There was without doubt, a lack of sleep for all of us on shifts, and the pressure of constant threats, from above, along with the fact that our circadian rhythm was totally altered, by staggered hours, made itself felt. We were stressed. After three months under bombardment, which seemed twice as long to us, we were gratefully given seven days leave. It was a bonus that Sally's leave time coincided with mine making it possible to share some of the journey and we left most thankfully, on the Underground together, connecting to a train in Paddington, each going on our different routes from there.

Leaving from Stanmore to Paddington, amid the usual kaleidoscope of humanity, an ever changing scene, we waited on the tube platform surrounded by their assorted piles of luggage, kit bags, duffle bags, suitcases and string tied packages. No sign of the night people who sheltered there at day's end. Air raids began at dusk usually, when the sirens sounded, but this was too early for the regular routine.

We each had a kit bag, gas equipment, tin helmet and a suitcase and when our train came in, and two helpful sailors aware of our plight, stepped up to help, telling us to hop aboard and they would take care of the luggage. Just before the doors banged together, closing with remarkable ferocity, an extra large portmanteau followed us in. Oh dear! Not ours! Through the window of the now departing train we glimpsed the apoplectic face of the owner, a bewhiskered Colonel, red and infuriated, he shook his finger at us, pointing to the whopping great luggage pile heaped at our feet. Last seen, as we vanished from his view, angrily, rapping on the door with his cane. Transferring our gaze to the sailors as we moved out, we beheld a look of spurious innocence mixed with barely disguised desire to erupt into laughter. "It would make an undertaker laugh," Sally said. I wondered what the Colonel said to the sailors?

It struck us as funny even though we had to go miles out of our way to the depot to get his luggage returned to the rightful owner, dizzy with collective fatigue, we laughed helplessly, all the way there, still chuckling when we parted ways.

At home, my parents killed the fatted calf in my honour, or to be more accurate, saved their bacon ration till I got home. Relieved that "home" was West Hagley now, well removed from the Birmingham and Coventry environs; it would be possible to rest, in peace, siren free. It would be a real luxury.

Anticipating my arrival, there was lots of mail for me, stacked in a neat pile on the hall table, and eagerly, I opened one from Joan, in Sketty. George, whom she had promised to marry, was now in France or Normandy (censored). After he was in the D-Day action, and revived enough, he had written Joan long, frequent letters, and then suddenly they ceased altogether. Not a word, as weeks went by. She worried herself silly, thinking he might be injured. Finally, he responded, explaining in detail, about his change of heart.

There was a girl back home who had always been special to him, and she had continued to write to him since he left the States, although while he knew Joan, in Wales, their correspondence had flagged. He knew now, that he had been lonely and anxious when he was in training, until he met Joan. She was very attractive and most important, she was there, and he so enjoyed being with her, that he mistook his feelings for love. His perspective somewhat restored, now that there was distance between them, and he was away from both girls, he realized that he really was committed to his girl at home, a childhood sweetheart. He hoped Joan could forgive him and try to understand. Not an unfamiliar story." It happened a lot, but a real blow to Joan. She had no inkling about an earlier attachment and was truly sunk.

George had succumbed to the human need to seek some kind of permanence in the impermanent uncertainty of war. The need to have it all, and do it all, while he still could; I understood, but all my sympathies were for my friend.

I wrote immediately to ask if she would like to come down for a long weekend with me at my home, but she thought it would be better to do that later, besides she was with her family now on leave, and they were very comforting, also wise enough to keep her busy, so there would be a better time in the future for me to help.

There were three letters from Frank, witty and descriptive, sometimes with little humorous sketches like the one of an American soldier tin-hatted, with a big shovel, digging his own tunnel under the ocean back to England and me. I shared some of the excerpts with my family who felt they got to know him better through these letters. They were much amused by one particular letter in which he replied to one of mine. He had written earlier asking for a new photo as his old one was a bit the worse for wear, he said, so I duly responded by enclosing one of me taken in civilian clothes and wearing three or four strands of smallish pearls. He responded with complimentary remarks about my blue eyes etc, but went on to add, "but less pearly attraction might lead to greater distinction." That earned a chuckle or two from my family at his delicate phrasing, and upon thinking it over I thought he was right.

Perhaps it was just as well that Joan decided to postpone her visit, as I was totally depleted and not my usual energetic self. Rest, in a threat-free environment was a great treat. Shift work made it difficult to adjust to regular hours even when I got the chance, but there were enough lovely, buzz-bomb-free nights, here at home where I gratefully slept, and slept and relishing the pleasure of it all, slept some more. Appreciating the comfort of my mattress with a down-filled upper layer, and my eider-down comforter on top, I floated away on my feathers, into that other world of peace and noiselessness. Tranquility itself!

Another bonus was an unexpected return of appetite. While in London, nothing had appealed, even chocolate wasn't tempting, but I noticed as dinner time approached here at home, it was a different story, by meal time I was usually so hungry, I could eat a horse and chase the rider.

There was enough time to do things with my sister, Norma, like going to a play, also to enjoy quality time spent with my parents. My two uniforms went for an overdue visit to the cleaners, and I managed a session at

Love Elizabeth. April 1946.

The Hudson Studios,   Birmingham.

"Less pearly attraction"

the beauty parlor for a new hairdo, also overdue, both were perks, restoring some normality to life.

One favorite indulgence was a visit to the Turkish Baths in Birmingham which had fortuitously escaped the Luftwaffe's notice, and the long building in the city, showing architectural Roman influences, was still standing, in all its peculiar splendour.

Norma and I entered promptly on the dot of our appointment time, to be met by a trim attendant in a short white uniform, who escorted us to our cubicles, handed us each a sheet and said to come out wearing it, when undressed. We were asked whether we wanted wet or, dry heat and chose dry, and then were conducted to the first of three rooms, each one keyed to a different heat setting, upgraded as we travelled towards the third room. Each room was tiled in pale green, floor, walls and ceiling, where we rested, either, on a long stone slab or chaise longue, as she timed our stay, progressing until we had finished our last session in the third, and warmest room. Next, we stretched out again on a stone slab, each with her own attendant, to receive a herbal oil massage, followed by a rinse, followed by a sea salt rub. Then, minus the sheet, we were told to stand against the wall to receive a hefty, full volume hosing down, first in warm, then cold water, after which, back on the slab for a delicious, scented talcum powder rub down. This was followed by our return to the cubicle for an hour of rest between lavender scented sheets while wrapped in a warm towel. When the attendant returned and we were up, and dressed, we were given tea and little sweet cakes (ersatz but good). When we left, our entire bodies felt as if they were silk clad and any sign of nervous tension completely obliterated. I never found another place like that one. Hedonistic? Yes, lovely!

Feeling considerably restored, all too soon it was time to return to the fray, making mental notes to keep in better touch with Mom and Dad, with special notes to Norma. Despite the age difference we were becoming more like contemporaries, but then the war made young people grow up fast and Norma seemed older than her years. I noticed this time, how all three kept up with the latest news every day, focusing especially on the London area, I must definitely send more letters, even if brief. How they must have worried about their daughter, and sister, in the thick of things.

In my favourite spot on the train, in the window corner, next to the corridor, I sat, feeling well put together in my clean, pressed uniform, shiny brass buttons, badge and new hairdo. Foregoing my latest reading material, I watched the passing scene flash by as we left the centre of Birmingham, travelling through the outskirts and bearing witness to its scars of suffering. Tall cube-like buildings showed large gaps here and there, like missing teeth in a child's mouth. Telegraph poles, their wires crossing at intervals, reached out across bomb craters and industrial buildings, revealing signs of incendiary damage, in big blackened patches. The Bourneville Chocolate Factory still stood, unscathed and alone, I was happy to note.

Waiting for an oncoming train to pass, we halted, and I saw a bombed out apartment building with scattered, missing sections, one of which exposed a jagged wall of uneven brickwork, joining the second and third storys. Someone's home, once; A door hung suspended at a crazy slant, part of a kitchen clock was still on the wall, and remnants of a window blind were hanging precariously. Strips of mirror were still adhering to the old plaster, oddly reflecting impossible shapes. Twisted pipes, pretzel-like, were making a strange, free-form sculpture, prominent against the aperture where a window had been. A silhouette casting its weird shadow in a broken mirror fragment opposite. It all reminded me of an Surrealist painting. A Salvador Dali perhaps.

Our trains passed and I turned my gaze to my book for relief, unwilling to dwell on more damage and loss.

Alighting in Paddington, it struck me as odd that I hardly ever saw any WAAF on my train journeys, but once in a while a few appeared in the Underground, or in a London club. We must have travelled different routes or at different times, I thought.

Stanmore in the early evening was quite balmy in mid September and pleasantly warm as I exited the Tube Station, so with only one suitcase to haul, no kit bag, and having left other excess baggage at home, I decided to walk. I had taken a bus and two trains by then, and thought the exercise would feel good.

I crossed the road to walk along the edge of a small field of empty land and out of the corner of my eye I saw it coming, and simultaneously heard that repetitious droning, sinister bzzzz bzzzz. There it was, tail light blinking, flying low over the roofs of buildings ahead, light still fiery red, as I watched, suddenly I was attacked from behind and thrown to the ground with someone on top of me, hat over my eyes, tin hat rattling, and furious. I kicked viciously, hit and flailed, finally struggling upwards to find a confused looking Sgt. MP standing over me. He thought he had saved me from the doodlebug. He used words like blithering idiot, and I, gung-ho fathead and finally, "look what you did to my new hair-do and my newly cleaned uniform." Then looking around I saw the freshly laundered contents of my suitcase spread out on the grass and leaves. The look on my face gave him pause and he began silently to help me pick it all up, kneeling alongside me in the soft grass and calmed a bit by this, I realized his intentions had been good ones. Slowly relenting, I told him a little about my job and that we in Ops knew a bit about buzz bombs, and if the light was still on, and they had passed you, it was probably okay to stay put, and see if it continued to travel. If the light went out, then and only then, it might be time to drop down flat if it was near, because the Tube Station was too far behind us to run for shelter. His name was John, and he walked me back to the HQ and offered me dinner to "make it up to me," he said. He was an interesting person to talk to, when he wasn't in 'attack' mode. Not knowing my schedule, and needing time to think, I gave him my telephone number at the house.

Sally was already there when I reached our billet, and she looked as if her leave had been a tonic too, and I complimented her, on looking terrific. She too, commented generously on my restored appearance, before she told me about the new and latest threat to life and limb.

The new weapon was called the V-2 (V for vengeance). We didn't know much about it yet, except that it was rocket powered, and travelled three times the speed of sound and carried a warhead of a 1,000 lbs. This meant that if you heard the gigantic blast as it reached its target, then you had missed it. You certainly couldn't hear it coming and by the time you heard it, it was all over and you knew you had lived to tell the tale. It wasn't possible to track them at that speed, so we were not able to plot them on the map, and the trajectory was such that it was invulnerable to anti-aircraft guns. They reached a height of 62 to 68 miles before arcing downwards and were mostly directed at London, where they did far more damage than the V-1s (doodlebugs). The crater was much bigger and results far worse, more widespread, and yet, it wasn't the war on nerves that the V-1s were, at least we, on the station thought so.

The V-1 was the world's first pulse-jet which required an atmosphere in which to work, whereas the V-2s were rockets, fuelled by ethyl alcohol and liquid oxygen and didn't. They were the world's first ballistic missile.

Much later it was discovered that Concentration Camp workers and enforced labourers who were employed at Penemünde, where these weapons were made, worked at great risk to themselves. A total of 12,000 lives were lost by those working on production. Many were Russian POWs and were, considered expendable, by their captors. This V-2 rocket was also extremely expensive to make, dangerous to launch, besides not being very accurate.

The last one of these exploded on Hughes Mansions in Whitechapel, in the London area, on 25 March 1945 with the result that 3,000 tons of materiel erupted into the air. However, that was yet to happen.

Right now, it was all new to us. We had to cope with the advent of this supersonic, ballistic missile, learning about it from scratch. Antwerp, and

Belgium were also, on the receiving end of these rockets and suffering a great deal, from loss and damage.

On duty in Ops, we continued to plot and tell plots on "hostiles," but of course, were unable to do so with the V-2 s. Too fast. We could hear the mighty blasts of those that dropped on London. It was a horrid feeling to know that so little could be done about them, except to eliminate them at the source, and our bombers were already hard at work on that.

We still went into London, though less frequently, but Sally was dating an American flyer named Mike by then, so she liked to go, when feasible. One evening, Mike together with two of his friends invited Charmaine and me to attend a dinner dance with Sally and himself, at the Savoy. We couldn't resist such a favourite spot, and arranged to meet in the bar there, called the River room, a few days hence and we looked forward to it. Wherever we were, on duty in Ops, rested, or not, sleeping, in the billet, or not, time passed as slowly as watching grass grow, but we always had this little jewel of an escape in our minds eye, to spur us on. The day finally dawned, and we left for the big city to find the Savoy intact, and waiting for us. At last, some fun.

"Not quite like pre-war," the aging maître de', commented, as we entered. Even so, everything was done with such grace and good service, and we could hear the upbeat sounds of a great band, in the background. Besides we were too young to compare how it might have been before the war and the ambience now, was a pleasure to experience. We all began to enjoy this glimpse into past peacetime splendour, immensely. Some civilians were in evening dress, probably on leave, if young, gliding under glittering chandeliers to the seductive rhythm of the music while mellow light from wall sconces gleamed on silver and crystal tableware, beneath. The very ambience spelled r-e-l-a-x and we certainly, did. Settling down to dessert after spending a happy time on the dance floor, as often happened, we talked about the war and were told the strangest tale, by Paul, the pilot who had been in London only the week before.

One of his crew, had attended a dance held on the second floor of a hotel in the West End of London, when a V-2 had rocketed in, nearby, not a direct hit, but the blast had achieved some uncanny results, ending in deaths of a select few. A couple dancing together had not been touched by any falling debris, but one had died, and the other had not. It seemed that the blast had somehow killed some, but not all, of the people on one side of the room, leaving those on the other side, completely unhurt. As if an invisible dividing line had been drawn, some in mid-stride;

Once before I had heard of similar results of blast, killing two airmen, on site leaving unscathed, two others, all walking together in a line. This was when one plane had crashed into another, on an airfield in the S.W. of England. It was so eerie. There was no sign of injury on those who had been killed, not a mark on them, they were just as if asleep, sometimes caught in mid-sentence, but dead just the same. Hard to imagine.

Shaking off these sobering revelations, we listened to the music, realizing that our evening had to finish before the last dance, even though we had late passes, we had to sign in before 2400 hrs. Our friends took us back to the Underground where we hoped not to encounter any MP's as we had left our gas capes behind in the billet. We hugged goodbye, and hoped we would see each other again. It had been a very successful event in our lives. I knew Sally would be seeing Mike again after that, but thought it was highly possible that my next posting would appear very soon, and it seemed unlikely that I could be a part of this group again, but we had discussed that earlier, so that it wasn't a surprise to anyone.

About a week went by, after our gala evening, of "stomping at the Savoy," with little let up of missile activity from the continent. Both V bombs kept coming, and the pace continued unabatedly, sleep becoming elusive once again.

During a lull one night, the Officer on watch told me what a good job he thought I had done," making no complaints, and always good for morale etc.", and how sorry, he and others would be, that I was leaving. That perked me up, but leaving? That was news to me, so next day I checked with the Orderly Room where it was indeed confirmed. I was to be once more on the move. Where next, I wondered?

7 – May Day in Scotland

Coastal command

RESIGNED, AS WE were to a world of noise and explosions, it came as something of a jolt to receive my next posting to Scotland (of all places). What could possibly be going on up there? True, Glasgow had been bombed but that was earlier and Oban was much further north. I was soon to discover that this was an important Coastal Station, for Sunderlands, namely four engine flying boats, and Catalina's, only two engines, both long range patrol bombers with Pratt and Whitney engines. Both, widely used sea planes useful for anti U boat warfare, convoy escorts, patrol bombing, air sea rescue and search and rescue, and that was what was going on up there!

Two Ops room friends saw me off, from Paddington Station in London, complete with kit bag, gas cape, tin helmet, gas mask, the lot, to catch what used to be known as the Flying Scotsman, more Scotsman than flying, these days. Despite the usual pangs of parting from familiar friendly faces as I waved farewell, I caught a glimpse of my own face reflected in the shadowy carriage window and recognized a look of relief, tinged perhaps with guilt at the prospect of leaving "a city in flames" (as Edward R Murrow so succinctly put it). I feared for my friends, still facing the newest menace, the terrible V-2 rockets. Pushing the feeling aside, knowing that retreat had not been my decision, I heard the whistle blow, the guard clanged the doors shut, waved his flag and we were off. As usual the train was crowded with uniforms, some sitting on their luggage in corridors, almost blocking off the loos. Carriages were divided into small rooms with two rows of seats facing each other, separated from the corridor by glass doors which helped keep out the cold in winter, if not the draughts. A jovial airman stowed my kit bag and I managed a corner seat next to a window.

The journey was long and foodless, unless you had the forethought and opportunity to bring a sandwich and I had neither, but I was lucky to have a seat at all, during the seven or eight hours it took to get there.

Just north of Glasgow a mysterious halt occurred outside a tiny station called Motherwell. It was early evening, already dusk, with enough light left to see little, but open rugged countryside for miles around. The bracken and heather, sprinkled with a few lone gorse bushes, spindly at best, were all that met the gaze. Minutes ticked by, and a half hour later, found us still there, stamping our feet to keep warm. No explanation. Not a peep! I imagined we were waiting for a train to pass, or perhaps there was a breakdown on the line, but no, that wasn't it! Sensing the atmosphere of general unrest, an RAF Warrant Officer wearing the wing of a Flight Engineer knew the routine, being a native of Scotland, his eyes glinting with amusement, confided rather conspiratorially, "not to worry, this is where the engine driver stops to whet his whistle with half a pint of mild and bitter. The local pub owner always has it waiting for him at this time of night." The response was immediate. Indulgent, understanding smiles, tinged with relief, and a touch of envy from the thirsty ones, spread thru the carriage like sunshine. After all, it was a long drive every day and somehow nobody minded the wait. This small human foible brought the omniscience of war down to manageable proportions. A far cry from the fast pace in London that we had left behind;

The Warrant Officer, Ralph Burnett tall, classically good looking, lively blue eyes and a lock of light brown hair tending to flop on his forehead, was stationed in Oban, where I was headed and amazingly, on the same coastal station, so he was able to clue me in about the area in general. Before we waved goodbye, he hauled my kitbag and small suitcase out to the waiting MT which bore me off to GHQ to sign in, then from there, on to my new billet. A nice welcome!

This proved to be a large hotel on the sea front overlooking the Bay and beyond the sea wall, a wonderful, briny, seaweed smell assailed my nose, and waves viciously biting the shore, sent up great arcs of spray as they hit the stone wall, the last rays of fading sunlight transforming them into a kaleidoscope of color. A photographer's delight! Rather better than the old, gaseous and leaky, Bethel Chapel in Wales, I thought.

Once inside however, there were some similarities as the room was enormous, even bigger than the chapel, also with only a few beds in it. Perhaps six, at most: A tiny fireplace on the long wall with a laughable, handful of coal burning brightly but inadequately, gave the room a glow. A little beacon of light, but not much real warmth issued from it: It was here I met Mary Wood, a lean Scot, who was soon to become my good friend. She also worked in 'Ops,' though here, this was known as Flying Control, since we were right above the field of action. Another girl present was a radio-telegraphist (R/T operator) and one other WAAF worked in Intelligence, while the remaining absent two girls, were doing their stint on night duty. Nancy made me a cup of coffee, a broad term for a brew which bore little resemblance to actual coffee, but it was all we had. It was brown, warm and sweet with lots of chicory and strangely I got to like it, much to my family's disgust. It was called Camp Coffee, a brown, chicory liquid contained in a bottle, to which one added boiling water. Still, it provided a moment shared, conveying a friendly welcome as well as giving me a chance to get the "gen" on my new room-mates and workmates.

Next day at 0700 hrs, buttons shining, nose not, uniform pressed, no tin helmet or gas equipment, there was I, at the hotel entrance waiting for M.T. to take me to my new post. A small air force-blue van came along, already occupied with four passengers whom I met and chatted with on the way to our destination. We travelled along the sea front, past a row of hotels overlooking the Bay called the Sound of Kerrera, a body of water separating the mainland from the island beyond.

The road we were on was between a low beach-wall on one side. and the hotels on the other. With few exceptions, houses, hotels or buildings in general, are to this day, not allowed to build directly on the beach in the U.K. as it would cut off the ocean view for everyone else. It was indeed a lovely view of the Sound, where I later discovered our planes took off and landed. Curving around the coast then veering slightly left, we travelled up a small mountain called Dungallon Hill, which I came to know very well, until we arrived at the entrance of a vine covered manse. This large stone building was our GHQ which housed Ops, Intelligence and Flying Control. It had once been a beautiful residence with a commanding view from the cliff top, of the Kerrera Sound, taking its name from the uninhabited island paralleling the coast, and Oban just beyond that. Upstairs, large bay windows enabled us in

Flying Control to easily monitor landings and take-offs of our Sunderlands and Catalinas as they spread out beneath us. Just behind Kerrera Island in the distance it was possible to see small boats plying back and forth between the Inner and Outer Hebrides and the Port of Oban. With pleasure I realized this would be a vastly different experience for me, with much to learn and no overhead threats to life and limb. I could stop waiting for explosions, and no tense muscles strained my body, stiffness between my shoulders, all gone. The fight or flight mechanism at rest; I fairly danced along trying not to think of friends still coping in Stanmore.

Already, it was apparent that there was less formality here, less spit and polish, less saluting, even a chance to rest on a rollaway cot at night, if there was an opportunity, as our nights were a great deal quieter here. My first impression of F/C was pure delight as my eye fell upon the huge, well fuelled, fireplace, at right angles to my desk, next to a large window. The Radio Telegraphist sat behind me. On my left was another bay window occupied by one of three, alternative Lieutenants, who rotated in shifts corresponding to ours. Behind his desk was a small sun room equipped to make hot drinks to keep us going through long watches, especially appreciated on winter nights. Next door to Flying Control housed Intelligence, staffed by younger officers some of whom were post-aircrew. They were a rather a lively bunch.

One of these ex-aircrew was a likeable Lieutenant now assigned to a desk. He was about twenty-two at most, when I met him. Kind hearted, always ready to lend a hand where needed, he seemed a little shy or perhaps introspective suited him better, despite his bright red hair which often denotes a more flamboyant character. In confidence I had been told that his record dossier had been tagged Lacking in Moral Fibre (LMF) nowadays it's called "battle fatigue". Between the age of nineteen and twenty-one, he had flown many grueling hours under heavy fire and flak, over enemy territory. This young man had been shot down twice, barely escaping with his life, and risking it again and again, finding his dangerous way back to his station, only to be sent back for more. Finally, suffering from stress his Medical Officer (MO) had grounded him and his dossier was branded LMF.

Stressed metal was treated with more respect yet a human being was expected to carry on past all endurance. What an appellation for a brave young man! I'm told that American aircrew reaching the burnout stage, were sent to a refuge called shack time, allowing them a period of rest, giving them dignity, followed by an opportunity to recover and carry on afterwards. Later on in the war I was glad to learn that the description LMF was justifiably scrubbed from the records, though not soon enough to remove the sting from those so categorized at first.

Part of my job was to hand over to Intelligence, certain data such as weather updates, or info on any emerging situation of note and another incidental part, was to log take-offs and landings, together with all pertinent facts. All personnel here were friendly, smart, and helpful but it soon became apparent to me, that my favorite watch companion in Flying Control, was a South African Lieut. from Durban named John Hayward. He seemed eminently capable, approachable, and enjoyable to work with. As time progressed we shared tea, sometimes chocolate rations if we were lucky, along with anecdotes, occasionally philosophizing about life in general, in that lengthy severe winter of 1944. The fire would be stoked, tea or cocoa at the ready and conversation flowed. On one such occasion I found myself confessing to a case of nervous apprehension about a play I had rashly promised to appear in during off duty hours. It was to be a comedy, directed by an illustrious professional who was well known in peacetime, one Hal Osmund. He had directed many plays, musicals too, and was associated with the George Black productions before the war so I assumed he could lick us into shape, if anyone could. The play was *Love in a Mist*, and I was to play the ingénue. Since there were only six in the cast, and the duration would be two and a half hours, there was an abundance of lines for each of us. John gave me much needed encouragement as he listened to my lines on a quiet shift, whilst adding that his younger brother had managed to do quite well in this field and "if that scamp could, then it would be a cinch for you" he said. Well, not knowing his brother it meant little to me, but good to have support anyway.

Soon the duty roster was changed to accommodate rehearsals. Usually we worked a morning shift from 8am to noon then again from 5pm to 8am next day. This long shift enabled us to have a day of rest plus the next morning off, after which we went in for a half day from noon to 5pm. Now, in order to accommodate rehearsals my night shift would begin after rehearsals at 11pm. Thus, began my late night toils on those occasions, up the icy mountain engulfed in the deep velvety blackness, which seemed to blank out space and time, with little sound to be heard. Luckily, I always had a companion, tho somehow, conversation became fittingly, hushed.

When the moon shone the scene was transformed, into an eerie photographically beautiful panorama. Of course, coming down that big hill in the daytime when the sun was just beginning to shine, brought everything into sharp focus and the view was quite spectacular.

One day, as I wearily came off a night shift in the early morning, a sight so incongruous transfixed my gaze. There, sailing down the mini mountain was a Chimney Sweep, face black with soot, tam at a jaunty angle, round brushes of his trade strapped to his back and grinning broadly, exposing teeth like a Hammond organ, he sat astride a very posh Harley Davidson motor bike. His compensation, no doubt, for a very murky job and he was obviously enjoying it to the full, radiating pure glee.

Because I had once expressed a desire to take a ride on a motor bike, my companions walking alongside, on the way back down the hill, dared me to ride with the Sweep, if he could be persuaded. And he could! It might be my only chance, they said. Needing no further urging, and amid many whistles and other shouts of encouragement, I climbed aboard the pillion, holding on to my skirt, jamming my hat on tight, and we were away. I had the ride of a lifetime back to my hotel, by this time, smiling and sooty myself.

The mail had been delivered, with a nice haul for me, including one from Joan. Much to my surprise she had begun dating another American, she said. Nothing like George, either in appearance, or in disposition, she continued. He was even tempered, knew what he expected to do after the war, when and where he planned to go into the orange grove industry with his Father. He very much looked forward to the prospect and seemed open, not as withdrawn as George had tended to be, at times. It was all quite different, she wrote. No immediate danger hung over them, and the war seemed to have taken a turn for the better. She would be careful not to go overboard, on the rebound, she assured me and had no immediate plans for the future. It sounded much more "feet on the ground" and I hoped this would be a happy relationship for both.

The night duty journey was always a choice of being either afoot, or wait for MT but waiting in a cold wind was pure misery. Better to keep moving. One night, neither duty nor rehearsals claimed my presence and I was actually free, so my 'train-friend,' Ralph, invited me to the pictures. He was however, a bit mortified to find that, that included carrying my stone hot water bottle (no rubber ones available). There was no heat in the ice cold stone theatre and blue noses were not my style, but he was good natured about dragging it along with us, and took the ensuing ribbing with good grace. The movie was *The Man in the Iron Mask*. For those who never saw it, it was a harrowing tale about a king who kept his brother hidden behind a locked iron mask, so that he couldn't be recognized as the rightful heir to the throne. The iron mask also hid a swashbuckling hero. Handsome, of course who, after many struggles, achieved justice at the end, becoming the rightful King, at last, with his ever loyal bride at his side. Naturally, the evil brother got his just comeuppance in a spectacular duel. On the whole, a satisfying respite from the grimness of war, and a brief escape into the world of make believe, and the world of the flickering screen.

Back at the desk that night, I briefly reviewed the movie with John, only then discovering that the dashing hero was none other than his brother "the" Louis Hayward, *the scamp*, at the time living a glamorous life in Hollywood and married to Ida Lupino.

On a more modest scale my little rehearsals were held in an old baronial-like hall known as Argyle Hall. It was a hoot!! Envision a huge high ceilinged room with all paneled walls, covered with glassy eyed, taxidermied, antler-headed beasts of assorted species. Hovering way up high, they cast their ghostly shadows on those beneath.

The controlling force of the upcoming opus, otherwise known as the Director, (Hal Osmund), was a small man with a powerful presence, who used it mercilessly to get the last ounce out of us. He handpicked our five in the cast, he said, taking the lead himself though the lines were quite equally divided, indicating a fair amount of memorizing for each of us. There were three acts with two scenes in the third, also two brief intervals, so it ran about two and a half, hours or a bit more. We had roughly six weeks in rehearsal with Christmas intervening, so the play would be presented on four consecutive nights. December 27, 28, 29, and 30th. Work proceeded as usual, though my duties in F.C. were adjusted for performances, leaving little time for anything else.

Roles in our Grammar school drama club, mostly classics, had hardly prepared me for this little caper, but what the heck I was in it now! Playing opposite me was a well built 6'2" aircrew member, modestly wearing his DSO silently emanating quiet composure, for the benefit of anyone watching.

I was 5'4", so we made a rather odd couple, with almost a foot of space between our heads making it an acrobatic manoeuvre when called upon to gaze into each other's eyes, it fairly made my neck ache. Lines came easily to me but stage love scenes weren't part of my repertoire, Shakespeare hardly counted. An episode in the script required that I get up close and tantalizing and wishing for a stool, I tried. Not a bit pleased, Hal, impatient as ever yelled, "move in, move in". So, leaving my feet where they were, about two feet away, I bent from the waist, just moving my top half over. From the back of the hall he bellowed "for Pity's sake Betty when you make love to a man don't leave your bottom sticking out". With that he stomped down the aisle, leapt up on the stage, gnome like, to demonstrate my strange position, much to the amusement of the rehearsal watchers who enjoyed my discomfiture no end. A bit miffed, I moved in with a vengeance, causing Howard to miss his next line. Just what the Director had in mind! "Good," said Hal, finally satisfied.

During the long weeks of rehearsal, I was in the habit of walking down Dungallon Hill, in the daytime as well, too impatient to wait for MT when December wind and elements were at their worst, rain created a penetrating damp, chilling you clear thru' to the bone. At night, one of the men usually accompanied me, as it was a two and a half mile walk in pitch blackness on moonless nights. Conversation kept us moving. The sea front caught the full force of the icy blast from tremendous winds sweeping inland from the turbulent sea, often turning a dark blue expanse into the colour of ripe olives Even clad in a heavy wool greatcoat, which felt as substantial as chiffon, I felt frozen to the core. At times my lashes froze. As a result I caught cold, which developed into an infection, namely fibrositis, and thus wound up in Sick Bay. Mess food, didn't help convalescence much. Powdered eggs, powdered milk, spam and the like weren't ideal for recovery. Once, we had canned beans on toast for breakfast for six weeks straight. I haven't eaten those watery, tomato-covered, soggy, wet beans since.

One shivery day at rehearsal, Hal took a look at my pasty face and said that if I could find a free evening, he would like to take me to a little known mystery Inn for some real food. Too good to resist! The very next evening, before night duty, we set off in a little van used for Drama Club purposes, into the country near the Falls of Lora. Nestled in rugged crags was a small, grey, stone Inn, covered in ivy and honeysuckle in summer. When it was warmer weather, the owners grew their own vegetables and some fruit, as well as a separate herb garden, freezing the surplus and thus were able to use their own produce in the kitchen year round.

Once inside, we found a red, carpeted, dining room with a little bar and oh Joy, a glorious fire blazing in the big fireplace burning a mix of coal and peat. Such lovely heat, I was warm at last! We were served a heavenly broth, accompanied by home baked bread, followed by beautifully cooked grouse, recognizable green vegetables, not the usual olive drab, stewed, concoction served in the Mess. Next, came a plum-duff pudding with an unbelievable sauce, then back to reality with chicory coffee or tea. Hal was a good host, full of anecdotes about his London life before the war, digressing periodically to tell about back stage gaffes, such as the time he was expected to make an important stage entry.

Duly banging on the door before his supposed dramatic entry, he found the door was stuck so he resorted to a push, with no apparent result, then getting anxious, a shove, and finally exasperated, a bigger shove, when to his horror the entire set caved in, exposing the wings and all those standing therein, whether fully clothed or not, leaving him looking totally gormless, holding the door knob aloft, and no door. The audience loved it.

Replete with food, at peace with the world, we travelled contentedly back to Flying Control. It had been a most successful restoration event for me and a pleasant easy going friendship had begun.

Another friend who enriched my life was Mary Wood who first endeared herself to me when she noticed how badly I mangled a shirt while endeavoring to iron it. Wordlessly she removed the iron from my hand with a shake of the head and took over, for the duration of my stay here. The good Chinese laundries in Wales and London that we liked, never made it this far north, leaving the iron and me in constant conflict with many a mangled shirt to show for it. Mary took over and luckily, there were a few things I could do to help her in other areas, instead.

Her life in north Scotland with an elderly, spinster aunt, had been a bit dour if not downright gloomy. Not much to laugh about, or people to share ideas with. As a result she was very shy and awkward in company, so with a little coaxing I persuaded her to attend a few social events with me. Sometimes she came to watch me rehearse, mingling with the cast, and things gradually began to change, as she relaxed and began to enjoy her off duty hours, revealing her wonderful wicked sense of humour, now and then. One ridiculous occasion that might have had a sad end, somehow struck us both as terribly funny, once we got over the fright.

As it happened, a room-mate had asked me to find out what had caused a blockage in an electrical wall outlet and not being very handy, I thought a good poke might do it. Unfortunately, the object nearest my hand was a fork. Not a good idea for poking. Of course, the current was still on, so the resulting gigantic flash which shot out of the offending outlet singed, and took off, the front of my hair, both eyebrows and even the tips of my lashes. When we recovered from the "shock," I consulted a mirror to assess the damage. The first sight of my bald face, suddenly struck us as hilariously funny and we collapsed on the bed in gales of laughter. Mixed with relief, at the narrow escape, I suspect.

Mary was also a serious scholar who was always studying some tome or other, the latest, being an enormous anthology of Dreams, dissertations by Freud, Kant, Jung, etc. An oversimplified version and summation of the contents is as follows: Philosophers indicate that only dreams of the past or future are of significance in analysis, as the present doesn't appear in dreams. Also, one must rule out those jumbled dreams caused by indigestion or other disturbances of the body, to properly research the quality or predictability of a dream. In order to avoid distortion of the dream, and therefore its significance, prompt note taking is necessary.

Mary determined to do her own research and come to her own conclusions. For this research she needed to keep pen and pad next to the bedside in order to write down her memory of the dream precisely at the very minute she woke, whatever time that was. Since we shared a room she asked my indulgence when the light went on at odd hours, but by then I was curious about results too, thus happily resigned to sleeping with a pillow over my face. Her study lasted for several weeks with little of major interest to report, until much later when we were both rather spooked, but that was yet to come.

In the meantime work went on as usual. Christmas came and went, without much ado, so everyone was ready for some entertainment before the big Scottish New Year or Hogmanay as it is properly called in Scotland. A very important event for a Scot,

The play was as polished as we could make it when the big night came. Sitting in the wings in unaccustomed civvies awaiting my cue, make-up in place, knees playing *God Save The Queen*, I wondered could one die of stage fright? Not a word, not a line could I remember. Looking around for comfort, there sat my cohort, Howard, looking intrepid as ever, well he was decorated for bravery after all, lounging on an upturned trunk, calmly reading a newspaper. The adrenalin would kick in and I would be fine, he told me. Mind you, I was even more reassured when I noticed that he was reading an upside down newspaper and there was a distinct tremor in both hands. If he could be nervous, it must be OK for me. True, once on stage, exhilaration took over, but no-one mentioned it would be just as bad every night, while waiting in the wings beforehand. Amazingly, the play was an overwhelming success. Tension had built up in all the right places, subsiding into laughter when it should, with curtain calls repeated over and over. Dizzy with relief but still wound up, we gathered to consider any possible refinements for the next performance. Four nights later was the final night which closed to a packed house and much applause, making us all very happy, indeed.

Pubs closed at 10.30 pm so the cast repaired to a club in a cellar unknown to most of us, but trust Hal to ferret it out for our little celebration. He had a nose for finding hidden gems. Leading all six cast members and two stage crew, down a flight of stairs, by tiny torch light, we saw a door with a tiny trapdoor in the top part, for ID, reminiscent of American speakeasy days depicted in pictures. Promptly identified by a face the other side, we were ushered in, whereupon everyone was invited to order a drink. Mine was a shandy, beer and pop mixed, with no ice of course. We feasted on real farm eggs I remember, and even half an ounce of bacon. The evening was a merry one embellished by a few renditions previously unheard of such as, *Eight Old Ladies Locked in a Lavatory* and other doubtful ditties, as our finale. A good thing we had late passes, as the night was no longer young when we reluctantly, parted.

The play was over and winter upon us, in earnest. One particularly bad night, in F.C. with winds howling at gale force, when no air traffic was expected, we flipped cots out, and my head was just down, when the R/T suddenly sprang to life. First came the tapping Morse code distress signal an S.O.S. coming in, then a voice, "Mayday---MAYDAY" peaking and fading over radio's crackling, intermittent static, desperately entreating once more, "Mayd-"--It's final call. Using a fix, established the pilot's position with barely enough time to give him some weather, we knew he was in deep trouble and coming down fast. Nothing more! No sound at all, the radio was dead. Silence filled the room for what seemed an eternity, before we scurried into action, each performing our separate tasks eliciting information from all available sources including the R.T. network and spotters. We discovered that a US bomber, a B-24, four-engine Liberator, had crashed into a mountain in the Outer Hebrides. These islands lie about 60 miles offshore, a very long way from Oban, when you consider that from Dover to Calais is only twenty six miles. They had crashed on Benbecula mountainside. That was all we knew!

Air Sea rescue once notified, immediately dispatched it's fastest, sturdiest, boat into the roiling sea, soon to be followed by planes, as the weather lifted. Even so, it was at best, slow progress through the roughest of waves and fierce winds, but struggling on, they reached the shores at dawn, where they were met by a few eager islanders waiting to help.

These boats were known as torpedo boats, and were the fastest afloat at 36 knots. Word had spread about them, revealing to US bomber crews, a history of their daring rescues of downed crews, off the coast of occupied France. Fliers, snatched to safety by our Air Sea Rescue crews, from right under enemy noses, in the English Channel. Fire and strafing didn't stop them saving countless lives. They were dauntless.

Islanders, made good guides, and were at the ready, so wasting no time, the boat crew, foul weather gear in place, hampered by cumbersome weather equipment, stretchers, heavy blankets etc., began its long trek up the barren mountain, stoic volunteers leading the way. Reaching their target, they found the pilot and one other, the navigator had been, badly injured, and sadly, both dead from exposure while waiting in vain on that bitter night. Rescue, came too late for them.

The rest of the crew were alive, some injured and those who were conscious, were given warming drinks before they were brought down the mountain, heavily blanketed, against the howling winds and into the waiting boat. Hours later, once they reached the shore, straight into Sick Bay they went for the best medical care we had to offer.

One week later, the Squadron and the townspeople expressed their feelings going wild with relief that nine young men had survived their ordeal, with only a few broken bones. They were an odd looking bunch in their borrowed clothes, balaclavas, scarves, odd hats and a few corduroy pants, some were sporting white casts, which bore written witticisms of varying brilliance. Supplied by us, naturally!

On the dark side, sad services were held for the two young men who didn't make it, in the beautiful, old, stone church, high up on a peak, looking out to sea. The sun glinted thru' the stained glass, lending an air of piety and hope, as it shone on the Minister beneath, while he read the eulogy. Such brief lives, so soon over, was a stark reality, especially to the crew who must go on without their leader and friend, with whom they had spent so many hours surviving together, as a team. Those nine men who were left behind waited, silent and forlorn, until the organ sounded the notes of a familiar hymn. Their voices, tentative at first, gaining strength from one another, swelled the choir to a crescendo, giving vent to their tragic loss and triggering the emotions of all who heard them. Sadness hung like a pall, and hit the gut like a sharp bodkin. Tears flowed abundantly. Very little was said, as all of us mourners, quietly left the church, under a pearly grey sky, dismal, gunmetal clouds in the distance, echoing our feelings.

Later, it would be time for them to move on, back to their American base in the south of England, but in the meantime the crew all, became frequent visitors to F/C and Intelligence, where their debriefing occurred. Results were then passed to proper channels, in preparation for their forthcoming return. We all got to know each other quite well in a short space of time. Danger does that to you, we found. It loosens the tongues of those involved.

During the interval, small parties, and two gala dances were given in their honor, during which I suddenly acquired two suitors. Both, from the downed plane; Gary and John began to wait at the gate, after I came off duty, to escort me back to my hotel billet, comically vying for my attention on the way, neither willing to back off, consequently I had two escorts up and down Dungallon hill, and we three, all attended the dances together. Were they serious? Maybe at the time, but not in a lasting way, Perhaps it became a game, bearing in mind, that many young men were unwittingly seeking the promise of a future, or the permanence of a partner, to get them thru' the sticky bits of every-day survival. A temporary affliction I thought. In the meantime, it was just fun for me.

We all set off together for the last dance. Gary far from being disadvantaged by his arm-cast, flourished it with gusto, to create space around him on a crowded dance floor, loudly bellowing instructions to "watch out for the arm." It worked! John, usually the more introspective of the two, decided to enter into the evening's frivolity with total abandon, cutting in at frequent intervals. Gary, feet flying at a dizzying pace, and forcing his partner to do the same, he twirled the floor till I thought my shoe leather was completely destroyed. But then, the Highlanders appeared in their kilts, and on we went, in a new burst of enthusiasm, to be challenged afresh by the traditional Scottish reel, and reel we did. One after the other. After that, tunics were off, sleeves rolled high and we were ready to attempt the Highland Fling. My friend, Ralph the expert, was there to demonstrate with unusual grace, the complex steps required, urging us on to greater heights. Well we tried, some succeeding, but earlier reels had taken their toll by now, and after several hours of not sitting one out, I had fallen by the wayside and was breathless and spent. Even a few hardy Scots had collapsed on chairs. Sporrans dangling, bodies drooping, sweat beads popped like petit pois, on some brows, but still eyes glittered, alive with merriment, and mischief. Incidentally, the Scots are not to be confused with the term Scotch as that is reserved only, for the beverage. People from Scotland are properly referred to as, Scottish.

Valiant souls still on the dance floor whirled, tapped, and kicked, never missing a beat, arms upraised, elbows bent, apparently prepared to continue indefinitely with nary a gasp out of any of them until, at last, the strains of Auld Lang Syne could be heard. Not quite dawn when a sudden hush fell on the entire assembly as we all held hands and formed circles in the vast ballroom. Quietly at first, a male voice began the haunting melody, picked up by the rest of us until the last few slow paced words were sung. Oh those bagpipes! "Auld Lang Syne" meaning," from long ago and now, may old friends never be forgotten." New Years Eve or Hogmanay in Scotland had been well celebrated this night. It always closed with this song, accompanied sometimes with kisses but in earlier times the last toast would require that all glasses be flung into the big open fireplace. What with the mistletoe and the mood, no glasses were thrown. We just threw in a few kisses instead, for good luck.

Inevitably, the day of departure dawned for our American flyers to leave and we felt sad to see them go, but by then they were ready to get back into the fray. They had made many friends who continued to write until war ended but too many demands intervened in my life, which was constantly changing, so I decided to stop after a while.

Sometime previously Ralph had asked me for a photograph of myself to put in his scrapbook, he said, and I had obliged, thinking that was the end of it, until one day to my embarrassment he explained there was more. A National RAF magazine published monthly, had requested photographs to be entered in the big nationwide beauty contest for Air Force participants, and he decided to enter my photograph. Ralph, a keen photographer made a copy of my original in suitable dimensions, and sent it in to be judged. Contestants from everywhere had entered, and the list was pared down to 50 finalists, then 25 than to ten, all the time, not a word to me. Any friends were sworn to secrecy, in the meantime the photographs of the finalists had been appearing in the periodical regularly. Blissfully ignorant until now, it seemed I was one of the ten chosen to be a guest at an elaborate lunch at the Dorchester Hotel in London, then and now, one of the top three hostelries in the city, where we would be interviewed and judged. No bathing suits! Fairly dignified, I hoped. The judges were a panel of three, comprised of two movie Directors and a well known star, Anna Neagle. The latter was impressive, as she had just won all the awards in a film called *Fifty Glorious Years*, depicting Queen Victoria from girlhood to old age.

What to do? I would like to meet Anna Neagle but I'd feel like Astor's plush horse parading around the place, to be judged besides how would I explain it to my family? Too much teasing would inevitably be my lot. Still, it seemed best to tell them at this point, and they could help me decide whether or not, to accept. My leave was due anyway.

Ralph thought I would be pleased, but I felt a bit silly about all the fuss. It seemed a bit superficial in the middle of a war, but perhaps people needed a little frivolity. It would be fun I'll admit, to meet Anna Neagle and I would like a peek at the Dorchester-a bit out of reach for my purposes. My friend John, in F.C. thought it, a bit of a lark and not too insulting to be thought beautiful, so I decided to go, if my family wasn't too horrified.

Once home, I reluctantly explained and produced the invitation to present myself at the Dorchester, much to my Father's amusement, my sister's delight, and my Mother's concern, over what in wartime coupon-dominated days, could I wear? They had just assumed my curiosity alone would induce me to go.

Since I wore a uniform there were no clothes coupons available for me, to buy something new, consequently, it had to be something I already had. There was a black silk dress or a newer, tailored suit in brown, not my favorite color, but that was the only fabric the tailor had, at the time I had been measured. Perhaps the suit with a pink blouse would work. That decided, the evening meal over, we sat around the fire drinking tea, when the doorbell rang. Much to my amazement, there stood Ralph Burnett, motor bike parked in the driveway, hat cocked over one eye, looking most pleased with himself. He had decided he would like to be part of my leave, with not a word to me beforehand, about any possible plans I might have, so with scrounged petrol coupons, and a few days leave, here he was! Petrol coupons were only issued for war work, essential travel, or transport to one's job, but I refrained from asking embarrassing questions. It was a long way from Oban in Scotland to West Hagley in Worcestershire, on a motor bike, but he was determined. However, there was something about his self assurance that he was to be included in family plans without any consultation with anyone concerned, particularly since he had never met my family before, that didn't go down too well with my parents. He was made welcome, given something to drink and a hot meal though not offered the spare room but instead referred to the little Inn nearby. I was a bit annoyed with my parent's unusual lack of hospitality, but then realized Ralph had been rather presumptuous in putting me on the spot, and anyway he seemed quite happy to inhabit the local Inn. Next day, not in the least put out, he jauntily appeared to be shown the sights, hence my second ride on the pillion of a motorbike. My last too, if my Father had anything to do with it. Still, the wind in my hair, no helmets required then, on a sunny day, balanced on this floating, swaying machine it was exhilarating, despite the vulnerability of human flesh on such a contraption.

We toured the countryside, stopping to explore an old castle, see a fortified manor, and enjoying the two days before my departure to London. Before leaving, Ralph confessed that he had fallen in love with me, and asked me to marry him, though he was not unaware of my commitment to Frank. I should have seen this coming but didn't perhaps want to recognize it, or to presume to think he thought of me that way, as he had frequently referred to himself as, "your good friend." It was most disturbing and rather touching, but he knew that Frank was very much in the picture, and that it might become permanent, when the war was over. I suppose my anxieties about the need to break family ties, if Frank and I married, gave him hope that things would change. Whatever happened to friendship? It was time to set the record straight and I did.

Unhappily, rather dejectedly, Ralph set off for Scotland while I prepared for London in a sober mood.

On arrival at the Dorchester, it was obvious that the way had been smoothed for the arrival of the contestants, with minimum formality. We merely signed the register in exchange for a discreet little name tag, before being ushered into a flower bedecked spacious room, where coats were deposited along with hat, gloves etc. Here, information was given to proceed to a special suite on the ground floor, where I was to meet the other nine contestants, judges and the press. I was a little nervous going down in the lift but decided to enjoy the experience to the full, and bearing in mind Dad's usual comments about any flattering remarks on my appearance, " Handsome is as handsome does." That jaded old adage certainly restored things to their proper proportion. Still, it was an adventure!

The girls were variously clad, some decidedly more festive than I, in my plain tailored suit, and generally, rather more heavily made up. We scattered around the room to talk to the luminaries. The girls were a handsome lot, nice figures, well groomed some tall, some my height and seemingly quite self possessed though on closer scrutiny a few tell-tale signs of nervousness, were discernible. Reassured, I turned to find Anna Neagle by my side who, upon introduction, appeared much younger, more glamorous than on the silver screen and, possessed of a charming presence. Easy to talk to, she answered all my questions about her life before movies and I was enthralled. Later, at lunch I was seated next to one of the movie directors who also proved to be most interesting and entertaining, making the time fly by. There was a waiter behind each chair to serve various courses and appropriate wines, but best to take it easy on the latter, I thought. No extra stimulation needed as the moment of decision approached. The panel of judges assembled in a separate room, then, one by one, each girl was invited in, to talk, stand, walk and pose as directed. Finally, two of us were asked to return several times for more instructions, before the final result was announced, which came as a relief, finally. Diane, another blonde, was first choice and I was second. We both smiled in relief and the applause was astounding. The whole thing had taken hours and left me feeling quite dazed and amazed at the outcome, oddly pleased after all, that the experience had come my way.

The prize was for each of us to be photographed in the studio of King George's special photographer, by the man himself. The photographer, not the King. Later, when I returned to keep this appointment, it was to be posed in all possible positions and photographed from all imaginable angles until self consciousness was eliminated by sheer fatigue. This time I wore my black dress as the artist told me never to wear brown again, as it was all wrong for me. Interesting, and to be remembered in future;

Hours passed, before at long last, he drew a satisfied breath promising wonderful, pastel results within the month. Copies were to be sent to me and would also be published afterwards, he said. Tea was served by the fire, bright lights doused as he turned into a human being again, while recounting his experiences behind the camera when photographing, shy King George VI, as well as other famed individuals. He was truly gifted in catching the essence of the person on the other side of his lens, as I saw by some of his photographs. I wondered what my essence would look like? This was the most exciting part of it all and I couldn't wait to see the results. Alas, it was not to be. Ten days afterwards I was notified that his studio and all in it, had been destroyed by enemy action. I don't know if the photographer survived, but I like to believe he did. No further news ever came my way, and I never had a response to my letters. No masterpiece photographs after all. I must admit I was very disappointed about this. Loyal friends raised their glasses at the local pub to my minor triumph anyway, and a few dinners ensued, before thankfully settling down to normal again. Somewhere, paper slivers of me, in my black dress, revealing my 'essence', are being blown heaven ward in the stratosphere, I thought.

A new play by J.B. Priestly, *Dangerous Corner*, was being considered with a role for me, Hal said, but rehearsals took every scrap of spare time, so it seemed best to think it over before committing.

My 'ironing' friend, Mary Wood had been home on leave in Inverary, further north in Scotland and while en route the train passed thru a small town, where a WAAF friend of hers, Fran Dale, had lived, before being killed in an air raid in London. Earlier on the dead girl had left a few personal possessions with Mary for safe keeping and she planned to return them. So on her way through Fort William she planned to debark there to take them to her family, before continuing her journey back to Oban again. She got off the train near the town, where she had never been before, yet following the map she had an uncanny sense of absolute knowledge of the street she found herself in. Knew it by sight, and even stranger, recognized the house before she saw the number on the door. It was as if she had returned to somewhere familiar, though she had never set foot in this place before. In fact she had never visited Fort William before. How odd! Dreamlike, she rang the doorbell instinctively knowing what the person on the other side would look like, seconds before the door opened, and what she would be wearing. Her logical mind could find no reason whatsoever, for this pervading sense of deja vu. and she felt spooked. Trying for a sense of serenity, she explained her mission to the grieving Mother, who ushered her into a small sitting room, welcoming her with home-made scones, cream, strawberry jam, after which, the mother said she had something to show Mary. The minute she stood up to leave the room, Mary already knew exactly what that would be and said aloud to the empty room, "a wedding dress." It was indeed the dress, never to be worn by its intended bride, the sight of which caused both, to shed tears and talk again about their loss. Soon after Mary left, still eerily shaken by the pre-cognizance she had just experienced. She couldn't quite shake it off, the whole series of events, staying at the back of her mind until she returned to her billet at the hotel, when her eye fell on the half-forgotten notebook of recorded dreams from the year before. Searching through copious notes, in her own handwriting, she found what she was looking for. There it was.

The visit to Fort William just as it really happened except there were no names in the dream, only places, faces and the wedding dress with its spreading train, draped over an older woman's arm. It was with reluctance that we finally turned out the light that night, unwilling to catch any more inadvertent glimpses into the future, in our sleep. It would have been hard to believe this strange tale, had I not been aware of Mary's notes and her passion for truth.

Letters from Normandy and elsewhere in France, were reaching me now with regularity. Frank had bravely survived the ordeal which was D-Day plus one, never to talk about it then, or later, which in itself revealed a lot. Now, he was impatient for the war to be over and even more impatient, to be with me. Magically he managed to get a brief leave, so I requested mine to correspond. He had already written my parents, expressing his feelings for me, a letter still kept, as it was most moving and articulate. In it he expressed his desire to marry me because he felt " Betty is essential to my life and all that is good and beautiful in it," these were his words.

My parents would be enjoying the countryside when not working and since my leave was no problem, I headed south on the long journey home to the village of West Hagley.

Frank arrived several hours before me, so he met my Mother first. Over tea and crumpets she did her best to persuade him to return to the States first, before making a decision to marry. She went on to say that there was a certain glamour and urgency implicit, about being in uniform, of dangers encountered, the wish for permanence that prevailed in this maelstrom of shifting sands, and never knowing what's next. All of which sometimes obscured reality. He might wish he had waited for an American girl, she said, and on and on. In other words, dump me, I remarked on hearing this later, and she cheerfully nodded. She told me that he listened politely without a word, all the time fondling our bulldog's ears, until at last, she ran out of steam. Then, looking her straight in the eye, he said quietly and firmly, "But I love her," as if that settled the matter. In his mind, it did.

My Father already liked him, despite the sacrifice it might mean to have a daughter go so far away, he recognized the quality of this man, but needed to add his two pennyworth, anyway. He then proceeded to express his own thoughts and fears, also at length. He mentioned the distance, the difference between the two Countries, and the cost of travel which would make visits home expensive, and at best, infrequent. He, also spoke of the closeness of our family. Frank's response didn't waver or change from his previous answer to my Mother.

These feelings acknowledged, the discussion was over, and they began to get to know each other, liking what they saw. Now the decision was mine alone.

I had received some warm and welcoming letters from Frank's Mother, who told me much about her family and a little about herself. She also said that she had wanted to send me an evening robe, and had asked Frank about my size but his answer was, "she is just about right," but that didn't give her much to work on, she said. She was much amused and it was a novel experience for her to see her son so 'over the top,' she said. It was easy for me to respond to her and I enjoyed her letters, very much.

I arrived home, happily anticipating the reunion with Frank, glad to be seeing my parents and Norma. She was a young teenager then of fourteen, who had managed to fall off a train that day, with a swollen knee to show for it. She and Frank soon formed a budding friendship over the band-aids and the inevitable tea, panacea for all ills.

Seven joyful days flew by, as we rediscovered the fascination of being together. My parents were secretly much amused by Frank's love-lorn bliss as he totally lost the thread of conversation when I entered a room and would stop mid-sentence to gaze in my direction, unconscious of all around him. My head in the clouds made me unaware of such details, though of course, I was much more sensible. Sure, I was.

We had a lot of time to talk about a future together until, somehow the long term reality of parting from family, receded into the background and I agreed to marry Frank after the war ended. A milestone for us both; the big decision had been made. Strangely, Frank just happened to have a jeweler's brochure in his pocket, illustrating a ring he particularly liked, and I thought it beautiful too, though probably too extravagant. "Not true", said he. It was a large emerald-cut diamond solitaire, flanked by diamond baguettes, set in platinum. It was truly beautiful. He must have ordered it soon after, just to be sure.

That leave travelled faster than the speed of light, and time was up, catching us unaware. Frank's leave terminated a day earlier than mine, so off we set for Birmingham railway station where he would embark for Dover then be transported back to France. There was a train leaving from Snow Hill Station leaving at 11.45am so we walked from the bus stop to the station, he in uniform toting a kit bag and all the usual paraphernalia, and I in civies with only a handbag. We arrived in plenty of time to find the train already in, so Frank decided to delay the final moment as long as possible and waited to get aboard at the last minute. The goodbye kiss took a giddy minute, during which time the guard called for the last stragglers to board, raised the flag, slammed the doors and off went the train, leaving Frank and me still on the platform seat. Alone!

A fluster of activity produced time tables showing that another train at New Street Station was due to leave in forty-five minutes, so we needed to hurry, as it was a long walk across the city centre. We started off, up the hill and through the churchyard scattering pigeons and threading our way through the multitude, across a busy intersection, luggage banging away behind, and finally New Street Station hove into view. Once there, I was totally unable to talk him into boarding, where we could continue to talk over the window sill, and once more, the train steamed out with Frank chasing in its wake, and not quite managing it.

Out came the time tables again, and since train departures alternated from both stations, we needed to struggle back, through the churchyard again. We laughed until we were near hysteria and I can hardly believe that it was not until the fourth try, and under threat from me, that if he didn't board this time, I would leave him behind and go home, that he got on the train. At last! By the time we made it through that churchyard for the fourth and last time, puffing a bit by then, the pigeons were so accustomed to two people constantly lugging their belongings back and forth, they hardly looked up and certainly didn't bother to scatter any more.

Knowing, he was safely on his way, I boarded a homebound bus in the gathering dusk and reflected on the leave we had just shared. Once home, I joined my family around the fire to speculate on the future and as always, they were so supportive. Next day found me on the train, returning to Oban, for just one more week, as it transpired, contemplating my life changing decision all by myself.

Back in Oban I had several letters waiting, one of which was a follow up letter from my friend Joan, telling me that Robert, her American love, had become very important in her life and that she had promised to marry him in the near future, asking me to be her only bridesmaid, and I felt honoured. Her parents knew him now quite well, she said, as he had been stationed nearby, giving them all ample time to spend in each other's company. Although, Joan and Bob had known each other for a mere eight months they were sure that this was the real thing for them both. Thoughts of being on the rebound from George had been addressed right up front, and painlessly dealt with, she wrote.

Bob's parents had been in touch with Joan several times, and had welcomed the news of their upcoming marriage. They understood that waiting for War's end would mean waiting for an indefinite period of time, but understandably only wished they too, could be part of the festivities and could meet Joan and see their son married. Unselfishly, love and best wishes came with their letter anyway.

I was glad to hear of a happy ending, or new beginning, for them both. Joan would keep me informed on the date, as soon as they knew it themselves, she said.

Again without warning, came the familiar envelope, summoning me to a new destination. I was posted! The usual railway ticket was enclosed, plus instructions to present myself to GHQ in Benson, an RAF station some distance outside Oxford, this time. Here, I would be dealing with Lancasters, four engine bombers, and Mosquitos, two engine fighter planes. All that remained for me to do was, pack the kit bag with the rest of my accoutrements, and make my farewell rounds, which would not be without quite a few pangs of regret, and fond memories. I would miss Mary Wood, Hal Osmund, and of course, Ralph Burnett who had all enriched my life in some way, not to mention many others whose lives touched mine.

Then it would be time to board the south bound train to Oxfordshire and find Benson. At least the climate would be a little milder, than up here among the braes.

8 – Bombers and Fighters

Manna for the starving

NEXT MOVE... a Bomber Station in a little town called Benson in Oxfordshire. Finally, finally! I was headed, where in all innocence, I had expected to be sent in the first place, either that, or a Fighter Squadron had been my naive assumption. Now, two and a half years later, I was actually on my way, full of curiosity and the desire to learn about the mysteries of a bomber Ops Squadron.

Arriving at the railway station, I saw sun filtering through high windows glinting sideways, creating shadows, and streaking across the entrance, setting the scene, backlit, as if on a stage. Moving figures about to begin a modern ballet, languidly, stretching, turning, carrying, and gracefully gliding, through the double doors. Fantasy figures, moving as if in slow motion in tune with the scene before me, I floated inside, then, slowly getting back to reality, common sense prevailing, I came back to earth, smiling that such a flight of fancy got the better of me. Steam trains also had their own mystery, but for now reality prevailed.

I saw with relief, only a moderate crowd waiting, as the train hissed in to the station, gasping and spitting great bursts of steam, before coming to a halt at our feet. Nobody seemed in a hurry here.

Gradually returning to the demands of the moment, fully awake by now,

I saw this crowd was nothing to compare with London hordes, where sitting on luggage, piled in the corridor, was a foregone conclusion. Perhaps this time, seats would be more readily available? Perhaps! Perhaps not! Allowing the press of others boarding to push me forward towards a door, I became aware of a hand on my shoulder reaching from behind, tapping for attention, then a voice in my ear said "Come with me, I've found some seats." Turning, I saw familiar Air Force blue, adorned with pilot's wings, above which was, a serious face, with bright blue eyes twinkling away. He looked reliable and I took, but a moment to decide it was worth a try, on such a lengthy ride. Following trustingly along behind, as he boarded a First Class carriage, and swinging my kit bag and his own luggage into the rack, he offered his hand. As I hesitated, showing him my ticket was for third, he raised his shoulders eloquently. "Not to worry," he said, I'll talk to the ticket collector. He won't mind." (Such faith.)

We settled into opposite seats, each taking a corner of the carriage all to ourselves, a rarity, then, introduced ourselves. His name was John Mills, which had a familiar ring, then I remembered the actor of the same name, but before I could comment, he said dismissively, "No relation."

No need to worry about the ticket collector, since he left us in peace throughout the entire journey, rather to my surprise. Perhaps occasionally, pilots had a little clout.

Gas cape, kit bag and mask safely stowed, settling in for a comfortable journey, with a chance to talk, was pure luxury and much appreciated.

Leaning back in his seat, John produced a sweet smelling tobacco pouch, and a well patinaed pipe, raising an eyebrow for permission, and given my nod he proceeded to tamp the tobacco down firmly. In between pauses to light it, he fanned the match out, and puffed away contentedly. No one had heard of smokeless carriages then. Peace reigned, and in answer to my question he began to tell me a little about himself.

A Fighter pilot, twenty four years of age, he had survived the Battle of Britain, a subject quickly dropped before it began, and I took the hint, and was now stationed in Reading, not far from Benson, where two of his closest friends were billeted. Both were bomber pilots, with whom he shared some of his off time, so John also knew the area quite well. He said both Lancasters and Mosquitos were on my new station, serving as bomber and fighter squadrons, respectively. The Mosquito was equipped to serve in either capacity, as bomber, or fighter plane, he told me.

When I asked him about his stay in Scotland, he mentioned his few days with relatives near the Falls of Laura, not far from Oban, which prompted him to ask about my own Coastal Station experiences in Oban. We regaled each other with various anecdotes and exploits, though I noticed he never once, touched on his own particular battlefield in the sky.

Time passed quickly and during a comfortable lull in conversation, he became introspective as his eyes lost some of their lively glow, he quietly expressed his more serious thoughts, "I think the impermanence of war prods us to live every day to the fullest, yet all the while, underneath, we still anxiously seek permanence and a future to look forward to. Nothing can be taken for granted."

Sensing his need to talk as I saw two lines in his brow deepen into a furrow, his shoulders were raised and tense, fingers tapping away as he glanced at me questioningly, almost as if for confirmation. Realizing a response was indicated, I mentioned my theory that hasty marriages, ones that I was aware of anyway, often seemed to be entered into primarily on that basis, particularly when a couple hadn't known each other very long. Perhaps any young man, or woman, going into the danger zone, facing the threat of death, would naturally feel a basic need for an anchor; a special person to return to, sadly, often mistaking the feeling for one of lasting love.

Unexpectedly, he laughed, albeit somewhat sardonically, and commented that his situation was just the reverse of 'hasty'. Only recently he became engaged, he revealed rather hesitatingly, to Fiona. Attractive, poised, smart, she shared many of his interests, and they never argued. What kind of interests do you have?"

"Well, collecting antiques, I suppose, playing tennis, politics usually, also we get along well," he said. "After all, we've known each other since childhood, and she lives nearby so it's easy to get together often, and we do. It seems only natural to assume a future together. It is what everyone expects, I'm sure".

"Did you actually propose?"

"Well, not really, in so many words." he said. "The relationship sort of gradually drifted into what it is now, just waiting, to set a date. Everybody expects it." he repeated. I waited for the "but" I felt hanging in the air. Almost apologetically he continued, "I don't know how I could want more, or even what is missing, but I find myself asking, is it enough?"

Two things caught my attention as he was talking, trying to give an accurate picture of his situation. The first, was that his fingers were never idle during all this time, either tapping away on the window ledge, or patting pockets for matches, removing non-existent hairs from his tunic, but never very still. The other, was the fact that never once was the word love mentioned during this recital of things in common, things shared. It was obvious that his mind was not at peace with the state of affairs as they were.

My comment was obvious, as a neutral observer, "It sounds as if you are wonderful friends, but only you know, if that is that enough? Is it possible you need something more?" "I always thought there should be more excitement, more longing to be together," he mused. "Neither of us has even mentioned a date, and she seems content to drift and go along, as we are. It really all seems a bit flat"…perhaps it isn't enough, after all.

"I wonder if she may feel something is lacking too?" I said quietly. He was quiet for so long, I wondered if he regretted his confidences.

Then I saw tension fade, his shoulders relaxed, he smiled as if a load had lifted saying, "It helped, to express it all, to hear it spoken aloud." He paused, "You have my thanks for listening, and posing the right questions. Now, I need to have a long overdue chat with Fiona." Out came the pipe…. In between puffs, leaning back and stretching out his feet, fingers stilled at last, he posed a question for me "So have you got your own future figured out and planned yet?"

Not sure I wanted to get into all that, made me think deep thoughts, but like proverbial ships passing in the night, never to meet in port, I knew the topic would not crop up with him again, and embarrass me. Bit by bit, I confessed to an ever present dread of leaving my family behind, in order to live in the US after the war, if I married my American. Once arriving in a new country the only person I knew, would be my new husband, Frank. No family of my own, no old friends, in fact no familiar faces at all. Was I up to it?

On the other hand, could I bear to part from Frank permanently? Those were my alternatives. This was my dilemma!

We bounced that ball back and forth a bit and in a nutshell his conclusion was, "Don't be in a hurry. Time may help. Wait and see."

Back in the moment, we looked out of the window to see our journey was near the end. It had passed so quickly. Already, Wallingford was the next stop, and there, I would be met by M.T. to be taken on to Benson. The stop after that, would be Reading, John's destination;

We had confided our problems like old friends which sometimes happened in wartime, and I silently wondered if we would ever meet again? As if the words had been uttered aloud, he said, "Do you think we shall meet again somewhere?"

Quoting his own words back to him, I said, with a smile "We shall have to wait and see, shan't we?" He leaned forward and kissed my cheek and I felt we had become friends during our soul searching journey.

With a wave I passed through the gate where I saw a tired looking M.T. corporal waiting on the other side. Together, we stowed the baggage. The air redolent with the perfume of night-scented stock, wafted under my nose, a reminder that we were well into the evening, and it would be too dark to see much en route. My driver, Phil was ending his shift and I was his last passenger, so he was not inclined to talk much, just happy to deliver me and my kit bag etc to the Orderly Room at HQ There, I was promptly checked in, and escorted to my new billet in "Married Quarters", a first for me in that setting.

"Married Quarters", intended for peacetime RAF personnel and their families, were small units arranged in rows, with a small plot of land for planting, or perhaps a sandbox. Some were semi-detached, but otherwise, all units looked pretty much the same as one another.

Each little house had three bedrooms and one bath upstairs. Downstairs, a small shower room with toilet etcetera, little living room and a minuscule kitchen, very handy for hot bedtime drinks on a cold night. All, conspiring to make a compact little home for a small family; There were two beds in my room, one used by my alternate, at present on night duty, who I would meet later, leaving me free now, to unpack and thankfully, settle in, in peace.

Refreshed and ready to start work next day I signed the log and was taken in hand by the Corporal on duty, and afterwards the Lieutenant on watch took over the task of furthering my education. I enjoyed both, and particularly liked hearing about planes on our Station. (Be careful what you wish for.) This developed into a pretty complete introduction delivered with enthusiasm by both mentors, in between our various tasks. I took notes, feeling appreciative that I had this opportunity to learn from experts on my first day here, and they gave me both barrels.

The Lancaster bomber had four Merlin X engines, attached to the underside of the enlarged wing section, and began life as the Manchester Bomber, in January 1941, but this was not a successful prototype. Improvements were promptly made, adding more powerful Merlin XX engines, along with other modifications.

It was tested and evaluated, before being declared successful, whereupon it was immediately snapped up by the Air Ministry. They put in large orders at once. The first production was on October 1941, and the first contract was for 1,070 aircraft. This was more than Avro could handle right away, so Armstrong Whitley, Vickers Armstrong, and Austin Morris combined to produce a final total of 7,377 Lancasters. Each one, heavily armed, with eight, 0.303 machine guns in various turrets.

Exceptions were made for the Dambusters raid later on, at which point the aircraft had to be specially adapted, to allow such bombs as the Grand Slam to be carried, on the plane. It weighed, 22,000 lbs. and this raid occurred in May 1943.

Many raids on Germany were made by Lancasters, but the Grand Slam missile was, no doubt, the heaviest to be carried in WWII. The raid on the Tirpitz happened in November 1944.

The Lancaster had a crew of seven, a maximum speed of 287 mph at 11,500 ft. Its ceiling was 24,000ft with a range of 2,530 miles. A well liked plane, from all reports. Altogether, the Lancaster flew more than 156,000 sorties during this War, dropped a total of 608,000 tons of explosives, and fifty one million incendiaries, but this information was only known generally, after the War, of course.

The Mosquito, known as "Mossie" to the crew, was a long range fighter/bomber aircraft, in use as early as 1941, gradually becoming better known in September 1942, after raiding the Gestapo HQ in Oslo, Norway. Before this, it had been used to photograph results of our bombing raids over Germany, and for reconnaissance trips. One raid mentioned in particular, to be photographed, was that of the 'Dambusters' in May 1944.

Then the Avro Lancaster was also specially modified in February 1943 to accommodate the kind of bomb that had been specially invented, to successfully disrupt the dams of Mohne, Eder, and Sorpe. Special raids, special equipment. In order to escape the torpedo nets, a cylindrical bomb was devised which, would skip along the surface, before sinking below the water line to reach the dam's base. This involved low altitude, precision flying, at night. A large challenge bravely met, especially since much of the usual armour and defensive weaponry had to be removed to lighten the load, also the bomb doors had to be eliminated, to make room for such a large explosive, which was then held in place by means of a crutch-like piece of apparatus. I bet the pilot of this plane sweated out the journey, devoutly hoping not to encounter any enemy fire before releasing his giant missive, experiencing heartfelt relief at its downward flight. Such a scary load.

It took multiple strikes to do the job. The dams then released a total of 330 million tons of water into the Rhur, reducing water supply by 75%. A big set back! However, the success was short lived as the German engineers fully restored everything back to normal by late June.

The Mossie was made by de Haviland Aircraft Co. Ltd. with two Rolls Royce Merlin engines. No statistics were ever released but unofficially, the speed exceeds 400 miles per hour for the MK11 and 376 M.P.H. for the MK1. The range estimated at 1,500 miles. Armament consisted of a 4.20 mm cannon in the nose and machine guns....Number withheld. A streamlined, swept forward craft, with engines underslung, and in line with the nose. It was a twin engine monoplane, with high wing and simple tail unit. It had a retractable undercarriage, with tapered, trailing-edge, wings, presenting a distinctive, easily recognizable aeroplane, which was also a big favourite with pilots. All this information was presented as we worked and took several sessions but it would have taken much longer had I struggled alone, and both tutors complimented me on my informal little test at the end.

Days vanished like autumn leaves in a cold snap, and slowly it dawned on me that, without noticing, I had settled in and learned a lot. Work was challenging, but manageable. I had made a few friends. And, we weren't being bombed in Benson. Oh joy!

London was another story. Earlier on, when I was in London the V-2s first were launched on September 8th, 1944. Now, a last frantic effort was being expended by the Luftwaffe to try to demolish the capital city, totally, and thereby ruin morale. Neither aim succeeded but my heart went out to all those living there, stoically coping, yet, still bandying cheerful quips about Hitler and his forthcoming downfall! The general viewpoint being that it was only a matter of time. Air raid warnings notwithstanding, people continued to show up for work, though the city of London was liberally dotted with great yawning craters, piles of debris and smouldering piles of ashes. For those travelling to work or school in the city, there were always several detours resulting in lengthy journeys to any given destination. It was expected as a daily occurrence.

En route were ambulances and Air Raid Wardens, wearing tin helmets and gas masks, hard at work with spades, flasks of hot tea and stretchers nearby, at the ready, hopefully for finding a living person to use them. Occasionally there was an unbelievable rescue and someone lived to tell about it, but all too often, it was too late. Just a body, or fraction of one, was all that was left.

Some had every reason to grieve, and of course they did, yet generally, even those bombed out of their homes, despite the often grim conditions, gave little indication of gloom, and no signs of giving up. Humour was still alive and well. A few moaned and groaned about shortages and queues, but that was an okay safety valve; expected, and allowed.

It was clearly apparent that Herr Hitler was now coming to grips with the tide-turning reality of the war and pulling out all stops to bring London to her knees, still vainly intent on trying to attain air supremacy. Simultaneously, his ill-timed conquest of Russia was to cost him dearly.

Back in Benson, a frequent visitor to Ops, Alan Jones, was being introduced to those who didn't already know him, and I was among those. He was a whiz at table tennis, where I had seen him play sometimes, as I watched him from the side lines at various Service clubs, I visited. He was blonde, pink cheeked, well built and rather shy for a twenty-two year old, air gunner, I thought. Watching him play a match, made me gasp. Table tennis at its best; The small white ball was dispatched so fast and so far, that both players were forced to move back about three or four feet from the table ends before bouncing that innocent white orb, high in the air and sending it spinning to the other end for a repeat performance. The little missive thus attacked would hit the table edge, ricocheting at an impossible angle making retrieval unlikely, yet amazingly, bending low it would be sent back rocket-like with lightning speed, just grazing the net, to gain a hard won point. Both players were impressive but Alan was usually the winner. It was then that I pondered about the half wing with the letter AG blazoned on the left breast of his tunic and I wondered if his split-second reactions in the air had helped his table tennis, or vice versa.

Afterwards, he brought me some NAAFI tea and briefly mentioned he was a "tail-gun-Charlie" in the rear of the plane, then rapidly changed the subject. He gave me some pointers on how to improve my game, not seeming in the least fearful of the threat I might present as a possible opponent. Strange! We began to share some of our off-time when our schedules permitted, enjoying the surrounding countryside and the conversation as we walked, to and from, a local pub after sharing a meal. I talked about Frank, and of D-Day and we speculated on how much longer it might be before a cease fire was declared. Alan confided his love of poetry explaining that on the rare quiet run home, perhaps after reconnaissance and over home territory, he would be inspired while travelling the 'wild blue yonder' to compose a small sonnet or perhaps a poem.

It boggled the mind to contrast the stress, engendered on a bombing run, while sitting in cramped quarters, engaged in the battering violence of being shot at, and then in turn, downing the enemy. From that maelstrom in the air, to the appreciative expression of beauty in the world around him, seemed impossible to conceive: Doubly anxious not to give me the erroneous impression that he casually put pen to paper, writing poetry, while dodging bullets, or in between taking pot shots at the enemy, he quickly stressed, "Not on the same run, of course."

Continuing, to explain that, sometimes, when there were no German planes anywhere near on a return run, the pure relief of finding himself alive, made him acutely aware of the 'beauty around him'. The silvery splendor of clouds tinged with gold, even the moody, threatening grayness heralding a storm, was appreciated, as he descended into safety to land among colourful wild flowers edging the perimeter, and the fragrance of purple clover underfoot as he trod the ground afterwards. "Everyday occurrences that are so taken for granted, suddenly seem special," he said. I was secretly amazed that he could find any serenity, and keep it separate from the violence that he encountered when on a sorti, but that was what probably kept him sane.

Conversation flowed. We didn't look back much, or forward either. Too precarious. We just enjoyed the present as we waited for peace.

Another person on the periphery of my acquaintance, also a shift worker, was Sonia (the Hon. after her name, signifying her abbreviated title) who later became a lovely addition to my life although I didn't see a lot of her even then. A true beauty! Brunette, with a dainty sort of small boned face, little nose, and graceful hands, she was very reserved, and worked in Intelligence. Our paths didn't cross until around the middle of this year when fate threw us together, and we had time really talk. In the meantime, we knew each other well enough, to pass on the odd bit of information when we casually encountered one another on some errand or other, always with a cheerful smile, a quip or small joke to herald the day, but brief.

Our duty roster was such, that when my other two cohorts were off duty, I was on watch, while the one being relieved would be due for rest, and the third one, enjoying her time off, between shifts, so our free time didn't overlap at all. Not much opportunity to get to know each other very well. That would change, if and when, we got our long expected, and overdue, relief. Our promised fourth member would make a big difference, we told ourselves, but when?

In the meantime, other WAAF living in our quarters who were not on shifts, consisted of Orderly room personnel, cooks and ACHGD's They all shared the same free time, making it easy for them to get together, having already found many common interests. No likely companions to be found there, to share my leisure time. Those of us on shift work all had the same problem. However, I discovered there was one live-wire girl, Vivian, secretary to one of the staff officers, and she was available now and again, when I was free too. Petite, sophisticated and amusing, she was very attached to her boyfriend, a Lancaster pilot. We managed to go out to dinner now and then, but most of her spare time was taken up with him. She was a little mysterious about their affair and they often spent time away together, yet she never mentioned future plans concerning him, and looking back, I suspect one of them may have been married, but I was too naïve to think so then. Our sense of humour was quite similar. We both enjoyed a sense of the ridiculous, and she had a gift for mimicry which was hilarious. Our times together were fun and dispelled all stress engendered by work and war. A light hearted sort of friendship We laughed a lot and were good for each other. I couldn't imagine living without a sense of humour. Life would be so bleak.

One day, coming off-duty in the late afternoon, tempted by the magic glow of a flaming sun, hanging low in the sky, a palette of vibrant yellow, and orange shot with streaks of rose, I decided to go for a walk around the perimeter. Strolling along I was again fascinated by the reflected, luminous, quality of a gold washed corn field, brilliant against the backdrop of the emerald hedge, bordering it, silently wishing for a camera, or an artist's ability to commit it to canvas, so that I could share it with others.

The shadow of two figures, bold against the sunlight intruded on my vision, blinding me temporarily. We almost collided, our bodies touching, but managed to stop just in time to avert a full on collision. Just my nose brushed a brass button on impact, but no damage done. For a brief moment it seemed as if we were the only humans left in this vast expanse of green and gold. It appeared to them, that my hair in the sunlight became the 'gold of my cornfield' and they professed themselves bedazzled. Poetic too! We laughed as I commented that I was glad not to remind them of a dowdy turnip field. Golden girl, was infinitely better.

Their names were Bob Jackson and Bouchier, both lieutenants, both pilots of Lancasters, on the Station, and great friends. Bouchier was the sole son and heir of a French father and English mother, he was usually addressed by only this one name and if I ever heard another addition, I have forgotten. He was the epitome of tall, dark and handsome with a distinctive dark moustache, matching strongly defined eyebrows, above deep blue eyes. Laughing eyes, set in an impish face, yet a fleeting glimpse of sadness showed in the set of his features I thought, after spending more time in his company, later. Right now, all I saw was merriment with a decided hint of devilry.

Bob on the other hand was a perfect foil, as he was just the opposite in appearance, blond hair, also tall, and very good looking, lively blue eyes of a lighter shade than his friend and a smile to advertise toothpaste. He seemed somewhat quieter perhaps, more thoughtful in a way. His father lived on the far side of Oxford, he said, but sadly, his mother had not survived the war, and I gathered it was due to enemy action. I didn't ask.

We barely noticed the shadows lengthening and time passing until I realized I would be late for dinner with Alan unless I scrambled. Regretfully, I made my adieux but not before we all agreed to meet, two days hence for dinner and more conversation. Just enough time to rush back now, freshen up and leave again to see my friend, the air gunner, cum-poet.

It was a boost to find there were interesting people to share my off duty time, after all. I kept my rendezvous in the cornfield, again, toward the end of the week just as the sun was going down, but still sending ribs of sunlight and shadows across the fields. Bouchier and Bob, already there, were sitting on a mossy log, feet stretched out in front, smiling at some reminiscence, looking up as I approached, to spring to their feet like overnight mushrooms at dawn. We just picked up, where we had left off, as if we had known each other for many moons. It all seemed so easy. Bob contrived to borrow an old 'banger' of a car, from some enterprising fellow on the station, with just enough scrounged petrol to get us to an old pub outside Oxford. I could well believe its touted old age dated back to Elizabethan times. The pub, that is, not the car. The old oak beams, bent in dog-leg shapes, and the hearts-of-oak front door, had become fossilized over the ages, with a bona fide patina of the centuries. Of course, both men had to stoop to accommodate the low ceiling. Outside was an archway extending over a cobblestone driveway, originally for carriages which once rattled over the old stones into stables beyond, in order for the coach driver to find the "ostler". The man who would feed and water the horses before bedding them down for the night.

This was one of a select number of about eight of the oldest hostelries to have survived the years, and still, with a little, sometimes a lot, of faithful maintenance, be in useable condition, although the loos left something to be desired. I wondered where the Elizabethans went to the w.c.? (water closet)

Inside the beamed dining area we studied the slate, and consulted the

Living Dangerously

chalked selections on the board, beside the bar. In a moment of daring, I bravely ordered a Henry VIII onion, not quite knowing what to expect. Bob ordered salamagundi which turned out to be sea food salad, served in a hollowed out cabbage, and Bouchier prosaically decided on fish and chips. In the meantime, departing from my usual shandy, I ordered cider. Cider is always hard in the country, and very good, but often strong, so it would last me all evening, I thought.

Somewhere between soup starters and entrée, we embarked on a discussion we were all vitally interested in....the end of the war. Looking back, as we did then, we began our own assessment of the past year. Of course, as Bob said, the biggest leap of progress had to be the Invasion, Operation Overlord, on June 6th which comprised the biggest amphibian landing force of all time. Remembering that over 160,000 Allied troops were deposited along the beaches of Normandy during Operation Neptune, which in turn, was a part of Operation Overlord, it beggars description.

In preparation for the main event next day, the Parachute division made their night jump the night before, proving to be both, difficult, dangerous, and costly. Many men were lost in this endeavour, but they had to try.

"A lot of planning ahead helped," said Bouchier, "look at the preparatory build up before any of those ships and troop carriers left our shores."

"Like what?" I asked. "In particular, there was a heavy air assault the night before, all part of the strategy," said Bouchier, "and prior to that on June 2nd Allied forces bombed oil refineries, transportation hubs, bridges and roads. A total of 81,110 tons of bombs were dropped on French railroads alone, depriving the Germans of the necessary transport of enemy troops and equipment." Air support, known as Operation Cover proved vital to the success of D-Day. Some of these facts were only made known to us, piecemeal, at a later date, obviously.

A subject dear to his heart, Bouchier had the floor and continued." On D-Day + 1, a total of six Divisions were sent in, made up of three American Divisions, two British and one Canadian Division. On D-Day + 2, they were followed up by two British, and one American Division, and on Day Three, the latter formula was repeated. Strong winds handicapped their progress on D-Day + 1 and blew them east of their target, thus all five landing sectors did n't connect until June 12th. Considerably later than hoped for, he said. It was a nasty set back. Landings were distributed between five Sectors, Utah Beach, Omaha, Gold, Juno and Sword Beach.

Omaha Beach with high cliffs, and heavy enemy gun emplacements made this an extremely difficult landing and the Allies met with the worst and bloodiest opposition at this point. Losses were heavy, but valiantly struggling on, the Allies prevailed, pushing forward, despite all odds". I found out later that this was where Frank landed and was glad I didn't know at the time." The beach needed to be cleared of many obstacles first, he said, such as wooden stakes, metal tripods, barbed wire and land mines, added to all the other hazards, including the weather he said, Actually the weather was a major obstacle, Bouchier, now in his stride went on, "Casualties were heavy and progress was considerably slower than predicted. Carenton, St Lo and Bayeau stayed in German hands longer than planned and Caen was not captured until July 21st.said he, and then he sat down after his long dissertation.

I believe the movie, *Saving Private Ryan* was based on this period and that the Director, Steven Spielberg won an award for its portrayal

Waiting for the dessert menu, I thought awhile, and then remembered aloud, that in March of this year many aviators (about 12,000) men dropped thousands of tons of explosives on Berlin with heavy losses on both sides, sadly. This seriously depleted enemy air strength but while Germany was unable to replace theirs, the Allies would be able to restore their former numbers.

"Even earlier," added Bob, "in February there was the Big Week." So-named, when combined Allied Forces waged a six day air campaign over Western Europe, targeting aircraft manufacturing plants, thus screwing up their production of aircraft, and other war materiel.

It was only weeks ago, we reminded ourselves, in August, that the Allies liberated Paris, forcing the Nazis to retreat across the Seine. A promising outlook for the future we thought, but perhaps a little too soon to 'count' our chickens just yet. Nothing, so far had been easy.

Back on home turf we were faced with the latest German threat, which began earlier, on September 8th with the V-2 Rocket. This is the very first long-range ballistic combat missile, ever created, and the first ever to achieve sub-orbital space flight. They were menaces exacting a heavy death toll, of both military and civilian casualties, and on detonation, left behind giant craters, wide and deep. Despite not being found to be very accurate, they were still, more deadly than the predecessors, the V-1s or doodlebugs. No warning air raid siren was possible There was no anxious waiting period, They were untrackable and unattackable. At first only one per day, possibly two, were deployed, but later the number increased to around eight each day. Untold damage was done when London was targeted by this weapon. Discussing the pros and cons of these two devastating missiles was useful but inconclusive, though we all agreed that the only way to bring about an end to one of those marauders was at the source. The launching pad *must* be destroyed.

Launching pads were portable, therefore hard to track down, somewhat similar to a ski jump in appearance, built in sections, so as to be easily dismantled and moved.

The V-2 was a rocket, whereas the VI wasn't. A big distinction! The V-1 was actually a jet propelled flying bomb, requiring an atmosphere in which to work. Our fighters frequently intercepted them over the Channel where Spitfires had perfected the ability to tip the wing of the V-1, which then obligingly plummeted down into the ocean. That must have been satisfying! Not a shot fired. Still, enough of them got through to wreak their havoc over land. Of course barrage balloons and ack-ack were also used, in defense.

In my opinion, the V-1 created a war of nerves, as well as being a bomb threat. Comparing my experiences with both Vs, I again realized that although the V-1 did far less damage to property, it inflicted another kind of angst to those on the receiving end. Beginning with the eerie drone of the air raid siren shattering the eardrums, to be followed by the staccato backfiring of a motorbike in the sky, then dwindling to a hiccupping cough, and ending with the cru-um ump announcing the explosion. In between, sometimes the missile would drop immediately and other times, there would be a long delay, perhaps carried by the wind. Plenty of time to hold ones breath in the uncertain interval. The seemingly interminable wait was hard, for those beneath, especially when not in a position to see the thing, perhaps only the evil, glowing red tail light as it passed overhead, barely grazing the roof tops. Nobody knew where to run for cover. If you were in bed, all you could do was listen and wait. And wait. The agony of not knowing its location in the dark, or the timing of its detonation as you waited was a kind of torture of the nerves. A torture repeated over and over. They usually came in clusters.

With a doodlebug, there would be another one along in a minute and you got to do it all over again, and again, throughout the day and/or night, or both. However, right now the V-2s were taking over as the main threat.

Well, we kicked these facts and ideas around for a while, drank our pretend coffee and decided that, though we couldn't quite win the war tonight, we were definitely on the right path. We left the pub linking arms, noticing the slight nip in the air, as we strode along to our O.B. Autumn leaves had already dropped, leaving bare branches and promising, winter would not be far behind in our neck of the woods. Not too soon, I hoped. It was already the end of October, however, so time to wrap up. My greatcoat had been in use for some time now, and underneath my Air Force tunic I wore my little red wool pullover. Not exactly K.R's, but warm, and only a bit naughty. Frosty Hollow could get very nippy and it would soon be Christmas, in about six short weeks.

It had been an interesting evening and by discussing our thoughts and sharing our knowledge, some aspects of the war seemed clearer to me. We agreed that we all felt confidence in the ability of our leaders, Mr. Churchill, Mr. Roosevelt and General Eisenhower, just to name three. The latter was head of the European Theatre of Operations, who worked closely with both others. We lifted our coffee cups in gratitude to toast a winning team.

Back in the old banger, all discussions over, relaxed on the new cushions, with Bob at the wheel, Bouchier started singing a lovely Edith Piaf song, knowing all the lyrics and putting them to good use. He had a beautiful voice and *La Vie en Rose* was one of my all time favourites too. We did our best to hum along as we wended our way homeward, feeling replete and mellow. It had been a stimulating evening.

On duty next morning, I could see the notice board had some reconnaissance sorties scheduled, and in conversation with the Officer on watch, I understood that we were earning a widespread reputation for our successful, clear, and accurate photography. This was invaluable for precision bombing, and very informative in other ways. It had been of inestimable value during D-Day, but we had already begun to earn some fame back in June of 1943 and would continue doing so throughout the rest of the war.

It's interesting to back track a bit now, to reflect on knowledge I didn't have then. In September, between the 17th and 25th 1944, Allies attacked occupying forces in the Netherlands sending Dakota aircraft, plus 500 gliders, towed by Stirling & Halifax bombers. They transported and dropped 35,000 men behind enemy lines in three areas, Arnhem, Eindhoven, and further south as far as Nijmegen. In the first stage not one RAF transport was lost. However, bitter struggle ensued when attempts were made to capture the bridges of the three rivers, all strategic points. One in particular met with fierce ground resistance. Over the following 7 days, aerial re-supply resulted in the loss of 238 aircraft and 138 gliders. A significant set back.

Eindhoven and Nijmegen were captured but Arnhem was a disaster. Out of approximately 10,000 men who were dropped 7,500 were killed and the rest evacuated after enduring nine days of desperate conflict. Incidentally, after the war, the movie based on this, was called *A Bridge Too Far*.

Head of Bomber Command at this time was Sir Arthur Harris ('Bomber Harris') who at an earlier date, said that he expected the bombing of German cities would weaken enemy forces obviating the need for D-Day but with less bloodshed, but this theory was found to be totally false.

What *was* true, was that proving the superiority of the RAF over the Luftwaffe was all important and decisive. More and more the British aviators demonstrated with impressive accuracy their ability to hit a target. New technology helped. Navigational and bomb aiming devices had improved greatly, thus enabling bombers to neutralize strategic and tactical targets in France, crucial to the success of D-Day during landings and subsequent advance of Allied ground forces.

The War machine clanked on, taking us with it, but we managed to plan distractions from time to time. It was important to take breaks from analyzing and stressing over every event we were aware of, and sometimes those we weren't.

On one such day, when there was no wind, and the sun pretended it was summer as it smiled benevolently down upon us, it was time for another adventure with my friends, Bob and Bouchier. They picked me up in the now familiar, ancient, chugging chariot and we set off for Oxford, and the river, bumping and jiggling, over the unevenly worn back roads, ignoring the sprung state of springs, no cushions that day. No complaints. Just glad to have transport and away from war duty for a while.

Powerboating, sailing and rowing on the river were not new to me, but punting was. The Thames in Oxfordshire is also known as the Isis and this was where our punt awaited, on a curve of the river beckoning and bidding us welcome, its little pennant waving us aboard in a light gentle breeze.

We climbed aboard and seated ourselves, settling in to enjoy the silent, floating ride, past the swans, the weeping willow and a couple of ambitious rowers intent on speed, eyes glazed in concentration, stroking effortlessly on to a distant goal.

Bouchier found waterproof pillows to support our heads, while we stretched out, absorbing it all in tranquil serenity. Bob was first to man the pole, setting off down river, gliding noiselessly along, handling the pole with a steady, graceful swing, and after a period of pure unadulterated tranquility, arriving at a predestined gap in the river bank where the water was fairly shallow. The pole was long and sturdy but the squish and suck of the river mud, made itself heard as the pole sank deep into the soggy, sticky, claylike, murk, and visions of disaster entered my head. If the pole stayed stuck, the punt with us in it, it would float rudderless and powerless down river, leaving Bob glued to the other end of the pole before it, and he, ignominiously keeled over, landing him squarely in the fast-flowing river.

The river dropped many feet at intervals along the way in the form of weirs, which would be a bit disastrous to undertake in a punt. Perhaps not as bad as Niagara Falls in a barrel, but not ideal, I thought, clutching the sides of our not too sturdy craft.

Bouchier took in the situation at a glance and quick as a blink, reached across the gap, grasping a firmly embedded shrub growing there, then with Bob still holding the pole, nimbly sprang ashore as if he had planned it all along. Catastrophe had been averted, leaving me limp with relief. Bob and Bouchier silently exchanged a look of triumph, liberally mixed with one of abject gratitude.

Over the teacups at a small café nearby, still serving at little riverside tables, 'weather permitting,' Bouchier commented on my horror stricken face telegraphing my thoughts, and he thought it would have made an ideal fright picture, for Halloween. Of course, all this reminded them both of true tales of other not so lucky punters, who had come unglued on a pole, mostly very funny stories. Bob happily proceeded to relate a couple. These were enjoyed all the more as we were served an unusual treat of scones, clotted cream and a tiny serving of strawberry jam. Lucky us. The owner must have a farm we decided, as we headed back to our old 'banger'.

En route to our billets, Bouchier mentioned the possibility of being posted soon, though he didn't actually have any information but he had been given a heads up by 'one who would know,' he said. Should this prove to be true, we must plan a special dinner, but would he be given official notice, beforehand, Bob asked? "Perhaps," wasn't a very satisfactory response and we parted company that night on a sombre note wondering when the axe would fall on our little trio.

November came in like a lion, roaring and howling, announcing the arrival of winter, then giving us a little breather it soon petered out into nippy nights and variable mild, or rainy, days. Before long, the frost would settle down to serious cold snaps and out would come the scarves.

London was still being pasted by the Luftwaffe, and the V-2s were arriving pretty regularly at the rate of about eight per day. Anyone passing through found themselves in a war zone and wondered how Londoners stood it and stayed so remarkably normal, even cheerful.

Early in the month we learned that President Roosevelt had accepted a fourth term as President. And that was a precedent, we heard, but it made sense for him to see the war through, so that seemed to be good news to us. I never was aware of any negative criticism in this regard.

On November 12th, Lancaster bombers from Squadrons 9 and 617 launched their third attack on the German battleship Tirpitz, anchored off the coast of Norway. This time 28, Tallboy bombs were dropped each weighing 12,000 lbs. The ship finally capsized.

They had fought a hard fight during earlier attacks, but now it was over. This was a serious loss for the German Navy as it was their last major surface ship in 1944. In retaliation, shortly afterwards the USS Intrepid was hit by kamakazees, and that was in our turn, a sad loss for the Allies.

Then just before the end of November, Himmler ordered all gas chambers and the crematoriums in Auschwitz, to be blown up. Too late for so many and hardly an effective cover up, if that was the intent, but perhaps it was an indication of his state of his mind. By then, so many prisoners had died there, buried without ceremony, en masse, and unclothed in communal pits, but the evidence of horror could never be completely hidden or forgotten. Perhaps Himmler thought it indicated a change of heart, or that the policy of exterminating all Jews had been abandoned? Perhaps he thought it was close to the end of the war for Germany? Who knows?

Adolph Hitler headed for his bunker in Berlin at this point, taking Eva Braun with him. Was this tantamount to retreat?

On my way to the Mess after night duty in Ops, I saw Bob headed my way with news that Bouchier had indeed received his posting, and the next day would be his last one before departure, so could I be available? How could I not? Luckily, my shift was early in the day so I wouldn't have to juggle my off time. We arranged to meet next day and in the meantime, it was time to go back to the billet for some welcome sleep.

Letters from Frank continued to come, usually a few at a time. He was already planning his next visit and eager to make things permanent between us. He seemed to think it wouldn't be long now. Somehow, I couldn't envision it all, and was experiencing a bout of the nervous Nellies. My letters to him were probably a bit remote, but I vaguely thought we could sort it all out together later, and in the meantime life was busy.

For the last time our little trio, Bob, Bouchier and I headed for one of our favourite pubs, fairly close to the station, intending to spend as much time together as we could. The meal came and went as we made an effort to be cheerful, but let's face it; we were parting from a good friend. The clock was ticking, our short time together coming to a close. It was time to say goodbye. I was very sorry to see Bouchier go, but I knew Bob would stay in touch with him by mail. Their friendship was special and by no means, new. Strangely, Bouchier was vague about his forwarding address, fidgeting with his cap, turning it around and around lodged between his knees, as he sat there, not looking at either of us, before saying uncertainly, that he would try to send that on to Bob, when he had one. He paused, and then he intimated that he might be 'away' for a while and that he hoped to be reunited with someone very dear to him soon. Who could that be? This information came in small spurts, as if he had to think about it first, and it all came out a syllable at a time, as if he was carefully censoring each word. Odd!

Looking at Bob I could see his bewilderment matched mine. Why hadn't he ever mentioned whoever it was, before, and why was it such a secret, only mentioned now, before leaving? "Was it a close relative," Bob asked? Bouchier shook his head and said she was close, but not related and that he wasn't free to tell us any more at this point. Later, much later, I wondered if he might even be married to someone in France, or expecting to be. For now, we were stunned into silence.

We knew his Father was French, and Bouchier had spent his early years growing up in France before the war. Supposing it was a woman, and if she was involved in the Underground, it would account for the silence surrounding her existence. It also explained his interludes, his sad, almost brooding periods of silence, when he thought himself unobserved. We were aware of these and noted them, from time to time. It was a mystery which we hadn't had much opportunity to solve. Questions about his future whereabouts weren't encouraged and we couldn't push. At evenings end, he gave us both enormous hugs, plus a kiss on each cheek for me, and I entered the billet feeling greatly puzzled and a bit lost. Bob and I planned to meet the following week sometime, when I hoped he might be able to shed a glimmer of light on the subject. Perhaps Bouchier would confide in him when they were alone?

My little circle of friends was diminishing. Not unusual in the Services but painful. Christmas was looming but no leave for yours truly this year. Instead I had a free evening on December 24th and some part of the day on the 25th, so now I needed someone to share it with, but I had a couple of weeks to think about that. A plan would emerge, I hoped.

Alan was away on a course, and Vivian was otherwise engaged with her flyer, but we had finally been blessed with a fourth member in Ops, so I may have a new pal,but that proved to have limitations. She too, was dating an air crew member though, so was only free when he wasn't available. Her name was Jean Wallace and she was a friend of Vivian. Very occasionally we managed a trio for dinner and that was a blast, if infrequent.

On the 23rd of December, after being badly hampered by bad weather, the Battle of the Bulge began as a desperate attempt by the Nazis to defeat the Allied troops, and they engaged in bloody strife to bring this about. Bombers dropped more tonnage on that day than on any other single day in the war. The 8th Air Force were able, at last to provide desperately needed air support for our Allies to win a terrible 'fight to the finish', struggle, thereby turning the tide of this major battle.

Next day was Christmas Eve. Coming off night duty, ready to fall asleep, Bob passed me, waving from a jeep and paused for a few words. I was glad when he asked me for dinner with a small group of his friends, meeting at the local pub that night. Since my usual chums were either away, on duty or already booked, this was perfect. I wouldn't have to spend Christmas Eve alone, after all.

The little house was quiet at this hour and I fell sleepily into oblivion, waking much later, refreshed with plenty of time to get ready for a nice evening in good company. My uniform was newly cleaned, buttons shining, and clod hoppers as dazzling as could be, and I was on my way.

Most nearby pubs had contrived to have live music of one sort or another and Bob had reserved a table at a familiar spot where we could hear ourselves talk above the chatter accompanied by haunting sounds from the sax. All around us our friends were distributed at small tables nearby and after exchanging Christmas greetings we sat down to discuss the mystery of Bouchier. Bob said he considered my theory was a possibility but would we ever know? After the war perhaps. We talked, danced and the time vanished like vapour in the hot sun, but the mistletoe proved to be our undoing.

Dinner was a long time in coming, and our friends soon left their tables, unwilling to waste the romantic music. I didn't lack for partners after Bob invited me to dance first. Many more men than ladies that night! Not really unusual considering the location and the date.

Since no smoking was allowed on the dance floor, this was a good place to be, I thought, looking back at the dining area, where little whorls of cigarette smoke were constantly circling their way upwards, becoming more dense as time passed, and creating a grey pall, which hovered overhead. Dancing past with an unknown to me, Navigator, I caught Bob's eye and could tell he was getting a bit fed up with losing his dancing partner every time we whirled around the floor. He coped, by cutting in from time to time, but then finally made it known that he wanted no more interruptions, and so we finished our dance in peace. He was by far the best dancer and I told him so, which seemed to restore the happy mood we had enjoyed when the evening began. Cutting in was tolerated sometimes, when there weren't enough women to go around, but it could be overdone.

Dinner appeared at last, and the occupants of a few tables, having been served earlier, were ready to sing some carols. One WAAF in particular, had a beautiful voice, keeping us all enthralled as she sang all the favourites, then, creating a sudden hush she began *Silent Night*, while the rest of the crowd joined in singing the chorus. We hated to leave it all behind, but a glance at the clock told us it was time we did, and so we rose and silently made tracks. The ambience that night was palpable and we basked in its warming glow as we navigated between the tables of those still enraptured eyes, riveted on the lovely WAAF who had captured the spirit of Christmas, with love and warmth. She fairly sparkled.

Reluctantly, we quietly headed for the door and as it closed behind us, Bob stopped abruptly, pointing upwards as his eye alighted on a large bouquet of mistletoe, complete with red bow. He lifted my chin towards his, and I was aware of his fragrant after shave, just before his lips descended on mine. It was not one of our usual friendly, quick pecks, but a heart pounding, *Gone with the Wind*, Rhett Butler kind of kiss. Breathlessly we agreed we'd better go, and beat a silent retreat, arms linked, brain buzzing, back to the old banger.

In the gloom of the car, I wondered what had just happened. I had not turned away and had responded with equal intensity. In fact I didn't want it to end. Oh dear!

Bob turned and looked at me with the depth of feeling I had felt in the kiss and his eyes, very blue and earnest, said it all, as he spoke "Now you know how I really feel about you, and I am aware of your commitment to Frank. You have always been honest about that, but are you absolutely sure?"

Here it was. On the table, and I didn't know how to cope. I was engulfed by my response to his kiss and in this moment, didn't know which end was up. I wasn't sorry at all. Conflicted? Yes, but not sorry. In fact I was wondering if I'd feel the same way if it happened again. And it did, and I felt just as enthralled as I dizzily said Goodbye at the billet door. We arranged to see each other three nights hence when I was off watch again. We knew we had to talk.

Why had I reacted this way, if I was in love with Frank? Sleep was elusive that night and still there were no answers in the morning. No brilliant resolutions at all. It was a relief to concentrate on the job at hand while on duty and necessary to keep a clear head to do that. Buckling down to work kept my thoughts at bay. For now!

Christmas day, I was on duty until 5pm after sliced turkey for lunch in the Mess, where I found everyone in a pretty cheerful state considering we were all away from home. Efforts had been made to put up a few well used paper chains and swags of holly here and there, plus a small tree with lights blinking away, signaling good cheer, so taking the hint, I went on duty with a smile.

There were a few sorties that day but my job was not very hectic at all, even a few lulls, here and there. It was business as usual, but slower. The spirit of Christmas, was abroad throughout the station, as if there was more to celebrate this Christmas than the last several war-torn ones. Optimism was rife. Those who were not on duty that night, had some kind of plan to make the evening as festive as possible. Some had gone to church to pray for the end of hostilities, hope bubbling just under the surface.

Even so, the bloodshed was far from over and thinking of the ravages of war and those still in the Battle of the Bulge area, and others who had loved ones in danger's path, including the terrible ordeals of the Russians, all made my own problems seem immeasurably small, by comparison.

It was a clear but chilly evening, as I made my way to the, by now, familiar old banger, mostly referred to fondly as 'old B', and there was Bob, resplendent in his pressed uniform and sporting a defiant sprig of mistletoe in his lapel. I asked him what he intended to do with that ? He said there was a waitress at the Inn that he rather fancied. I responded with, "That's alright then" and we climbed into old B, which was now done up with red cushions in deference to our bony bottoms and their encounters with sprung springs. Thanks be to our unknown benefactor/ tress.

Surprisingly it was easy to talk to one another with no feeling of strain and as we did, I commented on the fact that he appeared to live very much in the present and it seemed to work for him. Bob said it hadn't always come easily, but now it was a habit and a part of him, and he was always aware that, "Yesterday is over, and tomorrow hasn't come, so today is really all we have." He had discovered this was the way most air crew were able to cope better keeping this in mind since they were often reluctant witnesses to sudden, violent deaths of old friends. Sometimes, someone they had just had breakfast with that morning went down in flames on that same day. It struck a responsive chord in me. I got it. Today *is* all we have.

I decided that I owed it to myself and to Frank to find out how deep my feelings were for Bob and perhaps this chance was given for me to do just that. If Bob was willing, we should spend as much time together as we could, and find out? We agreed, and with that decided we began to enjoy the evening. Everything was brighter, even the stars.

For a brief interval this worked just fine and we saw each other in our off time, just walking, talking, having a meal or whatever there was time for, but the lighthearted camaraderie was not really sustainable. I felt like a cheat, and the feeling would not go away. Bob didn't press for anything more in the nature of a commitment, and that was appreciated, but then a letter from France would appear and I realized I wasn't able to cope with my conscience any longer, should Bob and I continue to meet. I needed to clarify my thoughts and feelings. I needed time alone before talking directly to Frank. A letter was not an option at this stage. It was obvious that I needed to see him and be completely uninvolved with Bob, until I had done so.

Well, I spent some worrying nights, not to mention many empty moments, soul searching, before meeting him on the perimeter, where first we met. It was all so different, even the weather was subdued. It didn't come as a complete surprise to Bob but that didn't make it any easier, to tell him what I had been thinking. As we strolled along in the faded sunlight at the end of the day, he confessed that he too knew it was only fair to handle things this way, but selfishly didn't want to suggest it, as he loved our time together. He then, very reasonably asked that I let him know when I expected to see Frank, and then to tell him immediately, what I had decided after that. We walked on in gloomy silence thinking our own thoughts, then to try to take the dismal parting feelings away he suggested a nightcap before seeing me home. Somehow it didn't help. It was still dismal. We said goodnight at my billet and I wended my way up stairs not quite knowing if I was afoot or on horseback.

Mail from France was becoming more frequent, more predictable and Frank was making optimistic noises about coming back to England should the war end in the foreseeable future. He wondered if my engagement ring had arrived. Pangs of guilt struck, and were only slightly assuaged by the isolation policy I had adopted. Time alone was essential for me to keep a clear mind and conscience, until we could see each other again.

Focusing on the letter and the ring, it should be there soon, Frank thought, and should arrive without penalty since he had consulted a lawyer about the legal prospects of it reaching me without heavy customs duty.

His careful descriptions of surrounding countryside had been censored along with any other words that would convey location, cut completely out, leaving a lacework of airmail paper, a challenge to decipher. Just enough room for love, a signature, and as always, well phrased thoughts of missing me.

In other letters, there were usually questions about wedding needs, and he thought his mother had sent on some chiffon, in case I couldn't find fabric for my gown. He mentioned writing to tell my parents and to let them know his leave dates, when he had them. He was anxious for the day to arrive when we would be together.

As I read these words guilt and anticipation mingled with earlier memories of our time together, surfaced, and I knew I had made the right decision to wait. Had I imagined the depth of our relationship then, or now? Perhaps the time at home would help me clarify my inner conflicts.

Knowing Bob was still on the station, when once in a while I would get a wave from a passing car or jeep, was really a strain but on the rare occasion when we bumped into each other, it made me feel almost furtive about feeling pleased to see him. Bob just looked serious and rather pale.

Days passed with ever increasing prospects of a cease fire, or whatever might announce peace. The winter had kept its icy fingered grip on us but soon it would be spring, and we would see the crocuses and snow drops, poking through the hard ground, followed by sunshiney, daffodils, narcissus and sweet smelling hyacinths and *then* it would be Spring. Consulting my calendar, I noticed that in two weeks my leave would be due and I would be homeward bound to celebrate my twenty first birthday. In between, the time dragged and I began to count the days until it was time to leave.

It was with a feeling of relief that I boarded the train for Birmingham, a day early for my big coming of age party. It felt as if I had been granted a reprieve from decision making for a while. But then, what did I know?

9 – The Decision

Coming of Age

SETTLING BACK ON the dingy upholstery, I opened my crossword book and five minutes later, the familiar whistles blew, doors banged, the flag waved and we were on our way. After a short snooze, I was wide awake, refreshed and looking out of the window to see a train coming from the opposite direction, rushing past us with a loud screech, making the windows rattle, clattering over points and passing through the station we had left behind. Watching the passing scene, with detached curiosity as we continued on our way, my mind projected to my upcoming visit. Seven days leave would go so fast and once home, there would be was much to do. My big birthday on the 18th of April meant that I would be officially declared an adult and we would mark the day together, among other things. A mature lady of twenty-one. Old enough to make wise decisions, I thought, hopefully.

A happy event to be shared with my family, but the big question, stifled at birth and shoved to the back of my mind, yet hard to ignore, was how much to tell my parents of my ambivalent feelings about Frank? Mulling and stewing about it to the point of exasperation, I finally realized that there was really no need to worry them unnecessarily, before I had talked to him myself. No decision could be made until then. I must see Frank first, face to face. Thinking about our meeting, it was as if I could barely conjure him up, in my mind's eye, yet memories of our ongoing dialogue, accompanied by a feeling of well being when we were together, assailed me now. Whether we walked the cliffs gazing at the ocean, or wherever we were, I remembered feeling so simpatico. This caught me unawares, and I smiled at the memory. We had been so in tune. These nostalgic moments, conflicted with my unresolved feelings for Bob, though thoughts of him were less vibrant at this distance, underlining the need to just hold my peace, for now. That decided, I couldn't wait to see my family, and began to count the hours. The journey from the train to the cab, then home, seemed as if it might take forever; but the waiting cabbie told me that the traffic was light, on our route, no delays likely. The day was bright for late afternoon in April, as the sun spread a mellow glow indiscriminately over the surrounding countryside. The pale yellow rays shining on the cab's polished surface creating beams of glistening dust motes, sliced across the seat, briefly catching my attention, until suddenly, interrupting my reverie, the driver turned into the driveway, and said, "This it?" And yes, it was. We were there.

My Mother opened the door, wreathed in smiles, and dispensing hugs. Behind her, in the living room, a huge fire burned brightly as Dad emerged to administer his usual a bear hug, followed by Norma, so grown up already, who embraced me, beaming with joy, when I squeezed her in return. Much to my surprise, as I turned around, there stood my old friend, Joan Nicholls from Swansea, still in uniform, here on a three day pass, and waiting her turn to be hugged. All of us were delighted to see each other again and ready to celebrate.

Parking my luggage in a convenient spot, we found comfy seats, arranging ourselves around the welcoming warmth of the fire, and out came the champagne, whereupon Dad popped the cork of a special bottle of Veuve Cliquot, thus officially launching my coming of age. Presents appeared, even a cake, a masterpiece, adorned by the required 21 candles, presented with a flourish, by Mom. I hated to think how many family members had sacrificed their sugar ration to create this appetizing treat, but from the moment I crossed the threshold, the tone was set for an intimate, happy time together. Time to talk and plan; As we clustered around the fire my mother produced the piece de resistance, a small, velvet lined box, which I thought, must be the ring, and quickly thought that Frank would be relieved to know of its safe arrival.

I hadn't expected to be so bowled over, but upon opening it, I found the most beautiful engagement ring I ever saw, which had arrived, by spe-

Joan in uniform

cial delivery, just days before I came home. It was indeed, truly lovely. The centre stone was a clear, white, square-cut diamond, about two carats and flanked by two baguette diamonds set in platinum. It fitted perfectly. How did he know my size? "Oh dear, it may have to be returned," but for now, I admired it on my finger, as it cast a small beacon of light, forming little sun spots flickering around the room. What a sparkler!

I felt worried, at the reminder of its significance, but perhaps a lifelong commitment was scary for anyone? Perhaps it was it all just nerves? Then I looked at my parents and Norma and wondered again, what it would be like to be separated? Strange that Joan, an only child, had made the choice to marry an American and seemed totally carefree and full of happiness, despite the prospect of leaving family behind. Shaking off these endless questions that I kept asking myself, this constant inner dialogue, I decided instead, to be 'in the moment,' and just enjoy this heaven sent opportunity to be at home with my family and best friend. My fervent hope was for clarity of mind and heart. And then I began to really relax, planning to enjoy each day as it came.

Conversation flowed and so did the champagne, a light-hearted mood prevailed as the topic inevitably turned to my wedding. Mom and Joan were full of ideas for preparations, while Norma and Dad asked some pertinent questions, because who knew when the next visit from France would take place they said? It could be anytime and we should be prepared.

Lists were made and before I knew it, like a galloping, runaway horse, plans were mapped out, without my even saying a word, leaving a few details left to be decided as the event got nearer. So speedy it made my head swim.

My mother had found someone to make my dress, using lovely cream coloured crepe which she had discovered in a store in the city earlier on. This delicate material was miraculously free from coupons, as it was designated for curtain fabric, and was wider than dress fabric they said. A mental image of the famous Scarlett, using curtains to make a gown, made me smile, also realizing my Mother's stroke of creative genious in her extended search for wedding gown material. Knowing friends and family were all pitching in with a will, touched my heart., and I fervently hoped never to disappoint them. Cousin Wynne offered the loan of her own wedding veil, and the church had been notified to call the banns. Cousin Douglas was to be best man, unless Frank had someone else in mind, and another two cousins, Margaret and Shirley would be bridesmaids, with dresses made from pastel silk, saved from prewar for a special purpose. Joan was happy to be my, matron of honour, though we had yet to find a dress for her, after more discussion soon. Norma was of course, chief bridesmaid. Other details could be decided later. Much had been accomplished, with very minor contributions from me. It was exciting, to see everything falling into place so easily, but still a sense of unreality hung over me, as arrangements were being made. As if it were all happening to someone else. What if I changed my mind? Was this actually a waste of time? It all seemed to be moving along so quickly. Perhaps all brides went through a similar jittery period, I thought? Friends and family seemed to be happy for me, and everyone liked Frank. The prevailing mood was joyous, sweeping us all with it, upward and onward. Best now to bide my time.

We stayed up way too late, reluctant to end the day. Conversation turned to events happening on Joan's station and then on mine, some of them pretty funny, like the tale of an unlucky WAAF who had the misfortune to empty out tea leaves, from an old pot of tea, in order to make a fresh one, pouring the dregs out of the window. In Sketty, the Ops room was on the second floor with the bay window extending over a rose bed and since she had heard tea leaves were a good antidote for aphids, and really didn't want to make a trip downstairs and down the hall, anyway, she decided to recycle them through the window and onto the earth below. Unfortunately the French windows beneath, were open and at that very moment the C.O.chose to emerge for a stroll outside into the garden for some fresh air. The soggy wet, tea leaves hit him squarely on his bald spot, plopped in a neat pile, mid pate and as he looked up, the cold tea ran down his hitherto pale face, now rapidly turning purple and he met the horrified gaze of the perpetrator. Guilty as charged! I missed it all, but Joan was on duty in the P.X. and heard the clamor in the hall as he strode past and up the stairs, two at a time, to confront the culprit.

This, and other mad moments kept us laughing for a while before everyone, but Joan and I, retired, yawning and weary. The soft lights from the lamps and glow from the fire were conducive to confidences and Joan had a chance to tell me all about Bob and his family who lived in California and owned a citrus grove, near the beautiful town of Carmel, and how she looked forward to being there. On being demobbed, Bob planned on working for his father, whom he loved and admired. Almost as an after-thought, she added that, her feelings for George were all forgotten now, since a deeper love had developed when Bob entered her life. This time, she averred, it was for keeps.

All too soon, it was time to see Joan off at the Station, but since we knew we would see each other before long, her departure was cheerful and full of promise for the future.

All relatives were duly visited after she left and plans discussed again, while I kept my fingers crossed, not quite knowing what I hoped for. Seven enjoyable days passed quickly, so that when it was time to hoist my kit bag onto the train and return, I was ready to get back to routine and be useful. I climbed aboard, feeling content. No overhead menace, constantly threatening us with extinction awaited me in Oxford I thought, with an enormous sense of relief. London, however was not so lucky and the V-2s continued their destruction.

Operation Manna

Operations continued with various sorties taking place, the emphasis now being placed on important photographic missions, and our squadron was credited with considerable skill in this area. Otherwise, nothing much had changed in Ops, although everyone seemed a tad more up-beat lately. News of war in Europe was good in general, but not in Holland where famine was rife. Winter of 1944 had wreaked havoc in Occupied Holland and became known as the Hunger Winter. In the Spring of 1945, roughly 20,000 civilians had died of starvation and those who were left were desperately trying to stay alive by eating tulip bulbs. At this time 120,000 German troops still occupied the Netherlands and the situation was grim.

Appeals were made by Prince Bernhard and Queen Juliana, at this time being sheltered in England, directly to Mr Churchill and President Roosevelt, urgently requesting help in alleviating the famine. This resulted in an attempt to establish a safe air corridor with the German High Command, allowing food to be delivered to the starving population. While this was being considered the RAF decided not to wait to begin Operation Manna, and braving the risks, were first on the scene, and right after that, between April 29 and May 7 the Allies dropped food, in bags, from a low level, rather than using parachutes from a greater height. These packages contained tinned food, dry food and chocolate. The first run was made by Avro Lancasters and later they were joined by Mosquitoes. Pilots from Australia, New Zealand Canada and Poland also helped, and the US Army Air Force also soon began their Operation Chow Hound, using Flying Fortresses. Operation Chow Hound made 2,268 sorties altogether, contributing four tons of food.

Operation Manna made 3,301 sorties dropping close to six tons of food. and what was so amazing was that none of these aircraft was armed, and none were damaged. Germans who had inadequate food supplies themselves, stood by and never encroached on the life saving sustenance being dropped in their midst.

The response by those on the receiving end was overwhelming. People in the streets and on roofs cheered and waved as aircraft came over so low, that those on the ground could see the crew waving from an open gun position. They danced and screamed, some fainting, from lack of food. A message of thanks was spelled out in tulips, on the ground and afterwards pilots and crew, voted those runs were the best of all their sorti's made during the entire war.

Still, when this wasn't enough food to resolve the prolonged need, the Allies followed up with Operation Faust and proceeded to send truck deliveries behind the German lines with supplemental food supplies, enough to see them through, until other resources were arranged.

514 RAF Bomb Squadron had been among the first to fly this mission, and some of the details filtered through to Ops rooms on many stations, all of us eager to learn of any way the Netherlands could be helped. Our sympathy for the Dutch people went without saying, and the heroic flights left us feeling proud of those flyers, and relieved to recognize the humanity implied in saving Dutch lives. The Germans acquiesced in making it happen, and no shots were fired on the rescuers, and that was their contribution.

I was kept busy on the job and it was odd not to have any contact with Bob, but any further meetings would be confusing, and unfair. I had accepted the fact that my first priority was to talk to Frank, but Bob had been my friend, for a long time, before the mistletoe episode, so of course, I missed the companionship. Our three way conversations and sharing ideas with Bouchier had always been stimulating, so not seeing either of them, left a big void in my life. Once again, there were so few people to share my off time, since our shift work hours didn't coincide. Alan was away on leave, so that just left Vivian who was not very available to play with, since she was only free one evening out of many, and one Ops WAAF was away on leave. In the meantime, I needed to stay busy during the next few weeks obviously, so I decided some self education might be useful, right about now. My new plan was to acquire information from the book store on what I might expect on my wedding night, 'just in case.' Perhaps there wouldn't be one, wedding that is, but its time I was better informed anyway, I thought. It seemed a bit odd to ask for specific details about marital sex, from any particular person, so I decided to investigate the well stocked bookshelves of the main Oxford book store, in private. Once there, I thumbed through a few available tomes and sat down to read the listed contents at a small table surrounded by armchairs. Since I didn't know, what I didn't know, I felt it necessary to take more than one book, and clutching my list of choices, I turned back to the shelves to return the rejects and in the process, brushed a passing shoulder, as I headed that way and glancing up I found myself looking straight into the familiar thoughtful eyes of Sonia. She too, was bent on the same pursuit, busy scanning titles and contents, and she too, looked as if she had been caught out in something spurious. I learned that she was planning to marry her pilot, and though she knew the basics,' we both did, or thought we did, but both of us were a bit in the dark about some aspects of actual sexual activity. Would it be painful? Did our sizes matter? No details were ever mentioned in our respective rudimentary, birds and bees talk, delivered by our mothers years ago.

Well, it was no good whispering in the store library, arousing raised eyebrows and stern looks, so we decided to go back to the billet and read what we had chosen, then afterwards, meet at the first opportunity and discuss what we had learned and see if we had any unanswered questions. Carefully wrapping the tell tale titles in brown paper bags, we left the book store, looking for all the world like two furtive spies, smuggling secret data out of 10 Downing Street. We arranged to meet later, during the week, at a little pub nearby.

When the time came, we arrived, without notebooks, and found a corner table where we could talk freely. It seems that neither of us had learned much that we didn't already know, about the sperm meeting the egg, however there were other suggestions that seemed ludicrous, concerning positions and measuring oneself. We decided, upon reflection, that it couldn't be all that complicated, yet somehow, I missed a link. It never said anything about erections, and how was a person supposed to know that was a factor? The subject never arose then, or at any time, beforehand.

We settled down to enjoy one another's company discovering we had much in common, but Sonia was being posted north to join her new husband after their wedding, which was to take place in about a week's time. Pity! I would be sorry to see her leave as I know we could have become good friends, given the chance, and I often wondered how things went for her, and where they would live after the war. We didn't see each other again, so I never found out.

Remembering the charm of the Bodleian Library, I spent some of my leisure time there investigating its history, while I was stationed so close to Oxford. It was something I could do alone, with pleasure, and an opportunity to learn about its subsequent development culminating in the famous structure it is to-day.

More than 400 years ago, the first building was given by the Duke of

Gloucester, the youngest brother of Henry V and in 1598 an important benefactor, Sir Thomas Bodley refurbished it with a new collection of 2,500 books. The library re opened again for business in 1602. Eighteen years later in 1610 a major historic agreement with the Stationers of London was reached, agreeing that the Stationers would give a copy of every new book they published, to be deposited in the Bodleian Library, by now bulging at the seams. Every new book over all those years provided an incredible scope of subjects, and an unimaginable volume of reading matter. By then, it was patently, necessary, to add an extension to house them all. The extended rooms were soon known collectively as Arts End, and were well frequented almost from the start.

In exchange for this largesse only one firm rule was made by the Stationers and agreed to, by the Bodleian, was that no book would be removed from the library premises, for any reason, and protection was provided to ensure this was so.

Looking around, I was interested to see for myself, that some of the exceedingly large tomes deposited upstairs, were attached to a reading desk by a hefty chain, just to make sure, also a few padlocks were in place in other areas.

One awkward moment mentioned in the history, and recorded in all detail, occurred when John Rouse was chief librarian, and the reigning King, (Charles I) at that time, was made aware of the library's extensive collection, and decided to try it out. He sent a direct order to the library Head, asking him to kindly forward the edition of *The History of the World*, by Agrippa D'Aubigne, for his immediate perusal. This, of course, threw the poor head librarian into a dither. What to do? After much agonizing over his duty as custodian of the library, it was obvious to him, that he must refuse to obey the royal monarch's command, since he was bound by the existing agreement, never to allow a book out on loan. How to convey the news? After more painful deliberation, and sleepless nights, he decided to present himself and the Book of Statutes to King Charles I and show him, in person, the written rule, fervently, hoping he would understand. Still in a dither, but determined nontheless, he arrived at the palace to face his sovereign. Kneeling, he made a deferential offering of the Statutes, with knees trembling in fear, he apparently so impressed the King with his courage and fealty, that John Rouse, chief librarian, was politely allowed to withdraw, with a proverbial pat on the back. He did so with immense, heartfelt, relief and left on winged feet, taking the Book of Statutes with him. He kept his head, in more ways than one.

In 1749 the Radcliffe library became the Radcliffe Camera a separate entity, for a while. Incidentally, the word camera is Latin for room. A century later, this was merged with the Bodleian Library which it is to-day, the former, adding considerably to its scope.

In 1842 not only all books published in England were collected, but overseas collections were also added, making a formidable total. Heating however, was not added until 1845, so we can only imagine how bleak and cold it was inside this building, for those reading hour after hour, for an exam, especially in winter. In 1909 in order to provide additional space for the incoming 30,000 books per year, an underground area was excavated beneath Radcliffe Square, going right under the road, and when the Library opened three years later, it was the largest in the world. The new main library building was designed by Sir Gilbert Scott, housing five million books. It was connected to the old Bodleian by an underground system using conveyer belts and pneumatic tubes.

During the Second World War in 1940 the Bodleian sent books to prisoners of war and made special maps for D-Day. They also provided a public air raid shelter, built in 1941 as part of their effort to "do their bit, towards winning the war."

The library itself fascinated me, and I intended to go back there, if I could, and spend more time, after the war, and perhaps explore the underground part, if allowed.

"After the war" was beginning to sound like a real possibility. Something was definitely in the air, a general upswing of mood prevailed in all areas of life. In shops, on the street, in the pubs little snippets of encouraging war news were passed around with an air of, "it won't be long now" attitude sometimes accompanied by a nod and a wink, and always a smile.

Then one day "the" long awaited day arrived. May 7 to be exact, the big news announcement was that Admiral Dimitz, President of the Third Reich had surrendered unconditionally, and the very next day May 8, 1945 the Allies officially accepted the surrender, and it became known as VE Day. Victory in Europe!

Celebrations broke out everywhere, and spread like measles, only pleasanter. By a fluke I was not on duty that day, so having secured a day pass and feeling unbelievably light of heart, I joined two friends, girls from Intelligence, and we set off for the capital city.

Mr. Churchill spoke on radio from Trafalgar Square where an incredible crowd was assembled and as he began, a great hush descended on this vast expanse of people, in tribute to this man who had been such a source of strength to us throughout six long years of strife. I wasn't right there myself, but heard all about it, in the evening, over dinner, from those who were present. Instead, I saw King George and Queen Mary on their balcony at Buckingham Palace but I didn't see the two Princesses, Elizabeth and Margaret when they mingled with the crowd. A rare event for them! I wondered if they were recognized as they wandered around, sharing in the boundless excitement of the crowds.

Battered but unbowed, London went wild that day, with a kaleidoscope of celebrants singing and dancing in the streets, some providing their own music on accordions, violins, guitars, mouth organs or just plain kazoos, and not to be outdone, some small tots had drums. Circles formed for the hokey kokey, and lines for the conga, arranged themselves, bodies of all shapes and sizes attached to smiling faces, wound their way around the throngs of singers. Spontaneous joy expressed itself, everywhere you looked. After almost six years of strife, we were ready, to kick up our heels.

Sometimes revelers performed against a backdrop of stark, skeleton, buildings, or alongside gaping holes in the earth, surrounded by rubble, where once, tall edifices had stood. Mute reminders of what, only yesterday had to be taken in stride. No more! One could almost see a phoenix rising from the ashes. It was hard to absorb the change all at once. Incredible to realize there would be no more shattered nights with mournful, all too familiar, wails of air raid sirens, strumming the air. No more tin helmets, gas kits etc to be carried around, and from this moment on, we could look heavenward and expect to see only an untrammeled sky, hopefully blue. No more fear of sudden death raining down on us. Surely VJ Day couldn't be far behind?

Most of us knew very little of happenings in the Channel Islands during the war, but were told only at war's end, that the German Garrison ensconced there, surrendered on May 9 1945.

After these major events, May vanished in a blur and now at the beginning of June. my mail was arriving in stacks. There had been a dearth of letters from Frank, but suddenly an avalanche of three arrived, with closely packed pages, detailing possible plans for the future but mostly speculating on probable arrival dates from France. His ideas were bursting from the pages, promising to let my parents know, as soon as a "ball park" date, could be more definite. His best estimate was the end of June, but that could change at any time. My feelings were hard to describe, perhaps an equal mix of hope and panic, says it best.

A letter from Joan arrived too, giving me an alert of one week. This particular week, in fact, was my actual alert, to plan on attending her wedding, a mere seven days hence, when I was expected to be her bridesmaid. The ceremony would take place in Sketty, South Wales but "What about a dress for you?" she asked. There were no coupons available for a new long gown, but I had a dress which I thought might serve the purpose. Worn once, it was pale green, silk crepe, form fitting, with a slight fullness in the skirt, and I already had silver shoes and matching purse, so that shouldn't be a problem. Just retrieving it was a challenge though. There wasn't time to wait for things to be mailed from home, mail being uncertain, so I must pick it up on the way to Wales. Accordingly, I asked for leave, merely a long weekend, but it would be enough. I knew I would soon need to request more leave when Frank came, so this must be a mini leave, This presented no problems with the officer in charge, of such sanctions. Two days later I was all set, and with pass in hand I managed an early train to Birmingham, conveniently linking to Hagley railway station. There would just be time for lunch with my family, then pack the dress, and I would be off to board the packed, Welsh bound train for Swansea, where Joan's Dad would pick me up. "Just in time for tea" he said, on arrival. And it was just after 4pm when tea was duly served

Joan fairly bloomed with happiness. She practically strangled me in a mighty hug welcoming me to this major event in her life. Bob was a bit more circumspect, kissing me on both cheeks, instead. He was a little shy, tall, fair-haired, blue-grey eyes and gentle attitude, towards life, I couldn't imagine him confronting Hitler, or his henchmen, with mortal combat in mind. Like so many others I knew, his role as soldier was not his favourite, but when the chips were down, he was ready.

Joan, who was more of an extrovert, seemed to compliment his nature and together they worked in total harmony throughout all the last minute preparations. Nobody seemed in the least, nervous, or edgy, so the rehearsal dinner progressed with no disruptions and a sense of calm. Not a single tantrum, no-one was late, no one dropped the cake. Everything flowed along as smoothly as liquid silver. It became a real celebration, with time to laugh, remembering tales of other peoples' pre-wedding fiascos.

Next day, the flowers arrived with a wreath of pastel coloured sweet peas artfully intertwined, for my head dress. Unusual, I thought, and a very pleasant surprise. There was also a small bouquet of the same flowers to carry down the aisle, surrounding me with soft fragrance. The bride's flowers, complimenting her gown, were more traditional, using white roses and lilies, with touches of lavender and it was a perfectly lovely bouquet. The groom wore a small white rose in his lapel and other men attendants, a white anemone boutonniere. Emily carried pink lilies and Nick, a pink anemone boutonniere. It was a truly beautiful wedding.

Joan's wedding to Bob with Joan's parents on the left and me on the right

Joan had no siblings, and very few relatives, so since the groom's family couldn't participate, it was a rather small wedding, but memorable. After toasts were drunk, and cake cut, the bride changed into a light suit ready to travel and the beaming couple, dallied just long enough to say their farewells and were swiftly on their way. I easilymcaught the bouquet as they entered the car. Well who else was eligible in this small gathering? The rest of us stayed to enjoy time with Joan's parents, Emily and Nick, who loved hearing comments from us all, agreeing that with at least, two photographers present, there would be enough prints for a sizable album. All too soon it was over, and time for me to set off to take the train back to Oxford.

They had made it all look so simple, this rearrangement of four lives. Just a few words spoken in a church and everything was changed forever, for all of them.

On return, there was barely time to draw breath before a letter arrived telling me to expect Frank on the 29th of June and right on its heels, a phone call telling me he was already there, at home, with my parents, and where was I? We had planned and expected to meet there, together, anyway, but the letter came after the event, leaving me no time to think. I was seized with a visceral thrill of anticipation, that fluttered like a bird in my stomach.

I knew he was coming and still I wasn't ready. Suddenly, like a startled gazelle, I was paralyzed with fear. Fear of making the wrong decision. Fright set in. I thought of pretending difficulties about getting leave, but that wouldn't work and wouldn't help. Ever positive, my parents and Frank decided to facilitate matters and using hoarded petrol, they said that they would come and pick me up, the next day, early. There was little use in trying to sleep that night, until at last in the wee hours, I made my big decision. I decided not to go ahead with the wedding. Worn out with thinking and analyzing, at last I fell asleep.

Compassionate leave was granted and I was ready, when everyone arrived to take me home. They were all in such high spirits, it seemed better to wait until we got home, to announce my decision. I couldn't drop my bomb en route, and knew when I did it would hurt, and confuse everyone. Best to talk to Frank alone, first, as planned, I thought. I don't remember the meal that followed our arrival but I remember pleading fatigue when asked about my quiet spell during conversation as they all happily discussed details of the forthcoming ceremony, the words barely sinking in, as I listened in mute silence. Not long after, my parents tactfully retired and Frank and I were left alone.

Fairly bursting with the enforced restraint, I plunged in and told him of my fears and doubts about the future, realizing as I did so, that my biggest barrier lay in leaving my family. Frank had yet to finish his training as an architect, and who knew about jobs available after the war? So many British men would be coming home, needing jobs in England, and would of course expect first priority, it didn't make sense to plan on our living in England, even if Frank were willing. We talked into the late hours laying bare our deepest feelings until bit by bit Frank realized that I wasn't going to have a change of heart and that there wasn't going to be a wedding. It was then I noticed how really thin and suddenly pale he was, and I had a glimmering of how much he must have been through and I hurt for him. It was sickening to know I was also causing him this much pain. Thinking of his ordeal in France I remembered that Omaha Beach had been Frank's landing point on D-Day + 1, and it was the worst hit, sustaining the biggest loss and damage, of them all. He never spoke of it, then or later, but it obviously took its toll.

We kissed a gentle, sad kiss goodnight and wound our way upstairs to our separate rooms, in silence. This time, I was so wrung out with emotions of the day, I became unconscious almost immediately. Sleep was no problem that night, but it seemed only moments passed before a new day was dawning. Bright gleams of sunlight sprayed the room filtering through the lacey curtains, waking me with the knowledge that I now had to give my parents the disturbing news. I bathed, dressed and went down the stairs to retell my story. Both of them were finishing breakfast and on their second cup of tea. Food awaited me, but I decided to postpone breakfast until all was told. Immediately I had their attention, as they knew at once, mine was not the happy face of a bride to be. It took a little while to relate my inner battle, my inability to see the problem clearly enough, and the need now to break my promise to Frank. Why hadn't I said so at an earlier moment? After D-Day wasn't a good time, nor was a letter a good option. Besides I didn't really want to say goodbye, and had tried to make sense of it all, as best I could. Why had I felt so clutched? I suppose it didn't matter, but it felt important to figure it out, as honestly as possible. There was little I could say to be any clearer. They completely understood my reluctance to emigrate, and only wanted to be sure I would have no regrets, afterwards. They were so unselfish in their reaction. Not putting their own self-interest first, knowing I would remain in England, if the engagement was over, would have been a bonus for them, but they set that aside, trying to consider my ultimate happiness first. Mom expressed for both of them, the sorrow they felt, knowing that Frank would find this very hard to take, and they cared about him. He deserved the truth, however and would naturally expect it from me. The pressure suddenly evaporated and though it had all left me feeling completely limp, I had totally shed a heavy load of worry. It had been rattling around in my head, or somewhere in my psyche, perhaps not quite as consciously as a thought, for far too long. The relief was enormous. I gave back the beautiful ring, though Frank offered it as a keepsake but to no avail. Then came the aftermath; The feeling of general let-down made itself felt, in a certain bleakness of atmosphere, a lowering of spirits, and despite our individual efforts to be normal, it was heavy going. Gloom clung to the walls.

The next two days were spent in disinviting guests, with sketchy explanations, at best. It was not an easy task, but everyone was kind, and soon it was over. Then, we disengaged all the services we had previously arranged.

After that, we shared the responsibility of calling the dressmaker, the Vicar, the florist and the organist, also the photographer, undoing all the happy planning that had gone into those preparations, but we managed to get it all done by the end of the day. It had been a long twenty four hours and we were all tired out, and feeling the need to retire early. I think Dad succumbed to two whiskies instead of his usual one, in the evening, and Frank kept him company. Mom, Norma and I were too tired to care, and the evening became an early night for all.

Two days later, Frank and I took our bulldog for a stroll in the village and on errands. On the way, we picked up rolls for dinner, each of us lost in our separate thoughts. There had been little conversation, barely a peep out of Frank, but breaking the silence on the way back as he touched my hand, he announced his decision to return to Base. He told me that he would be leaving tomorrow, so "We may as well say our goodbyes, now," he said, all in one breath. This should come as no surprise, but somehow it caught me left-footed.

I looked up at him, squinting in the shaft of sunlight and feeling somehow dazed by the finality in his voice, and I wobbled.

It suddenly hit home, that this might indeed be very "final." The last time we would ever see each other. "Wouldn't we be able to stay friends?" I asked. After a long pause, his eyes dulled, evading mine, when he said, that he thought that was not a possibility for him, and it would be better under the circumstances, to make a clean break. There was a bench a few yards ahead, and suddenly feeling the need to sit down, I headed over there. Frank stood next to the hedge flanking the bench, idly reaching out to fiddle with a twig of hawthorn, drawing blood from a small thorn, as he snapped it in two. He appeared to be looking without seeing, somewhere into the middle distance, already absent in his thoughts. Already, somewhere else.

It flashed across my mind that I would never see him again. What had I expected? Dummy! The idea was truly impossible to imagine. He had been in my mind for so long, I couldn't even think of the void he would leave. A permanent void; Could I really bear to part now, for always and ever? That was my choice and it was obvious, of course. The answer was just as obvious, "No, I wasn't"

Without stopping to analyze matters further, or worry about the implications, or the inconsistencies, I said, "If you can take a chance now, on this being the best and right decision, after all that's gone before, then I would like to say, yes to our future." The seconds passed and the world stopped revolving, as I waited for his response, and then I saw the shine in his eyes. It was like a bright lamp had been lit and the rest of him visibly, came to life, in a quick whirl of movement. With a smile that left no doubt he said, "I'll take that chance," as he enfolded me in both arms with a kiss to stop traffic. We did cause a few raised eyebrows among the occasional passers by, but it was an emotionally charged moment, that had to be recognized and just took over All that mattered was this totally unexpected revelation, after all the uncertainty and pressure, it was now truly resolved. Both of us on the same page! Then with buoyant steps we set out for home to break the life changing news, to my long suffering parents.

The first response was one of disbelief, naturally, then laughter at the ignominy of having to turn everything back on again, after which my Mother wanted a word in private. I followed her upstairs. In my room she closed the door and stood with her back to it, as she asked if the feeling of pressure had anything to do with my change of heart and I told her exactly how it had all unfolded. She was satisfied, and relieved, realizing that it was in fact, the lack of pressure that helped me make the right decision, finally. All she and Dad cared about was my happiness, she said. Of course I knew that, and felt fortunate that they were my parents. Their tolerance and caring love was never more in evidence than during this last week of soul searching. The house came alive again that day, with renewed hope and humour.

Oh dear, back to the church we must to go, to restart the vicar, so that the ceremony would take place in a few days on July 10. Looking at us, with great forbearance, and infinite patience, the vicar said he would marry us in the middle of the night if that became necessary. Not so, the organist who was not to be found anywhere, though we tried. Would we have to go without music?

Next, the dress had yet to be finished, entailing a final fitting, so we made an appointment to go to Handsworth, home of the dressmaker, that same day. It was a distance of about thirty miles, to designer Pat, who would need as much time as possible, she said, if it were to be ready by the day before the wedding. She would go to work on it as soon as we left, and sew into the night if she had to, she told us. We felt most appreciative and very blessed. Somehow we felt renewed, and ready to conquer all obstacles, now that we were all united in our desire to make this wedding happen. The flowers were re-organized with minimum difficulties, the Best Man alerted and the bridesmaids and the guests re-invited who in turn, responded with a few jocular remarks, about bridal nerves.

Out came the ring and back on the finger it went, placed there with a firm touch and appropriate words to the effect that this was where it belonged, always.

One thing that couldn't be helped was that my dear friend Joan didn't have time to find a long gown to be matron of honour, on such short notice but she would do her utmost to be there in uniform she said. She would be there for the ceremony. Her presence was what mattered most, of course and so next day she had her ticket, and would come even if she only had two days. I heaved sighs of thankfulness.

Unfortunately the delayed decision, now posed a problem of shortening the time to make honeymoon plans. Our time together was reduced to four days, with only three days notice, hardly enough time to make a booking we were told. We each took turns phoning various resort areas that were not too far distant, requesting hotel accommodation, but found little available, due to short notice. Eventually, a reservation at a small private hotel materialized in Blackpool of all places! This was a strange spot to go for a honeymoon, I thought, where the main attractions were the so called, 'illuminations,' in peacetime, and it's Fun Fair, a large one, only partially functioning now, due to fuel rationing. Not exactly what we had in mind, but still, it had the advantage of being not very far by train, and on the ocean, with well kept promenades overlooking the beaches, so we could take walks along the front. It was a spot neither of us would have chosen, but we were grateful to be assured of good accommodation so near the sea, and with little advance warning.

Having arranged this much for the honeymoon, we addressed the next item on the list and turned our attention to finding appropriate help to serve a wedding lunch after the ceremony, then made plans to parcel out the groom on the eve of the wedding, so that he would not see the bride before the service, honouring the old tradition. We were finally able to spend some happy relaxed moments together, with family, at day's end, congratulating ourselves on our prowess.

July 10 would find us ready. On that day, I was subsequently told by our friends, that Frank had been ready at a very early hour, at dawn, just to be sure. The Nightingales, where he was staying, said that he was anxiously checking the weather, and had been up for quite a while, when they joined him at seven thirty am.

It did sprinkle with rain at first, but the clouds obligingly parted to let the sun through, as we reached the church and no-one got wet, on our big day. The church seemed about half full, surprisingly. Altar flowers were abundant and beautiful, but alas no music, which I really missed. Frank

Bride in full regalia

however, told me afterwards that he didn't even notice. Besides my bridal regalia and bouquet of roses with trailing ivy, I wore, something old (the veil) something new (my gown) and something borrowed (a bracelet) and something blue (a garter). My chief bridesmaid, Norma, looking elegant, played her role as if it were an everyday occurrence for her. Margaret and Shirley followed suit, and as we turned to retrace our steps down the aisle, a happy peal of bells rang out and over my shoulder I caught a glimpse of the minister. Was that a look of relief I saw on his face as he looked heavenward?

My wedding ring was a complete surprise, rather symbolizing the times we lived in. It was a silver American quarter fused into a circle by a German prisoner of war, made in France for an American to give to his English bride. An international symbol I thought. It fairly gleamed on my finger (a higher content of silver was used in quarters then), and I continued to wear it even after I was presented with a platinum one to match my engagement ring, early in the following year. The quarter ring was always my favourite and I wore all three together later on.

Wedding guests. Mother of the bride number three from right. Douglas, best man and math whiz next to groom

We lingered at the reception for a while, long enough to have a visit with friends and family who had all made a long journey to be there, then I went upstairs to change into a pale blue silk crepe suit, bought with family coupons, and a small, blue, matching hat with an ostrich feather, no coupons, that I rather liked. A nice change for me, from collar and tie, worn for so many years, either in school uniform, or as a WAAF! At the foot of the stairs, I tossed the bouquet, and think Norma caught it. Out came the hoarded, confetti, and we were liberally sprayed. I even found it in my shoes afterwards, then along came the limo opening its sheltering doors to take us to the station. Last minute kisses bestowed, a chorus of good wishes followed us, more confetti thrown at the car, and we were on our way. Our train seats were half way down the carriage and it was a full train, so we threaded our way through the crowds, trying to look long married, composed and matter of fact, but trailing tell-tale confetti, as we went. We were surprised to see so many soldiers aboard, where we were soon spotted as newlyweds. Toasts were made and songs were sung, barely quieting down as we reached our destination. So much for anonymity, and privacy! There, at the station, we were lucky enough to get a taxi but as soon as I sat down, the door was flung wide and five more soldiers hopped aboard, and my seat became Frank's lap. More songs and quips ensued before this jaunty, jam-packed ride was over.

It was dusk when we disentangled ourselves from the taxi, where we were deposited on the pavement along with our light luggage, and backed up by enthusiastic shouts of goodwill from the Army. Hoisting bags up the few entry steps, we entered a long skinny, brick building, noting the crisp white trim at the door, as we passed by which looked freshly painted, with paint saved from pre-war days, we were told. Once inside, we were aware that no chink of light escaped, heavy, wine, velveteen, blackout curtains, creating a welcome sense of comfort, besides deadening noises from the busy road outside. Well tended plants placed in strategic spots around the room, and near the windows to get daytime light, thrived, and also separated the seating into small groups, enhancing areas of privacy. As we took it all in, the proprietress herself emerged from a room further back, behind the staircase. A motherly figure, with lovely complexion, beneath grey blonde hair, and startlingly blue eyes, now trained on us, she was clad in a soft pastel, longish dress, which billowed out behind her as she moved. Smiling when she saw us, she invited us to follow her up the thickly carpeted stairs to our room, chatting without pause, along the way, she said she was available any time, should we need anything. Giving us a happy weather report for tomorrow as she went, she assured us that, we had a room with a view, then flung open the door to our room with a flourish, as if she were revealing Aladdin's cave. Not lavish, but charming with simple furnishings enhanced by a skillfully arranged vase of fragrant, old fashioned roses, sitting next to a fruit bowl, atop an old chest. The room exuded a soft pinkish glow of light from shaded wall sconces. Candles and matches, nearby. Best of all was a tray bearing a cold supper, flanked by two wine glasses and a bottle of wine already chilling, in a cooler. With another beaming smile she said goodnight and vanished with a swirl of skirt.

Left alone for the first time that day, we sank into armchairs, looked at each other and laughed at the day's events. Kicking off our shoes, and removing our jackets, we lit the candles and had a little wine before our meal, then finding we both were hungry, neither of us had eaten much in all the excitement and it had been a long day, we began our supper and before long, bed time with my new husband had arrived. When he departed to the bathroom next door, to shower and change, I too disrobed, cleaning my teeth in the little wash basin in the room, then taking my turn in the bathroom, I returned to feel Frank's loving embrace, as he gently steered us towards the bed. It was a wondrous time to be together but not knowing all the secrets of the boudoir caused some bewilderment, on my part. Notwithstanding that, it was a happy time for me, but more complicated for Frank. All the uncertainty of the off-again, on-again wedding had created major tension that was hard for him to dispel completely, and he found that erectile dysfunction was a problem for him, but not knowing what that was, or what didn't occur, I didn't know what was missing, therefore I didn't realize how stricken he must have felt. Otherwise it was all very warm, loving, and intimate.

Next day, we enjoyed a combination breakfast and lunch together before going to investigate the so-called Fun Fair, further along the promenade. Many of the rides had necessarily been discontinued due to lack of petrol but there were other 'attractions' left to capture a spirit of adventure, in the dodgems cars, and the ghost train, but no Ferris wheel for me. Dominating the area was one great, daredevil slide, which seemed to rise high in the air, heavenwards, attaining the height of a three storey building and looming over all it surveyed. This seemed to tempt Frank, so we headed for that. On arrival, I positioned myself nearby to watch, but no, that was not the way it's done said Frank. Together, or not at all, Surely I wasn't chicken? Of course I was just that, chicken with feathers, but not about to say so, and before I realized it, all bravado, I was at the top looking down a steep chute, with a restless queue behind me waiting, impatiently, for me to "get aboard.

Please!" Heart in mouth, I sat gazing down at an almost vertical slide, stuck! I couldn't move, welded to the spot, perfectly immobile, eyes closed. When I could no longer bear the pleas, to "get going, hurry up," I let go and was off at breakneck speed, like a speeding bullet and wound up with skirts billowing, at the bottom of the slide where Frank patiently waited, oblivious to the panicky descent. Now, the only trouble was, the slide was wood surfaced and somehow I had collected a few splinters when I sat down, and as we wended our way home, I was painfully reminded of their presence every step of the way. First aid was indicated. Lying face down on the bed, I waited while Frank went to work with a sterilized needle, to remove deep-seated pieces of wood, but the light was poor, so we tried to figure out a way to move my posterior nearer the window, but I couldn't stay unsupported in a bent over position long enough for him to work, so we moved a chair closer for me to bend over and hold onto. While in this embarrassing pose, I happened to look sideways out of the window and saw with horror a double decker bus on the other side of the street had halted to let passengers off, and our little tableau was being avidly watched by all on the top deck, with gleeful fascination. Frank was at first, equally horrified but then he saw the funny side and after brilliant attempts to stifle his laughter, he said he thought those people on the top deck had never had such an interesting ride, and not to worry, because he'd get all of them out before the next bus came along.

In no time our few short days evaporated, and it was time to journey back, Frank, to his Base and I, back home, where I would once more change into uniform and head back to Benson. Frank had yet to achieve complete conjugal bliss, and was mightily upset about it, though he said little, but considering the time pressure and other stresses it didn't seem too surprising to me. Getting the idea, but not fully realizing the difference I could be much more philosophical.

We travelled as far as Birmingham together where we both had to change for different connections. Frank saw me off first, wearing a very sad face indeed, and desperately needing to be reminded that I would see him in the US next time we met. "Surely, the war with Japan will be over 'ere long," we said, almost in unison. His lone, hatless, figure, slowly waving, dwindling to miniature size as we gained speed, was the last I saw of him, on that platform. It would be almost a year before we met again on the other side.

Once more in my quarters in Benson, the first task was to let Bob know what had transpired, as promised, so I phoned him and was lucky enough to reach him on my first try. I offered to meet him to explain in person,

Rolling a hoop

but he said that he had guessed what had happened, when my absence was prolonged, and that there was really no point in our meeting again, besides he would be leaving next day he said, to a new posting, at his own request and had a lot to do beforehand. We wished each other well, and that was our closure. Dragging the undertow of loss, I proceeded with my list of things to do, realizing that I had lost a dear friend, but had at last gained clarity of mind.

As a married person, I could request demobilization, now that VE Day was over, and that is what I did. Benson, as a station, had already shrunk with some of its personnel having moved on, and newcomers had taken their places, however there were enough familiar faces around to speed me on my way. We managed a nice farewell dinner also a spur of the moment lunch, before it was time to for me to depart.

The resulting formalities of discharge didn't take long, and by August 2nd. I was on my way home to be a civilian. I had hardly had time to get the hang of it again, when there was more major war news.

Four days later, on August 6th Enola Gay dropped the first atomic bomb ever, on Hiroshima, and three days later on August 9th the second bomb was unleashed on Nagasaki with results so devastating that Japan speedily surrendered unconditionally, on August 14 1945. Next day, August 15 became VJ Day. This was formally signed and officially accepted on September 2nd, on the USS Missouri, then at anchor in Tokyo Bay. Celebrations followed everywhere, there were servicemen and women and especially among our American Allies, and not forgetting those on the home front.

Frank was soon among those to be sent home and then began the long wait for transportation to the US for me. I received word from US Immigration authorities that I would be notified when this would be, after filling out my application papers. Documentation on Frank, and his family was to be filed, well ahead of time and this I did, after Frank had done the same on the other side of the "pond". Determined to enjoy my time with family, we planned many enjoyable occasions together and it was a special period of closeness for us. As the months rolled by, Frank exasperated by the long delay, was exploring other complicated ways for me to get there sooner, such as via Portugal to India, then Canada to New York and etc., etc., very complex routes, but Dad laughed aloud on hearing that and I wasn't exactly sold on doing this alone, so we waited and waited, with my family making the most of our time together. Civilian transport to the States was just not possible from Europe, as the troops had first priority, understandably enough. We spent a happy Christmas together and New Year too, before word came that my passage was assured and the dates finally set for late February, when I must present myself to the authorities on the hospital ship, USS Huddleston, in Plymouth, now to be used for brides travelling to the US It was a bitter sweet occasion when I visited each of my relatives and friends to bid them farewell, but we did that together en famille, and suddenly the departure time was upon us. The information also mentioned

Shopping with Norma in Birmingham, while waiting

was that due to the poor weather expected at that time of year, we would be taking the southern route and it would take sixteen days for us to arrive at our destination in New York. Dad wanted to know if we were going to row across? Sixteen Days!

The memory of that journey by car, which we shared en route to Plymouth, and my Mother's tears as they dripped off her chin, will stay with me, always, so I will say no more about that final step we took together and the subsequent parting, on that emotion filled day.

The USS Huddleston was filled to overflowing with English brides, and my stateroom was one big ballroom-like space in which there were forty bunks. Forty room-mates! I felt lucky to occupy a corner bed so, no neighbor at least, on that one side. It was an eventful trip in many ways, with two male English stowaways discovered after we left port, hiding in the lifeboats. We waited while a cutter was dispatched to take them back to shore, before we were under way again. The brides assembled were a complete mix of all sorts, but I soon found two like-minded ones, to share adventures. The first day out, I was slightly sea sick, after breakfast and until noon, as were my new friends, and that was all, but the rest of the ship was awash with prostrate forms who continued to be, oh so very sick, and lying in the aisles. Meeting one, on my way down to the Mess, I thought she was wearing green make up. She was truly green, and I thought she was fooling but a second look told me otherwise. My two cohorts and I stayed on deck in the open air as long as possible, sometimes eating lunch up there, and somehow we were fine. We played board games or just talked, trying to stay away from the stateroom, where the suffering was all too audible. Many days passed before other passengers, besides ourselves, were able to bear the sight of food, or even think of going below to the mess.

It was barely dawn when some of us were on deck, as our ship sailed past the statue of liberty, and I was duly impressed by her size, and presence. It was easy to see why people from oppressed countries found her to be such a symbol of hope. Looking around and seeing all those faces, I wondered what they were feeling at that moment ?

Soon it was time to stuff the last items, toothbrush, nightie, into my steamer trunk and comb my hair and wait for the formalities to take place on deck.

When we were, at last ready to disembark I wondered if I would recognize Frank from a distance in his civilian clothes, and what our new lives together would be like?

10 – Channel Islands

WHILE WAR WAS waging in Britain, not many knew of the fate of The Channel Islands, or even of their loyalty to the crown. These islands consisting of four main ones off the coast of S.W. England, with two, tiny little blips of islands called Herm and Jethou, so small they were little used and seldom visited. Jersey is the largest, and lies only ten miles off the French coast at Cape de la Hague, and next in size is Guernsey, followed by Alderney, only eight miles from France, and last the smallest, inhabited island is Sark.

These islands were originally part of the Duchy of Normandy, when the Duke of Normandy conquered England in 1066, at the Battle of Hastings. A date known to every English schoolchild. Oddly enough, this entitles the islands to call England their oldest possession, though they tactfully refrain from doing so, as a rule. However, when the Norman Duchy reverted to France the Channel Islands opted to be independent and became the States of Guernsey. They then, stayed loyal to the English Crown, though not so loyal as to pay taxes to England. They govern themselves now, though they have kept many English laws, customs, and names. Strangely, a Medieval language still survives. A kind of local patois, which Islanders claim William the Conqueror used himself.

Jersey and Guernsey cows are famous the world over, and originated on these pleasant islands, and they still remain two of the main dairy breeds in America.

Tourists are a good part of their economy, attracted by the history, and the fiefdom still existing in Sark, but millionaires are enticed also, by this sanctuary for modern tax dodgers, bent on escaping the British Chancellor of the Exchequer.

Jersey, is the largest of the islands and also the capitol. Ruling the States of Guernsey is the Bailiff of Jersey, and during the German occupation, throughout World War II Mr Alexander Coutanche, was in charge and it speaks well of his character that he was again elected to the office of Bailiff, after the war. The title encompasses a combination of Lord Chief Justice, Speaker and Prime Minister, all in one person. When presiding over the States, or local parliament, his chair is placed exactly seven inches higher than that of the Lieutenant Governor, representative of the Crown, clearly indicating the fact that he is the is the most important man on the island.

There is also a Bailiff of Guernsey, who was at that time, Mr Victor Carey, with family history on the island going way back to when his antecedents first came there in 1340. There was also Judge Frederick Funch who presided over Alderney and last of all, the little island of Sark which was, and still is, very different from the other three. The Dame of Sark may be the only feudal ruler to ride a bicycle, maybe the only feudal ruler. She is also traditionally, a power and a presence on her small island, a kind of benevolent Dictator.

The Dame of Sark inherited her title from her Island Grandmother, widow of a Guernsey businessman, who bought out the Seigneur of Sark, when he went bankrupt. This island is a separate entity with the feudal system still prevailing. No cars were allowed on the island. The Dame, Mrs Hathaway, was the widow of an American who flew in the RFC in WWI. and after he died she re-married. Her second husband then became Lord of Sark, however the Dame was always the final authority. During the war he was sent to an Internment Camp in 1943, leaving his wife to rule Sark alone. This she did, with intelligence, wit, and a knack for getting people to do her bidding, and during WWII she even kept the German invaders in their place, when they occupied her home. Recreation for the 600 peacetime inhabitants included bridge, scandal and liquor, it was said.

When the Germans landed on the island, the Dame sent one of her officials to meet the officers at the harbor and instructed her maid announce them as guests when they arrived, as she herself waited in a long room seated behind her formidable desk. The 'visitors thus, must approach her, after being admonished first by the maid "to wipe your feet," over a long stretch of carpet. As time passed, she was able to use her influence with the Commandante to get German doctors to treat her tenants, on occasion. At war's end when VJ Day was declared, there was a shortage of British personnel to organize the occupying force's removal from liberated Sark, so the Dame took charge of the 275 Germans left there on the island, making sure that they cleared all the land mines before leaving. The British Government honored her with an award after the war and in their records she was dubbed, "a lady of unusual personality."

During the Occupation, the four Rulers became a strong force in the lives of the people living there. Before the Occupation of the Channel Islands, the German invasion of Norway, Holland then Belgium, had occurred, followed by the famous Dunkirk evacuation, but there was a lesser known evacuation after that. The aftermath of Dunkirk in which islanders were very active.

Mr. Coutanche, Bailiff of Jersey, was secretly told, by General Harrison in Government House that help was desperately needed to rescue those last ditchers, the remaining BEF, still trapped in the port of St Malo, France. After BEF tried to assist French forces, the weakened French line had disintegrated, leaving, thousands of BEF soldiers stranded, high and dry.

Responding to the urgency of the situation, all small boats in Jersey were asked to participate in the evacuation, to which there was a heart-warming response, and though the number of those saved was not disclosed, perhaps it is enough to know that the operation was hailed as eminently successful. Most, were returned safely to England, and a few of them to Jersey.

Now with the enemy on the doorstep, the question was, how to keep the Islands as safe as possible? British troops were sent to Jersey in the form of an Anti-aircraft Battery, a Machine Gun Battalion, and two Hurricane Fighter Squadrons but alas it couldn't last, and wasn't enough. Manpower was desperately needed elsewhere, and they were spread too thin. Britain was also fighting for survival.

The Chiefs of Staff in England, after due deliberation, recommended to the War Office that the islands be de-militarized in the best interests of the population. Mr Churchill loudly protested, trying to find another alternative, but he too finally realized nothing else, was feasible. A choice was offered in the form of evacuation by sea, for all those who wished to leave in order to find havens in the Britain.

The total population was about 90,000. It was interesting to note, how in each island the Ruler, exerted a profound influence on the inhabitant's decision to go or stay. Bailiff Coutanche and Dorey were both against evacuation so only about one fifth of the population opted to leave. However,

Carey and Major Sherwill in Guernsey, left the decision squarely up to the individual resulting in fifty percent who chose to go.

Sark as usual was a separate entity and since the Dame, Mrs Hathaway, was against evacuating, almost all stayed. She had acquired a deep knowledge of the German people, and was fluent in the language, which she expected would help.

Judge French in Alderney, favoured evacuation and thus almost all, left.

Alderney was closest to the approaching Germans, so close that they could see the French people burning oil-storage tanks. It was also cut off from its neighbours, with no telephone to Guernsey, since the undersea cable was in disrepair. Messengers and, believe it or not, the 'town crier,' and the wireless, were the sole means of communication. Even so, using wireless was discouraged for security reasons. On a clear day, coastal road traffic in France, also could be seen, sounds of battle, flashes of gunfire, followed by explosions as the Germans came nearer and nearer.

Before the general exodus, from the islands, all manner of pets, cats, dogs and others had to be taken to the animal shelter to be put to sleep, numbering about 6,000 in all. Such a mournful sight to behold, during which, endless queues waited their turn, outside a veterinarian clinic, as those in line tearfully cradled their pets for the last time. Such sad goodbyes emphasized the ache of departure.

Before the last Brit soldier left, a detachment of Royal Engineers arrived and after smartly saluting the Bailiff of Jersey, the Officer in Charge cheerfully announced, "We've come to blow you up, sir."

Further enquiries elicited a few more facts from said RE about what, and why, the need to blow up facilities, such as docks, installations, airports, gas works, power stations, waterworks. It was, he said, in short, anything of value to the enemy. However, Bailiff Coutanche, pointed out that since there would be about forty thousand people still living in the islands, these facilities would be very much needed; vital in fact, and he would much prefer that they didn't, so a very disappointed officer and his Royal Engineers executed an about face, saluted and nothing more was said about that.

By this time the two Fighter Squadrons had already left Jersey, and all too soon it was time for the children to be evacuated. Their quick little footsteps could be heard long before dawn, echoing on the pavement as they headed for the docks, their arrival coinciding with some departing troops. Two entire schools and their teachers marched to the waiting ships, all wondering what lay ahead. When and if, parents would follow?

It was a hard decision for parents to take, and the choice wasn't great. On one side they had explosions and war sounds from the French coast, and on the other, a choice of air raid shelters in England, and of course, one other option was the unknown consequences of German Occupation when they arrived on the islands.

Because it was not known how many ships could be spared for the lift off, it had to be on a priority basis, and that meant children first, with parents endeavouring to put up a brave front, as they waved farewell.

About 5,000 children left during this period, leaving in their wake a giant void. In the ensuing silence where no children's laughter sounded, Major Sherwill commented, "No children play in the streets and Mothers mourn their loss and will not be comforted."

Making amends somewhat, not long afterwards, free sea passage was available to any person who wished to leave. Six small cargo ships were sent to collect them and Alderney church rang its bells to summon all passengers. One woman, on hearing the first peal left home without bothering with breakfast dishes, commenting, "I'll just let the Gerries do the washing up."

Most household valuables had to be left behind, but some were buried and often survived intact after the Occupation was no more.

Each individual was allowed two suitcases. Judge Funch left his 30 ton yacht in port, so that he could sail with his wife, toting his two suitcases like everyone else, as they all headed for the unknown in Weymouth.

Those inhabitants left on Alderney were few, and many of the ones who stayed, moved to Guernsey later. It was only days, after the last boat left, before Guernsey was the first island to be occupied when Major Sherwill formally handed over authority to the Luftwaffe officer who came to meet him, escorted by an Island policeman. After the war the Major was knighted for fine work accomplished during that time.

Major Albrecht Lantz took over then, as German Commandant, proving himself to be a good soldier in command of an Infantry Battalian. He was educated and cultured and established a rapport with Major Sherwill and the feared Occupation lost some of its terror. It began well, but the five years to follow involved many changes, not all of them, good.

One day later Jersey was occupied, under different auspices, and after that Alderney and Sark. Eventually Major Sherwill was shipped off to the Cherche Midi prison in France, and afterwards sent to Laufen Internment camp in Germany.

Little is known about what happened in certain areas during the period from 1940 to 1945, and is yet shrouded in mystery. In September 1942 a notice was posted in Jersey that certain people were to be deported to Germany. Anyone who was not a permanent resident in the Islands qualified. Males between 16 and 70 not born on the Islands, were to be shipped out within 24 hours. Single men were sent to Laufen, families and single women sent to Biberach and Wurzach, and relieving the grimness of incarceration they were sometimes recipients of Red Cross food parcels.

It wasn't until after the war in 1970 that I had a chance to visit the Channel Islands and was better able to visualize what had happened there, and to learn what it might have been like. I stayed with friends on the island of Guernsey and read all I could find, to be more informed. I was astounded to see that Guernsey was a rabbit warren of underground installations, which I believe still exist today. There, it is possible to see gun emplacements, ammunition storage areas, living quarters, and hospitals of some size, throughout the island, all deep underground. These stretched for miles, burrowing under the earth.

Guns from the Mirus Battery had once been camouflaged by the shell of a dummy cottage on wheels. Guernsey was indeed, a fortified stronghold.

Special mention should be made in this extremely brief summary, of Alderney which became the hell hole, of all the four islands, under German rule. This island was the site for four prison camps, with more recent data, indicating a fifth existed. Therein were incarcerated between 5,000 and 7,000 slaves, many dying of dysentery and worse. Inmates represented Russia, France, Spain, Poland, Yugoslavia, Holland Algeria, and Belgium. The words, "horrifyingly pitiful," come to mind.

The four camps were recorded as follows:

Heligoland was mostly used for Russians, later evacuated and burned in October 1943.

Norderny, housed civilians of various nationalities and was broken up in July 1944.

Borkum, held Germans working in specialized fields.

Sylt was used for 500 political prisoners. Guards and Staff were provided by S.S. Totenkopf, known as the Death's Head unit in Nevengamme. This was a Concentration camp of the harshest and most horrifying treatment.

Todt Labour Org. handled discipline at the other three camps. Todt was the largest force on Aldernay. The other two forces came under the heading of, Civil and Military.

Alfred Herzka of the International Red Cross, along with other interested organizations discovered the existence of Citadella, the fifth camp but not much is known about it.

The first cargo of unfortunate prisoners arrived in July 1942. After that, thousands were brought in to be housed in dreadful inhuman conditions. Many civilians had been press-ganged, or snatched off the street for no apparent crime, and often were wearing summer clothes which wore out and were never replaced. Not even shoes. For sustenance, they were given watery cabbage soup for lunch and dinner with occasional ersatz coffee without milk or sugar. Of course, no meat; Two desperate men, found behind the butchers, digging up animal entrails, with their bare hands, were shot. Besides enduring regular beatings, on this starvation diet inmates were compelled to work in heavy construction lasting twelve hours per day, seven days a week.

Rations meant for the prisoners were sold on the Black Market for gold by the infamous Todt organization. Russians were particularly singled out for the most brutal treatment and when they fell, were often clubbed to death.

Two Aldernay men who had moved to Guernsey, decided to return to their homes in Alderney. They were namely, Mr Pantcheff and Mr Doyle, and they described what they saw. Terrible lack of nutrition, resulting in skeletal like bodies, and at some point, they reported seeing blood running down the legs of prisoners, no doubt, as a result of dysentery. They worked almost naked with only sacks for cover, they said. Since the prisoners were herded to work at dawn and only returned under cover of darkness, captives were almost never seen. The horror of it all, hidden from general view.

The purpose of all this horror was to induce prisoners to carry out Hitler's decree to make the Channel Islands an impregnable fortress. To this end, shipload after shipload of cement was dispatched to Alderney accompanied by slaves from the aforementioned Countries, but always, principally from Russia.

A small blow for justice was struck after the war when Hoffman's inhuman treatment of the prisoners under his rule who worked there, particularly Russian Slave workers, was revealed. He was hanged in Kiev watched by 40,000 Russians. Hardly enough to level the score of depravity that had been endured, but 'something,' denoting a small measure of justice.

Alderney was fortified out of all proportion to its size, because of its position in the Channel, just eight miles off the French coast. The man in charge was the aforementioned Herr Hoffman, who instituted elaborate networks of fortifications. Even preparations for flamethrowers and Artillery were made there. Three heavy coastal defense batteries manned by Naval personnel and two anti tank walls were built. All beaches and cliffs were wired, booby trapped and mined with 37,000 mines in all. Earthworks with underground concrete emplacements were stacked with food supplies, and drinking water. These hide outs were built to survive intensive bombardment, over long periods of time in case of invasion. A network of underground tunnels, some hundreds of yards long, were added as well as elaborate air raid shelters.

According to Monsieur Delauney, a Frenchman who was picked up by a press gang in St Malo in February 1943 to work as a carpenter on Alderney, prisoners there saw nothing other than work and the camp. They were marched each day at dawn, from camp to work and back again at night after dark. Mr Delauney managed to escape while being transferred from Alderney in October 1943 by this time his sturdy build after eight months of existence in camp, had dwindled to a pitifully dangerous sixty four pounds and barely alive. It was unthinkable depravity to see a man thus treated by so-called humans beings.

During the German Occupation, dead secrecy descended on the Island,s camps, with many crimes committed in silence. A former Spanish, Republican. Army Officer, named John Dalmou was put to work as a slave in harbour maintenance from 1943 to 1944 and later wrote a book about his experience, entitled, Slave worker in the Channel Islands. He wrote about Germans baiting imprisoned Jews, as a pastime. He told of their practice of throwing bits of carrot just to watch the pitiful wrecks of men, fighting for them, their humanity debased, with only the instinct for survival left. He saw political prisoners on the quay at Braye working with no boots, only sacks tied with string, and when one stopped to tie a loose string, an SS Guard shot him through the head. The body was then tossed over the cliffs into the sea. Others who were digging gun emplacements on Fort Albert front, who collapsed from malnutrition or sickness, suffered the same fate. Senor Dalmau reported that the glut of bodies in the area, lead to a macabre invasion of lobsters, crabs and octopi in Braye, obviously attracted by the human scource of food. What diabolical abysmal monsters could be guilty of such horror? Germans had many names for Alderney, but during the war it was known as the Gibraltar of the Channel because it was so excessively fortified. Guns, guns and more guns were left behind, lining the island everywhere after the Germans surrendered and vacated the island in 1945.

At war's end, Alderney was a terrifying example of what Hitler would have inflicted on the world, had he won the battle. It was stripped of its natural beauty, ruined and silent, the epitome of corrupt power, used to torment helpless human beings, in secret. Even the birds refused to witness the abject terror and degradation, and they abandoned their nests in Alderney for the entire occupation from 1940 to 1945. They simply flew away. All of this was happening so close to England, yet still closer to France. Alderney, only eight miles from that coast, was on its own. The Islands were kind of a middle ground, I suppose and yet so few of us in England knew anything about the Channel Isles, or the role they played in the war. During the Occupation it is doubtful that the British government had any source of reliable information either, about what was happening during that time. It existed as a deep, dark monstrous secret. Those islanders evacuated from Alderney were kept in the dark as well. All was silence!

Bibliography

Battle of Britain by Patrick Bishop (Foreign Correspondent)

Wings on my Sleeve by Captain Eric Brown CBE, DSC, AFC, KCVSA

Islands in Danger, by Alan Wood and Mary Seton Wood. Specifically written about the period between 1940-1945. (One of several good books written about the fate of The Channel Islands during the Occupation and a book I read more than once.)

B-17s Over Berlin edited by Ian Hawkins

Slave Worker in the Channel Islands by John Dalmou

Made in the USA
Middletown, DE
28 September 2018